THE HBC
BRIGADES

Culture, conflict,
and perilous journeys
of the fur trade.

THE HBC
BRIGADES

Culture, conflict,
and perilous journeys
of the fur trade.

Nancy Marguerite Anderson

Ronsdale Press

RONSDALE PRESS
125A – 1030 Denman Street, Vancouver, B.C. Canada V6G 2M6
www.ronsdalepress.com

Book Design: Derek von Essen
Cover Design: David Lester
Map design: All maps in this book created by Eric Leinberger, unless otherwise noted

Ronsdale Press wishes to thank the following for their support of its publishing program: the Canada
Council for the Arts, the Government of Canada, the British Columbia Arts Council, and the Province
of British Columbia through the British Columbia Book Publishing Tax Credit program.

LIBRARY AND ARCHIVES CANADA CATALOGUING IN PUBLICATION

Title: The HBC brigades : culture, conflict and perilous journeys of the fur trade / Nancy
    Marguerite Anderson.
Names: Anderson, Nancy Marguerite, 1946- author.
Description: Includes index.
Identifiers: Canadiana (print) 20240336720 | Canadiana (ebook) 20240336771 | ISBN 9781553807018
    (softcover) | ISBN 9781553807025 (EPUB)
Subjects: LCSH: Hudson's Bay Company. | LCSH: Fur trade—Canada, Western—History—19th century. |
    LCSH: Fur traders—Canada, Western—History—19th century. | LCSH: Pack transportation—Canada,
    Western—History—19th century. | LCSH: Indigenous peoples—Canada, Western—History—19th century. |
    CSH: First Nations trails—Canada, Western—History—19th century.
Classification: LCC FC3207 .A48 2024 | DDC 971.2/01—dc23

At Ronsdale Press we are committed to protecting the environment. To this end we are working with Canopy
and printers to phase out our use of paper produced from ancient forests. This book is one step towards that goal.

Printed in Canada

CONTENTS

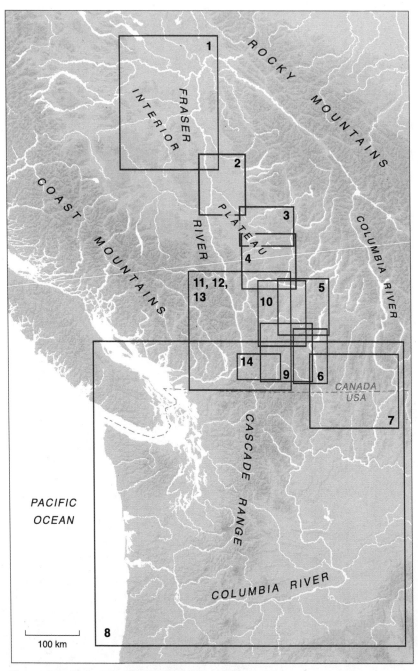

The numbers above correspond with the maps in the list of maps.

LIST OF MAPS

INTRODUCTION

A man stood on a flat of land overlooking the frozen Fraser River, watching as its icy surface shifted and broke in the sun. He heard tremendous explosions that echoed through the deep valley as large cracks shot across the ice. A short time later, the well-worn footpath that crossed the river to the Hudson's Bay Company post on the opposite bank began to crumble as the ice broke into large chunks that were swept away by the Fraser's strong current, spreading chaos and ruin everywhere.

That afternoon, while the brown Fraser still rumbled with the noise of the ice's passing, the first bateaux of the New Caledonia (modern-day British Columbia) brigades rushed downriver, the flat-bottomed boats filled with Métis and Canadien *voyageurs* (travellers) pulling the long oars. All was noise and chaos once again as the men in what their observer called their "wild mountain dress" leaped ashore and pulled the bateaux onto the beach below the fort. The men from the post ran down to greet them, and all worked together to unload the precious cargo from the boats. Soon hundreds of leather-wrapped packs of furs lay in piles on the beach.

While the clerks stood guard, the men packed their valuable loads into the safety of the fort. Then Peter Ogden, gentleman in charge of the northern posts and leader of the New Caledonia brigade, climbed the slope to Fort Alexandria, to be greeted by Ferdinand "Red River" McKenzie, the post's clerk-in-charge.

The man who watched was Frank Sylvester.[1] He was a packer, a member of one of the many pack trains that in 1859 brought provisions and tools into the goldfields around the Quesnel River and Barkerville. Thousands of gold miners needed their goods, and they needed them yesterday—yet Sylvester stopped to watch the flurry of activity around the Hudson's Bay Company (hereafter HBC) post as the men carried loads into the fort. He knew that the Old Brigade Trail he and others like him followed north had been built by the HBC men, who had been here for fifty years before the packers followed gold miners north into the HBC's New Caledonia district, with its headquarters at Fort St. James. He was also aware that he

Men with horses loaded for a long pack journey into the wilderness.

and the other packers could only reach the northern goldfields because the HBC men had already opened the territory for them.

Both the HBC men and, before them, the partners and voyageurs of the North West Company (hereafter NWC) had developed the natural paths that First Nations peoples had shown them into ten-foot-wide pack-horse trails. Although the fur traders never considered themselves packers, they spent at least five months every summer carrying furs or trade goods in brigades to or from headquarters, or transporting the same trade goods and furs between their home post and tiny outposts in the wilderness.

From early years, the brigades were an important transportation system in New Caledonia and on the Columbia River. The furs that the traders took in at their far-flung posts had to be shipped to London in time for the fur sales: like any other business in the world, there were no profits made if no sales occurred. In order to get their furs out to seaports, each company developed its own brigade route.

The Nor'Westers were the first to build trading posts west of the Rockies. By 1813 they had four posts scattered around the northern district (Stuart's Lake, Fraser's Lake, Fort George, and Trout [McLeod] Lake), with no trail connecting them to posts farther south—Fort George (Astoria), Spokane

House, and two small posts to the east, and the Thompson's River post at modern-day Kamloops.

Until 1821, the NWC canoe brigades took the furs out to Montreal every summer. The gentlemen traders and voyageurs from New Caledonia would travel by the Peace and Athabasca Rivers to Clearwater River and Portage la Loche. Then they continued on as far east as Rainy Lake, returning with their trade goods and some of their provisions before the rivers they travelled became impassible after freeze-up. Those from the Columbia district paddled in wooden canoes called Columbia boats, up the Columbia River to Boat Encampment (where the NWC geographer David Thompson had built the first Columbia boat in 1812), then crossed the mountains on foot via Athabasca Pass. If they were leaving the district, they travelled by birchbark canoe on the Athabasca and Clearwater Rivers to Portage la Loche and beyond, in the canoe brigades that had brought their trade goods and provisions west.

New Caledonia was provisions-poor (the nearest moose or bison were on the Peace River near Dunvegan, on the east side of the Rockies), and the Nor'Westers in the Columbia district felt that growing vegetables was not part of the fur trade, so they imported much of their food. Because of the distance from the east, however, sometimes provisions failed to reach New Caledonia before winter set in and everyone suffered. In some years the NWC men would travel to the mouth of the Columbia River with unloaded horses and empty boats, meeting the ship that carried their provisions and trade goods, and return heavily laden with provisions to keep the men alive over the winter. As they did not carry furs and did not travel out every year, they were not true brigades as we understand them today, although the NWC's provisioning trips to the Columbia River laid the groundwork for future HBC fur brigade trails leading south to Fort Vancouver, built in 1825 on the north bank of the lower Columbia River at what is now Vancouver, WA.

When the HBC took over the NWC in 1821 and moved into what is now British Columbia and the Pacific Northwest, it was also carrying furs to the east each year. For a time, the HBC men west of the Rockies carried on the NWC tradition of taking the furs over the mountains via Boat Encampment and Athabasca Pass to Jasper's House, handing off their loads to the HBC brigades that ran down the Athabasca and other rivers; from there, the furs were taken by York boat to their headquarters on Hudson Bay.

In 1824, however, Governor George Simpson made changes to the trade west of the Rocky Mountains. In 1826, the brigades that carried furs east to York Factory by the old NWC route was discontinued, and the York

Factory Express was created. The annual express was a fast-moving, lightly laden brigade that left Fort Vancouver in March, carrying passengers and papers over the Rocky Mountains to Hudson Bay. At the end of its seven-month-long journey, the express—now called the Columbia Express—returned to the Columbia district in late October or early November, bringing the news from Canada and London. Its unique history is told in this author's book, *The York Factory Express: Fort Vancouver to Hudson Bay, 1826–1849*, published by Ronsdale Press in 2021.

The second important change that Governor Simpson made in this district was the creation of the HBC brigades that brought the packs of furs down to Fort Vancouver, their new headquarters on the lower Columbia River. From Fort Vancouver, the furs were shipped to London via the newly reorganized London ships. New brigade trails replaced the old NWC trails that brought the HBC men down to the Columbia River. In the 1840s, the HBC men built brigade trails to the new post of Fort Langley on the lower Fraser River. From there the company shipped its furs by small sailing ships that could enter the shallow waters of the Fraser River to the safe harbour of Fort Victoria, where oceangoing sailing vessels, known as the London ships, carried them on to England. The brigades used many trails over the years, but the trail Frank Sylvester called the Old Brigade Trail was only opened in 1843. In short order a new Cariboo Road would replace the Old Brigade Trail, but that had not happened yet.

Just as they had different brigade routes, the two fur trade companies had differing administrative structures. The NWC had wintering partners, the traders who lived out in the trading posts and bought furs from the First Nations peoples, and agents in Montreal who sold the furs in Europe. Agents and wintering partners shared equally in any profits. Beneath them were the clerks, who were salaried employees, and hundreds of Canadien and Métis voyageurs, who were the backbone of the early canoe brigades. When the NWC was absorbed into the HBC, the agents and partners expected to lose everything. But Governor George Simpson of the HBC wanted them on his side, and to their surprise almost all were granted positions of power.

The HBC was set up differently: the "gentlemen" were divided into three classes—chief factors, chief traders, and clerks—all of whom were responsible to Governor George Simpson, who was in turn responsible to the HBC directors, known as the London Committee. The entire district west of the Rocky Mountains was called "the Columbia," but it included both the New Caledonia district in what is now north central British Columbia, and the more important posts along the lower Columbia River and its connecting rivers. In this massive district were two chief factors, one at Fort St. James, the company's northern headquarters in today's north central B.C., and the other at Fort Vancouver on the lower Columbia River. Under the two chief factors were various chief traders, who were responsible for their own territory and who reported both to their own chief factor and to the governor and chief factors at the HBC's annual Council meeting at Red River or Norway House. Under these traders were the clerks, who were placed in charge of smaller posts in their assigned districts. Some gentlemen went out with the brigades, but many stayed behind at their home posts to keep things running while the district's chief factor was absent.

Those gentlemen who travelled to headquarters with the brigades had work to do while they were there. They attended meetings; they organized their trade goods for the year and saw them packed; and they shared information and discussed problems that they expected the chief factor to solve. They often complained about the shortage of horses or men and were scolded by the chief factor for raising these apparently unsolvable problems. At times the chief traders fought among themselves, and on a few occasions they disagreed so strongly that they came to blows. The chief factors imagined the worst, but the traders patched up their differences and worked together, or separately, to solve the problems that were specific to their territory. The chief traders ensured that new trails were

The brigades did not pass Okanagan Lake as close to the shoreline as is shown here, but on the benchlands above. Oil painting by John Innes.

discovered and used; old trails were improved; curves in the trails were straightened; new switchbacks were carved into mountainsides when necessary; and bridges were built over turbulent streams to allow the horses an easier crossing in high water. The bogs, however, remained as stubbornly resistant as always, eating up the wood laid down to make the crossing easier. Every year this old problem was addressed anew.

Separate from the HBC gentlemen were the many employees required by the fur trade: Scots from the Orkney and Shetland Islands or the Highlands; Canadiens, French Catholics from Quebec; and Métis from the Saskatchewan district or Red River.

The Scots were employed mostly for their agricultural skills and were often blacksmiths or millers. As one clerk put it: "The chief characteristics of the highland Scotch and Orkney servants are honesty and providence. They make excellent fort and farm labourers, but indifferent voyagers."[2] They were thrifty, especially in comparison to the more excitable Métis, who had no familiarity with money, nor any use for it. The men from Scotland and the islands were more likely to remain behind in the posts when the brigades went out, especially if they were farmhands. But some of them also travelled out with the brigades. The pay was better, and most of these men hoped someday to return to Scotland.

One clerk noted that "the Canadians are generally noted for hard swearing and are excellent voyageurs."[3] The Canadiens were adaptable and creative workers: one Fort Alexandria gentleman commented on his employee's "marvelous piece of workmanship. In those days of makeshift, and appliances, to turn a Canadian voyageur into a mill-wright was nothing."[4] They were natural-born watermen who knew their rivers and the canoe-shaped boats they used on the Columbia and elsewhere. As they had always done, whenever they arrived at their destination the Canadiens celebrated with song, dance, and regales, and they played their traditional games of strength or agility. The men were proud of all the work they had done to make their journey possible, and their pride demanded that they arrive at headquarters fresh, as if their trek had been nothing but a jaunt.

The Métis had been on the periphery of the brigades from the early years, and by the 1840s they were a prominent part of every brigade, replacing the Canadiens, who no longer joined the HBC's fur trade because of better employment in Quebec. They adopted many of the Canadien traditions their fathers had taught them, but they also carried with them the stories of their Indigenous mothers. More than anyone else, the Métis were noted for their love of voyaging, and for their antics at headquarters.

One clerk noted: "Let a half-breed be ever so tired [but] if he but hear a discordant jingling of an ill-tuned fiddle he must be up and capering with ever and anon an inspiriting 'Hi! Hi! Hi!' inviting the others to join in the dance."[5] For the Métis, voyaging was an adventure, and they celebrated the journey as long as they were well-fed and had shoes to wear and horses to ride. If they were unhappy, however, they caused chaos at whatever headquarters they arrived at. Often their complaints forced change, as when the gentlemen in the interior districts and those at the coast were compelled to ensure that their men had sufficient food.

The Canadiens and Métis sometimes travelled with First Nations men, visiting villages or fishing camps to trade for salmon and furs, or hunting for game with the relatives of their First Nations wives. It was most often the Canadiens or Métis men who learned the secrets of the districts they worked in.

The First Nations peoples played an important role in building the trails and working in the brigades. When the HBC men invaded their territories in the search for new trails, First Nations families greeted them and gifted them with more food than they could carry away. At the posts and elsewhere, First Nations men listened politely as the HBC gentlemen harangued them; everyone understood that the "harangue" was a tradition among First Nations peoples everywhere, a tradition borrowed by the HBC men. First Nations men guided the HBC traders over their footpaths, and on occasion they explored for new trails they hoped would work for the brigades. First Nations men who regularly worked in the brigades often loaned their horses to the HBC men, and when these horses died of exhaustion on the trail, the company men replaced them with horses from their own depleted stock.

Unfortunately for the HBC men, the First Nations peoples along the Columbia River soon recognized the increased value of their horses and stopped trading them for a single blanket, as they always had done. In the 1840s the "Indian Wars" that occurred in U.S. territory forced the HBC men to build new trails when their old route down the Columbia River was closed to them. In years when the Fraser River salmon run was poor, the First Nations had few salmon to trade with the HBC men, causing worries of starvation in the New Caledonia posts. One year, the Nlaka'pamux rustled the HBC's stock of horses from the horseguard at Campement des Femmes, forcing the company to bring out their resident bully (an official position in the fur trade). In starvation years, First Nations men hunted the HBC's cattle, and once again the HBC bully rode out with the brigade. But in 1848 the Nlaka'pamux and Stó:lõ First Nations and others were entrusted with the job of searching for lost packs and returning them to the brigades; on this occasion they proved entirely trustworthy.

For many years after 1848, these groups worked together to build the trails that connected the interior posts with those on the coast. The Scottish gentlemen, and their Canadien and Métis employees, were a natural part of the HBC community. They had come to the territory as members of that community, and the work they did reflected their commitment to the shared values of the HBC community. At times some men wavered in their commitment and resisted, and some members gave up entirely and escaped. But while they worked for the HBC they were committed to the overall community.

Some First Nations men, such as N'Kuala and his nephew, Tsilaxitsa, or Black-eye and his son, were tied to the HBC community because of their personal connections and trust in individual fur traders. These men took on the responsibility of being supporting members of the traders' community and gave aid whenever it was needed. But other First Nations men, who lived distant from an HBC fort and had little connection with the traders, also sometimes took on the responsibilities of the HBC communities when the fur traders travelled through their territory or when they asked for their assistance. They all supported one another to ensure that the furs were taken to the coast and the trade goods were brought to the distant interior.

But while this is partially a story of building and co-operation, it is also a story of conflict between the many characters who inhabited the territory at this time: the powerful chief factors, the overworked HBC traders, the hard-working and hard-partying Canadiens and Métis, and the First Nations peoples who had lived in this territory for millennia.

For many years, the HBC men were the only "settlers" in the district. In the 1840s, stories of a wealth of resources in a land of promise brought Americans west to Oregon Territory (Idaho, Washington, and Oregon), and in the 1850s they also brought British colonists to farmlands around Fort Victoria. But the story is larger than colonies and settlers: it is the story of the formation of British Columbia in the years before 1858, when the gold rush brought in hordes of American, Chinese, and Australian gold seekers. More than any event in the preceding fifty years, the 1858 gold rush and the invasion of American miners into the goldfields of the Thompson and Fraser Rivers changed the lives of everyone who lived in this territory. The First Nations peoples, who had lived there for ten thousand years and who had welcomed the HBC men and shown them their trails, suffered the most. But the invasion also created opportunities that even the First Nations peoples were eventually able to take advantage of.

From early days, the history of what are now British Columbia and Washington State is composed of stories of invading peoples. The early North West Company changed the lives of the First Nations peoples, but those Indigenous people also changed the NWC men, making them more like themselves. Then came the Hudson's Bay Company men, who imposed their changes on top of or as a replacement of those the Nor'Westers had made. In later years the HBC was forced to change when British colonists arrived at Fort Victoria, and when the Americans flooded into Oregon Territory from the east. Eventually these same Americans moved north over the brigade trails, changing the lives of all those who lived in British territory: the HBC men, the First Nations peoples, and the Métis. As we will see, the history of British Columbia and Washington State is made up of stories of people forcing change on other peoples, altering their lives forever.

PROLOGUE

In 1824, George Simpson, the HBC governor, toured the Columbia district. He viewed the crumbling headquarters on the coast at Fort George (in what is now Astoria, Oregon) and made changes to ensure the HBC grew its own food instead of importing provisions as the NWC had done. A new headquarters was to be built a hundred miles upriver, where there was an abundance of rich agricultural land. Chief Factor John McLoughlin began construction of the new Fort Vancouver that winter, and by March 1825 its twenty-foot-tall palisades enclosed three-quarters of an acre. Inside the walls were dwelling houses for gentlemen and clerks, storehouses, an Indian hall, and temporary quarters for the employees. A great deal of work was needed to finish the buildings; nevertheless, a good start had been made.

On that 1824 visit, Governor Simpson decreed that when Fort Vancouver was ready, the New Caledonia gentlemen would deliver their furs to

Fort George, at the mouth of the Columbia River, was the HBC's Pacific coast headquarters before Fort Vancouver was built in 1824. Painting by Henry James Warre, 1848.

the new headquarters rather than ship them out to Hudson Bay via the Peace district. An HBC ship would bring trade goods from England to Fort Vancouver, and it would take the furs to London on its return voyage. With that decision, two important HBC transportation systems were created and organized: the London ships and the HBC brigades.

Both had complicated schedules. The London ships carried trade goods and mail to the Pacific slopes, and returned to London with the furs that had been collected over the previous year at HBC posts that might be a thousand miles distant from Fort Vancouver.

Dr. John McLoughlin, who until 1845 was the chief factor at Fort Vancouver, ca. 1850. Artist unknown.

One of two London ships stocked with trade goods would sail from England in late summer and, after rounding Cape Horn during the southern hemisphere's summer, would arrive at Fort Vancouver in spring of the following year.[1] Furs that had reached headquarters with the brigades were repacked and loaded onto the same London ship that had brought their trade goods. The ship would leave the coast in the autumn, rounding Cape Horn in the southern hemisphere's summertime, passing the second ship, which had left London in late summer, and arriving in London the following spring.

The outgoing New Caledonia brigades began their journey south to Fort Vancouver as soon as ice left the northern rivers and snow melted on the trails. They arrived at the southern headquarters in June, delivering their packs of furs and picking up the trade goods they had ordered two years earlier. At Fort Vancouver, there was lots of work for the gentlemen to do. The clerks shook out the furs and repacked them in barrels for shipment to London, while the chief factors chose their trade goods and organized them for transport upriver. They also prepared their orders for more trade goods from London—goods that would be delivered to Fort Vancouver in two years. They attended meetings and discussed problems that affected their business, suggesting improvements to the brigade routes and receiving orders from Chief Factor McLoughlin. They arranged for the Columbia boats to be repaired and restocked with lines and sails, organized the provisions for the brigade, and loaded the boats with dried salmon, fresh-ground flour, and freshly butchered beef. In their free time, clerks and chief factors read newspapers that were already a year old and wrote personal letters that were delivered in England nine months later.

Meanwhile, the voyageurs had few responsibilities at Fort Vancouver, where they enjoyed a well-deserved rest. They slept and drank and danced and played their fiddles or challenged each other to competitions of strength, such as throwing the hammer, "putting" the stone, or playing quoits with metal or rope rings. They enjoyed foot races and wrestling matches, and the strongest man at the fort earned the name of bully. They flirted with the Chinook women who came to the post, and they were sometimes successful in obtaining sexual favours. The voyageurs dressed in their most colourful clothing, decorated with feathers and ribbons, and pranced around the post, annoying the hard-working gentlemen as much as they were able. Charles Wilkes of the United States Exploring Expedition wrote a vivid description of the voyageurs he saw at Fort Vancouver in summer 1842:

> During my absence, Mr. Peter [Skene] Ogden, chief fac-
> tor of the northern district, had arrived with his brigade.
> The fort had, in consequence, a very different appearance
> from the one it bore when I left it. I was exceedingly
> amused with the voyageurs of the brigade, who were to
> be seen lounging about in groups, decked in gay feathers,
> ribands, &c., full of conceit, and with the flaunting air of
> those who consider themselves the beau-ideal of grace
> and beauty; full of frolic and fun, and seeming to have
> nothing to do but to attend to the decorations of their
> persons and seek for pleasure; looking down with contempt
> upon those who are employed about the fort, whose
> sombre cast of countenance and business employments
> form a strong contrast to these jovial fellows.[2]

Eventually the gentlemen's work was done, the goods were sorted and packed, the boats repaired, and the brigades prepared to return to the interior. By early July the New Caledonia men were ready to retrace their route up the river, and they reached Fort St. James by late September. From there, they would distribute trade goods to other posts in the territory. In the fall, First Nations trappers came to the newly restocked HBC posts to trade for traps or ammunition for their winter hunts, and so the cycle began again.

The HBC men were not the first to travel from New Caledonia to the mouth of the Columbia River. In 1813, provisions were sent by ship to the Columbia, and Nor'Wester John Stuart led a brigade from Stuart's Lake to collect these supplies. He travelled light, with nine men in two birch-bark canoes. Somewhere around the future location of Fort Alexandria (built on the Fraser River in 1821, south of what is now the city of Quesnel), he hired Secwepemc men to guide him to the NWC post on the Thompson River. His route is unknown, but it does not appear that he travelled over the Thompson Plateau to the North Thompson River. In 1817, fur trader Alexander Ross described the North Thompson River valley as "a large tract of wild country never before trod on by the foot of any white man."[3] There are, however, stories of brigades travelling down the Bonaparte River valley to the Thompson River post at the confluence of the North and South Thompson Rivers, and even stories of gardens existing near a small post at today's Vidette Lake. Stuart might have been guided over First Nations trails that connected these points.

From the Thompson River post, a well-used land and water route to the Columbia already existed.

"John Stuart, an explorer with Simon Fraser," artist unknown.

It was not until 1820 that the NWC again brought provisions to New Caledonia from the Columbia. Hugh Faries began his journey home from Fort George (now Astoria, WA) in June, reaching Stuart's Lake on October 20 with an enormous load of provisions.

In 1821, Stuart started off in February, using dogs and sledges until he got to Fort Okanogan. We don't know when he arrived at the mouth of the Columbia, but he departed Fort George heading north on June 7 and reached Stuart's Lake on October 12. Later that year the NWC men learned that their company had been absorbed by the Hudson's Bay Company, but no immediate changes were made. The next year, Hugh Faries left Stuart's Lake for the Columbia on May 1, and his brigade returned to Stuart's Lake in early October.

This was the fastest journey yet, but it was also the last of the provisioning brigades.

—◆—

Although we may not know the exact routes Stuart and Faries took, the traders who came after would have been familiar with them, so John Stuart's trails no doubt laid the groundwork for future brigade trails leading south from Fort Alexandria. His early trail was abandoned for a better one that led across the Thompson Plateau to the "North River," now the North

Thompson River. William Connolly travelled this route for the first time in 1826, described in Chapter 1, and it was used every year until 1842, when the HBC men opened a new trail to Kamloops. In 1828, Governor Simpson tested the theory that the New Caledonia men might be able to bring their furs to Fort Langley via the Fraser River, but the plan was soon discarded (see Chapter 2). Five years later in 1833, a herd of cattle was driven from Fort Okanogan to the Thompson River post and then to Fort Alexandria (see Chapter 11), and nine years after that, in 1842, a new trail was discovered that led from the south shore of Drowned Horse Lake (Horse Lake) to the Kamloops post, avoiding the old trail's deep swamps. Chapters 3 to 6 tell how, in 1846 and 1847, exploration parties set out to find a useable route between Kamloops and Fort Langley. In 1848 a new trail to Fort Langley was opened; it proved a disaster (Chapter 8). One year later it was replaced by another trail to Fort Hope, which the HBC men used for more than a decade (Chapters 9 to 19).

1826–1847:
OLD BRIGADE TRAIL TO FORT VANCOUVER

Two surviving Fort St. James journals reveal what occurred on the brigades travelling south to the HBC's new headquarters at Fort Vancouver (now Vancouver, WA) and returning in the years between 1826 and 1847, when everything changed. The first journal, written by Chief Factor William Connolly in 1826, records the departure of the New Caledonia brigades for Fort Vancouver. Quotations in this section are from Connolly's journal unless otherwise indicated. Page numbers from Connolly's journal and other journal quotations in this book are given in parentheses after each quotation.

Connolly's journal begins with the words:

> May 5th Friday [1826] ... The Brigades Consisting of three canoes, were dispatched for [Fort] Alexandria on the 3rd Instant [May]. And myself with Mr. [James] Douglas (who is to accompany me to the Columbia) embarked from Stuarts Lake at one o'clock PM to proceed to the same place. The weather was fine and we encamped at half after seven PM in Stuart's River. The water is very low, None of the snow in the Mountains being yet dissolved, and the Current is therefore not strong and our progress, altho' we have a crew of nine Men, is not so great as might be expected.[1] (3–4)

In autumn 1825, close to sixty horses had been delivered to Fort Alexandria from HBC posts on the Columbia River, but because of the long, cold winter of 1825–26, more snow than usual had fallen on the grasslands that surrounded the post, and all but fourteen of these horses had died. In early 1826, horses were generally hard to find: the cold winter that had killed the Fort Alexandria horses had also caused horses to perish at other HBC posts as well as among the American Indian tribes such as the Nez Percés, the usual supplier of HBC horses.

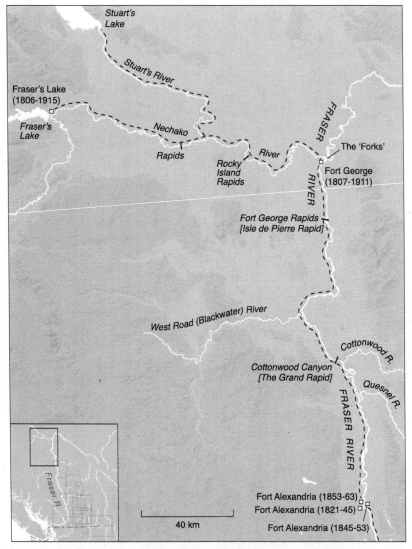

Map 1: Fraser's Lake to Fort Alexandria. The river route from Stuart's and Fraser's Lakes led to Forts George and Alexandria, via the Nechako River and the Fraser.

Connolly's outgoing canoes arrived at Fort Alexandria on May 8, and his journal for that date read:

> Mr. [James Murray] Yale had returned from Kamloops on the 1st Instant [May] with 49 Horses, 29 of which had been furnished by Mr. [Francis] Ermatinger, who is in charge of that Post, and the remainder were hired from the Indians for the voyage hither and back again, at the rate of Eight [beaver] Skins each. These added to 14 which have escaped the general destruction, and five that are hired from the Indians of this place for the whole Summer, forms a Total of 68 which number will just answer to carry out the Returns and provisions requisite for our Supplies from here to Kamloops, where a supply of fresh Horses will be furnished in lieu of the Indian Horses, which are to be returned there to assist us on from thence to Okanagan. (3–4)

Connolly noted that many of the animals were lean, but he hoped that with care they would be able to carry their loads—two packs that weighed from forty-five to eighty-five pounds each—as far as the Thompson's River post. He had his men load the horses carefully, matching the size and strength of the individual horse with the load it carried. The next day, "at an early hour the Horses were mustered, but before their loads were adjusted (a duty with which most of our Men are unacquainted) it was ten o'clock" (6).

The brigade consisted of Connolly and two clerks, with twenty-four men and sixty-eight horses carrying eighty-three packs of furs and fifteen of provisions. "For the greater Convenience of Travelling," Connolly said, "the Brigade was subdivided into twelve Brigades of two Men each, with from five to Six Horses each" (6). Connolly hoped that this would prevent confusion and make it easier for the men, who were on foot, to look after the horses that were assigned to them. But, as Connolly notes, there were problems. "Some of the Horses having never before carried a load, did not much like their Burthens, which they contrived by kicking to throw off their backs. Some time was therefore lost in readjusting their loads" (7).

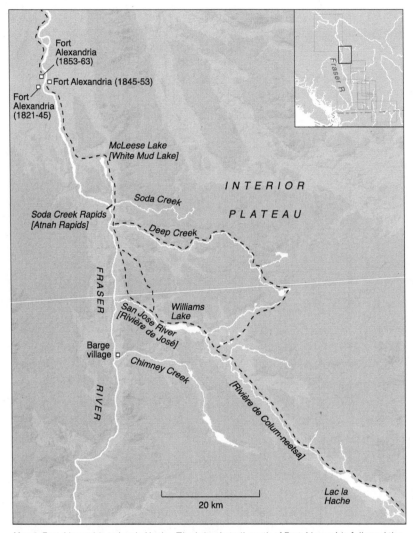

Map 2: Fort Alexandria to Lac la Hache. The brigade trail south of Fort Alexandria followed the Fraser and San Jose Rivers by various routes to the north shore of Lac la Hache. The trail along Deep Creek may also have been used as a brigade trail after 1831.

Their trail led them south from Fort Alexandria along the banks of the Fraser River. They passed modern-day Soda Creek and turned east, riding through the grasslands north of today's Williams Lake and Lac la Hache. From the east end of the second lake, they followed Salmon River (now Watson Creek) south and crossed the ridge to what is now Little Bridge Creek, continuing along that creek to the Beaver Dam River (Bridge Creek). The brigade horses swam across the river, while the men carried the packs across the natural bridge (a beaver dam). In the morning they "baited [fed] the Horses at the Drowned Horse Lake" (Horse Lake), which was named "from the Circumstance of 18 horses having perished in it by breaking through the Ice some years ago."[2] Later they found Lac Tranquil (Bridge Lake) frozen over. Beyond that, Lac des Rochers was also covered with ice. After a short rest, they continued their journey, "and reached the foot of the Mountain at 5 o'clock PM when we Encamped. The road we passed through this day is very rugged, and many obstructions occasioned by fallen woods occur" (11).

They had reached the eastern edge of the Thompson Plateau; ahead of them lay the steep downward slope they called "the Mountain." Between the place where men and horses now stood and the North (Thompson) River lay the morass they called "the swamp." It snowed as they approached the Mountain, and the snowfall continued while they set up their camp at the top of the hill. On the following day, May 19:

> It being impossible to cross the Mountain in one day, and there being only one place, about midway, which affords food for Horses, we did not therefore leave our Encampment until twelve PM & just to have time to be able to reach the above place, which we did at about 7 o'clock. Our route was through Marshes & very deep snow, in the former of which the Horses Sunk in many places up to their bellies & were with difficulty extricated. This is the most fatiguing march they have yet performed, and they were entirely exhausted when they reached the swamp, which unfortunately afforded but very poor means of recruiting their strength ...
>
> 20th Sunday. Early in the Morning we pursued our route in order to reach a good feeding place for the Horses as soon as possible. A man was sent to see after the one we left yesterday, he returned shortly after & reported that he had found him dead. Another of our Horses being unable to rise, we have therefore under the necessity of leaving him behind. At nine o'clock we reached the heights from whence we had a view of the North River. In our descent the Horses fatigued a great deal, and when we reached the small River [Eakin or Philetta Creek] it was necessary to Halt, in order that they might rest & replenish themselves. (11–12)

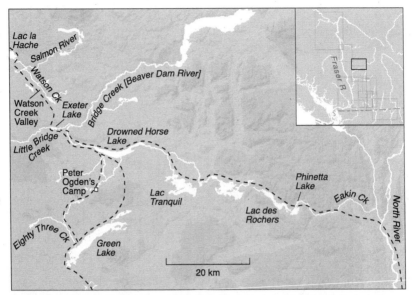

Map 3: Lac la Hache to Green Lake and Little Fork. The brigade trail from Lac la Hache to the traverse of the North [Thompson] River, via modern-day Exeter Lake and Bridge River. Also shown is the beginning of the 1843 trail to Green Lake and Kamloops. A continuation of the latter trail appears in Chapter 11.

After a short rest, the brigade men and horses made their way to the North River, where five Kamloops employees waited with canoes to transport the property across the river. By night all the packs had been taken across, but the exhausted horses remained on the west bank. To lighten the horses' loads, twenty-four of the original eighty-three packs of furs were sent to Kamloops in the canoes, and the horses were swum across the river. The next morning "at nine o'clock we left our Encampment & proceeded along the Banks of the North River which are extremely rugged and fatiguing to the Horses" (13).

> At one o'clock PM we reached a small plain where I resolved on passing the remainder of the day in drying the Furs that were wet & for which purpose the weather was particularly favorable. A thorough examination of the Packs was made, and a smaller quantity of Furs was found wet than I expected. At Sun set they were all dried & repacked. And at day break ...
>
> 22nd Monday. The Horses were collected, and as soon as they were loaded we set off, and at 10 o'clock we reached the Barriéres [Barrière River], where was a camp of

Indians from whom I procured a sufficiency of Trout for a meal to the whole Brigade, in exchange for Tobacco & Ammunition.[3] (13)

After allowing the horses a rest, they continued their journey, camping that night at a place they called "the Pineaux." The brigades reached Kamloops the following afternoon, where a fresh batch of horses awaited them. Connolly was displeased that "the Horses from Spokane which are here are fat, but from bad usage on their way from [Fort] Okanagan to this place, they have very sore backs, which is even worse than being low in flesh" (13). There were enough horses, however, to allow the brigades to reach Fort Okanagan without much difficulty.

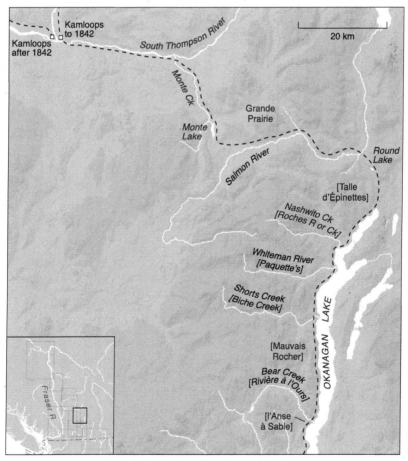

Map 5: Kamloops to the top of Okanagan Lake. From Kamloops to the Okanagan Lake, the brigade trail led the HBC men to Monte Lake, the Grande Prairie, and Round Lake, before continuing down the west side of Okanagan Lake.

The next stage of their journey would take them via Monte Creek to Okanagan Lake. All the Kamloops men travelled out with the brigades this year, and the preparations for the temporary abandonment of the post took some time:

> [May] 25th Thursday. Although the Horses were crossed early in the Morning, yet before they were caught, tacked & loaded it was Eleven o'clock, & we therefore were not able to proceed farther than the Monté, where we Encamped. For want of Cords to tie them with, I had to leave about 1100 Salmon, with a few Appichimons [saddle blankets] & Pack Saddles, at Kamloops, which were put in charge of an Indian called Nicholas [N'Kuala], who is said to be an honest fellow; & possessed of sufficient influence over his Tribe to secure them from being stolen. The weather was fair & warm. (15)

In these years, the valley that Monte Creek flowed down was often flooded by the freshets, and the brigades may have followed a different route over a saddle or through the benchlands to Monte Lake. (Paxton Creek, and its benchlands east of Monte Creek, has been suggested as a possible alternative route to Monte Lake.) Beyond Monte Lake, the Grande Prairie's Salmon River wandered through wide marshlands, and when the freshets overflowed those marshes, the brigades followed along the extreme northern edge of the Grande Prairie towards its more heavily treed eastern end.[4] This year they made good time and camped for the night at the farthest extremity of the Grande Prairie. The next night they camped on Okanagan Lake, at a place the HBC men called Talle d'Épinettes, or "sharpened spruce." Their trail led down the west side of the lake:

> 28th Sunday. Set out as usual. Our route lay along the Okanagan Lake, which is rugged & fatiguing to the Horses. We reached Red Deers River at 11 o'clock AM, where we remained until 4 in the afternoon, from which hour until seven we proceeded on, & passed the Mauvais Rocher without accident—a little beyond that we put up for the night. (15)

South of Talle d'Épinettes the horses had waded across the Roches (Nashwito) River and gone south again through Paquettes (Whiteman) River and past Paquettes Point. Near modern-day Fintry they stumbled through

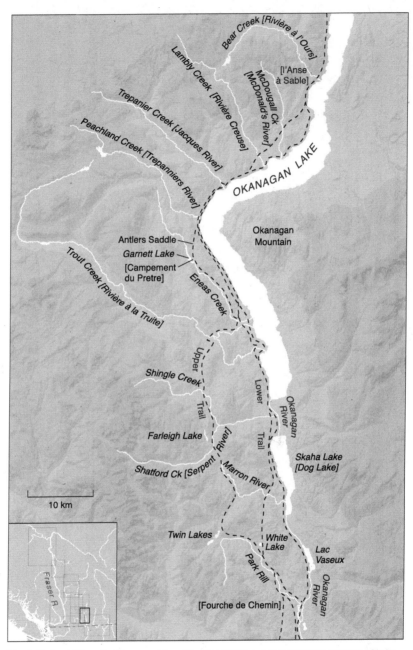

Map 6: Rivière à l'Ours to Okanagan River. The first HBC brigades followed the shores of Lake Okanagan until they passed Lac Vaseux. Later brigades took various routes that led them over the benchlands above modern-day Summerland, avoiding the deep mud of the bulrush-clogged river banks south of the lake.

Red Deer's River (Biche Creek, now Shorts Creek), named for a doe elk. This was just north of the section of trail they called the Mauvais Rocher, or Bad Boulders, a particularly rough and rocky section that often caused problems for the unshod horses. Once they were past that obstacle, they crossed over Rivière à l'Ours (Bear Creek) and reached l'Anse à Sable (Sandy Cove) on the west side of Okanagan Lake. McDonald's (McDougall) River came next, and then Rivière Creuse (Lambly Creek). The summer weather along Okanagan Lake tends to be hot, but this year it rained:

> 29th Monday. Rainy weather, which retarded us much, but as it increased towards the afternoon we were obliged to Encamp at an earlier Hour than usual.

> 30th Tuesday. At an early hour we moved off but stopped for some time at Jacques river [Trepanier Creek], where the Packs were examined from a suspicion of their having received some damage during the late rains. They were however all in excellent order. After this we pursued our route, and Encamped a few miles from the Prairie de Nicholas. Weather fine. (16)

South of Jacques River was Trepanniers River, now Peachland Creek (not to be confused with Trepanier Creek, mentioned in Connolly's account). From the place where a landmark called the Lone Tree stood on the shoreline, the trail led along the lakeshore and river past Dog (Skaha) Lake, and muddy Lac Vaseux:[5]

> June 1st Thursday. On leaving the Encampment much delay occurred in passing through a Long Miry Prairie in which the Horses sunk to their Bellies, and many of them could not be extricated without being unloaded. They were allowed to rest at the Little Okanagan [Osoyoos] Lake, from whence we proceeded in the afternoon to the Barrière, or entrance of Okanagan River, where we encamped after having crossed the Property & Horses to the opposite shore. The former was crossed over in Canoes, which a band of Indians we found here lent us for the purpose. These people also supplied us with some fresh Carp, & roots. (16)

The fish were not the common carp (*Cyprinus carpio*), but some other carp-like fish such as the large-scaled sucker (*Catostomus machrocheilus*) or

"Early History of the Okanagan: The Fur Brigade," oil painting by George Henry Southwell, an early B.C. artist.

bone-filled but edible members of the minnow family, possibly the northern pikeminnow (*Ptychocheilus oregonensis*). The roots were bulbs such as camas, which when roasted in a covered pit were not only edible but sweet and delicious.

Neither William Connolly nor Peter Warren Dease, whose journal we will read in the second half of this chapter, spoke of an Okanagan chief guiding their brigades through the valley. Indeed, in 1826, the young chief, who was referred to as an honest Indian, was left behind at Kamloops to caretake the fort. Yet it is a well-known tale among brigade trail historians that the grand chief of the Okanagan people, N'Kuala (Hwistesmetxöqen, or Walking Grizzly Bear), met the outgoing brigades at what the HBC men called Prairie de Nicholas, or Nicola Prairie (Summerland), and guided them south through his territory.

N'Kuala was still a young man when, in 1811, the incoming Pacific Fur Company (hereafter PFC) trader David Stuart described him as head chief of the Okanagans; Alexander Ross, who in 1811 was in charge of Fort Okanagan, also had a close relationship with N'Kuala. Although the PFC reports appear to be true, there is some conflict with the dates: in November

1822, John McLeod, then in charge at the HBC's Kamloops post, tells the tale of N'Kuala's father's lingering death by murder, and the son taking over the position of grand chief. It is also clear that the tradition of N'Kuala's guiding of the brigades through the Okanagan Valley did not begin with William Connolly's journey in 1826; nor did Peter Warren Dease mention his presence, even though Dease traded for furs and horses with various First Nations men on his way through the valley.

In 1835, Peter Skene Ogden took over the New Caledonia district from Dease. In 1837, as he rode south towards Fort Okanagan, his good friend, Samuel Black (then in charge of the Thompson's River post of Kamloops) met him and warned him that the Kamloops brigades had experienced some difficulty with the Okanagans. An Okanagan man had stolen one of the Kamloops brigade horses, and in a conflict that arose out of a subsequent negotiation another First Nations man was killed—no one knew how. Then, as Samuel Black and Peter Ogden shared this information, First Nations men emerged from the brush to attack them, killing an HBC man and shooting Black's horse out from under him. Ogden rushed his brigade men to safety and they made it to Fort Okanagan without further conflict.[6]

It becomes clear, however, that in 1837 N'Kuala was not riding with Ogden's brigades to prevent conflicts such as this, and it is quite likely that on their return from Fort Vancouver in August, Ogden and Black connected with N'Kuala and arranged that he accompany them through his territory, keeping them safe from attack. By taking the brigades under his wing, N'Kuala made the New Caledonia and Kamloops brigades part of his community and thus prevented further conflict with the First Nations in the valley. By the 1840s the tradition was well established, and N'Kuala regularly rode with the HBC brigades.

From the south end of Osoyoos Lake, William Connolly's brigades continued their journey south through the wide, grass-covered valley where the Similkameen River flows into the Okanagan River. They crossed the Okanagan at the junction of the two rivers, where there was an active First Nations fishery. Here Connolly left the brigades behind and rode ahead to Fort Okanagan, which stood on a big flat of land north of the junction of the Okanagan and Columbia Rivers.

Connolly's brigades arrived on June 3. Three days later the New Caledonia men were joined by the Fort Colvile men, coming downriver from their Columbia River post east of Fort Okanagan. Connolly's journal continues:

7th Wednesday [June 1826]. This Morning the Brigade, consisting of Six Boats manned with seven men each, & loads of 35 Pieces left Okanagan for Fort Vancouver, under the Guidance of an experienced man, Pierre l'Etang. The passengers are besides myself Messrs. [John] Work, Douglas, [Pierre] Pambrun & [William] Kittson ... The day was fine, & the strength of the Current being proportionate to the usual height of the waters, we went on with much rapidity until seven o'clock PM, when it was necessary to Encamp in order to Pitch some of the Boats that are very leaky. From some Indians we saw, a few Salmon were procured of an excellent quality. (18)

The boats they travelled in were Columbia boats, originally designed by the NWC explorer David Thompson as a substitute for canoes. When John Work entered the district in 1823, he wrote a good description of these unique boats:

Embarked at 9 o'clock, and proceeded down the Columbia River, in three boats or kind of wooden canoes, worked by 8 Men each, who row with paddles and not oars. These boats will carry about 55 pieces and are made of a light construction so that 12 men can carry them across the portages.[7]

The HBC men added two boats to the outgoing brigade at Fort Nez Percés and left on June 9. The next day the brigades reached the Chûtes, the first of three major obstacles they had to overcome as they made their way through the Cascade Mountains. The next morning they passed through the three rapids of The Dalles, where strong westerly winds delayed them. The boats finally crossed the portage at the Cascades on June 15. Having seen his men safely past this dangerous section of the river, Connolly went ahead in his boat to Fort Vancouver, reaching it that evening. One day later his men rounded the last corner in the river, their voices raised in song.

———————

Five years later, in 1831, Chief Factor Peter Warren Dease led out the New Caledonia brigades in their birchbark canoes, leaving Fort St. James on May 7 and arriving at Fort Vancouver in Columbia boats on June 11.

Fort Okanogan [American spelling] stood on the east bank of the Okanagan River a little above its junction with the Columbia, and the image looks up the Okanagan River towards Osoyoos Lake. Artwork by John Mix Stanley, 1853.

By this time the latter post had been moved from its location on the bluffs above the Columbia River to a piece of land in the valley that rarely flooded when the Columbia overflowed its banks. Dease's brigade left Fort Vancouver on June 27, and one month later it reached Fort Okanagan, where the men loaded their goods on pack horses. The course of the trail they followed from Fort Okanagan was up the east side of the Okanagan River. Their first stop might have been at the Rivière à la Grise, or Rat Lake. On the next day the men and horses encountered rocks that blocked their trail and forced them to travel up a gorge that was later called McLoughlin's Gulch. They emerged on the highlands above the river and rode north until they reached the banks of the Okanagan once again. At the Similkameen Forks, they were sixty miles north of Fort Okanagan.

This section of Dease's journal begins with these words:

> 29 [July 1831]. Baited the horses at the Forks where Exchanged a worn out Mare for a horse with one of the Natives from the camp we found at this Place. Traded some salmon & berries and proceeded to Tea River [Testalinden Creek] where we put up for the night.

> 30. Stopped at our usual hour at Fourches de Chemin from when we proceeded to Serpent River & put up having passed a River Called Rivière la Cendri previously.[8] (14)

Fourche de Chemin translates as "forks in the roadway," and this was the junction of the upper and lower trail in the hills west of Lac Vaseux. The upper trail was new and was the route the brigade followed as it swung up the slopes via Park Rill (Meyers Creek) to Horn Lake (Twin Lakes), where the HBC had a horse park. This trail continued along the west side of Marron (Wild Horse) Valley to cross Snake River (Shatford Creek) where, near Farleigh Lake, they had a campsite. From there the brigades followed the valley of Beaver River (Shingle Creek) north. Crossing over a large flat, they descended a hill to reach Trout Creek, which they forded above its canyon. From that crossing they followed Eneas Creek, avoiding the hazards of brush-filled streams and high water, if any, by riding on the benchlands through another back valley (Garnett Valley) to the ridge now named Antlers Saddle. From Antlers Saddle, the trail led them down the long sloping hillside to Nicola Prairie (Summerland).

Dease's journal continues:

> 31 [July]. Passed Beaver River, Trout River & Stopped at Rivière Prairie de Nicholas from whence we put up at the Tree along the Lake. (14)

Prairie de Nicholas, or Nicola Prairie, was a long-time seasonal village used by the Okanagan people, under Grand Chief N'Kuala. It was a safe place; to the west a chain of fourteen extinct volcanoes, called the Penticton Chain of Volcanoes, provided protection to Prairie de Nicholas. On the east side, high silt cliffs abutted much of the shoreline of Okanagan Lake. To the south, the Trout Creek Canyon blocked easy access to the prairie; to the north, Goats Bluff also provided protection. Only three gulches led into the prairie itself, and there were perhaps six narrow, easily defended access points through the silt cliffs. Today all show evidence of burial sites from ancient battles.[9]

The "Tree along the Lake," or Lone Tree, stood at the place where both the upper trail and the lower reached the shores of Lake Okanagan, north of Nicola Prairie. Dease's journal continues as he led his brigades north from the Lone Tree:

> Monday [August] 1. Passed Rivière à Trepagnier, Rivière à Jacques, Rivière d'Ours, the Anse à Sable and put up at Sunsett. (14)

Today's Peachland, or Deep Creek, was called Rivière de Trepannier on Alexander Caulfield Anderson's 1867 map, and Trepannier River on

The rocks that formed Okanagan Falls, on the Okanagan River south of Okanagan Lake, are the result of one of the many volcanoes that belong to the Penticton Chain of Volcanoes that encircle modern-day Penticton and Summerland. Photograph by GHE Hudson, ca. 1912.

Samuel Black's 1839 map. This river was named for a medical operation, a trepanation, carried out on its banks by Pacific Fur Company trader Alexander Ross, who saved the life of an Okanagan man by trepanning the head injury he suffered in a bear attack.[10]

Dease's journal continues:

> 2 [August]. Stopped at Rivière la Biche [Shorts Creek]. The roads in this part bad, 2 horses broke their loads, by which ½ Bag Flour & ½ Bag Corn were lost not having good Wrappers for such Pieces & the Cords very bad.
>
> 3. Passed Okanagan Lake. Stopped at Lac Rond [Round Lake]. On passing the strong woods found fire Raging in all directions, and had to pass very near it, the smoke so thick as almost to darken the atmosphere. Some of the Horses were Sore galled, 2 of them were unloaded. Passed Salmon River and put up at East end of Grande Prairie.
>
> 4. Some of the horses were not brought up until a late hour. Lolo [Jean-Baptiste Leolo] and Party took the lead to go on to the House [Kamloops]. Put up at Campement du Poulin for the night. (14)

Remnants of the Old Pack Trail remain visible at Monte Lake, B.C., many years after the last HBC brigades passed through the area.

Both Round Lake and Salmon River bear the same names today, and are six and ten miles north of Okanagan Lake. As seen in Dease's journal, the brigade crossed the Salmon River and followed it west to their encampment on the northeast side of the Grande Prairie, possibly setting up camp in a grove of aspen that grew on a bench above a spring.[11] Their next camp was the Campement du Poulin (Colt Encampment) on Monte Lake. From Monte Lake it was a short ride over the hill to Monte Creek (or Paxton Creek), which they followed down to the banks of the South Thompson River. Dease's journal tells of the brigades' arrival at Kamloops:

> 5 [August]. Reached the [South Thompson] River at 9AM, and got to the crossing place by the house at 3PM. With the assistance of the Natives & their Canoes 7 of the Brigades Baggages were Crossed over to the Fort. The others remain until morning. All the Horses were driven across except one.
>
> Saturday 6. This morning the remainder was Crossed & find that 4 of our horses Cannot continue the voyage, they are therefore left here. Hired 5 from the Natives to take us to North River, and 6 of those Mr. [Samuel] Black has lent us leaving 4 of them here and 10 Pieces remain here until they can be sent for by Mr. [Alexander] Fisher. Sent off the Brigade at 3 PM. (14–15)

On August 7 the brigade rested at Pineaux Point, and the next night they put up at the Grand Prairie south of the Barrière, where a fire raged in the woods. They crossed the North River at the Grand Traverse (Little Fort), where they stopped for the night. The following night they camped on the patch of grasslands in the swamp, the only place in this section of the trail where there was grazing for the horses. By August 11 the brigades had topped the Mountain and passed Lac des Rochers, putting up for the night at Lac Tranquil (Bridge Lake). And the next day they stopped to rest at the junction of what appears to be Bridge Creek and Little Bridge Creek:

> 12 [August]. Put ashore to bait at Rivière la fourche, but a heavy Shower of Rain obliged us to stop all day. Some of the horses being much Galled & Exhausted, intend to proceed in the morning for [Fort] Alexandria in order to send the mares that are there to assist them on. Take one Man with me.
>
> 13. Left the Brigade under Care of Mr. [Francis] Annance & Gregoire, and Stopped for 1 ½ hour. Had a violent shower of Rain towards Evening. Put up for the night at Dusk.
>
> Sunday 14. Arrived at Sunsett at Alexandria, where find Mr. Fisher and all his people safe and well. (15)

At Fort Alexandria, Dease discovered his canoes were "in a very bad state and require a thorough repair to be able to take up Cargoes" (15). He had the dried-out canoes sunk in the river so the fragile birch bark would become strong and flexible. As there was no birch bark, gum, or *wattap* on hand, he sent men out to locate these necessary items.

The gum was pitch, which was mixed with grease and used both as glue and as a waterproof shellac of sorts for the canoes. Wattap was threads of harvested tree roots used to sew the birch pieces together. It was easy to collect pitch, grease, and wattap, but Dease complained that "want of bark for the Canoes is a great obstacle to us at the present moment, for which the Worst of the canoes could not be done with today, and but 2 men capable of doing that work properly" (15). Good birch bark was scarce on the west side of the Rocky Mountains, and a birch tree, once harvested, could not be harvested again for another decade. In addition, the birch trees that grew in New Caledonia were much smaller than those in the east, and their bark was thinner.

The difficulties of repairing the canoes delayed the men for five days, but they finally loaded their fragile craft and headed north. They broke three canoes on their way upriver, and one became so unmanageable in the Big Rapid (Grand Rapids in Cottonwood Canyon south of Fort George) that they abandoned it. On September 13, Dease's party finally reached Fort St. James.

Dease left New Caledonia in 1835. When Peter Skene Ogden took over the territory, he replaced the birchbark canoes with wooden boats called bateaux. These were relatively flat bottomed and carried a heavier load than the Columbia boats, but they were heavier altogether and could not be portaged easily. The largest were thirty feet long, seven feet wide, and two and a half feet deep. Like the York boats used on the east side of the Rockies, their keel was laid first, and the *varangues*, or ribs, were bent with the use of a steam box before being attached to the keel. When all was ready, the boat was turned and the sawed planks were bent around the ribs and nailed into place. Finally, the bateaux were caulked and sealed with *oakum* (old rope, shredded) and pitch. These clinker-built boats were sturdy and much more able than canoes to handle the rough waters of the Fraser River.[12]

Only Connolly's and Dease's journals have survived from the years the HBC travelled over the old trail, but before 1847 the brigades used the trail every year on their way out to Fort Vancouver. However, later HBC men considered sections of the heavily wooded and swamp-ridden trail over the Mountain so inconvenient that they looked for a new route that would bring them from Drowned Horse Lake (Horse Lake, near 100 Mile House) to Kamloops. Any new trail had to also avoid the bogs along the Bonaparte River, which the HBC men were already all too familiar with. Chief Trader Samuel Black of Kamloops was put in charge of the project of finding a new trail. By 1842, Secwepemc men had told him of a trail they called the "detour," that brought them from Lac Vert (Green Lake) to Kamloops via Rivière à l'eau Claire (Criss Creek) and Carabine Creek. In winter 1842, HBC clerk Alexander Caulfield Anderson rode over that trail on his way to Fort Alexandria, and in 1843 it was used for the first time as the brigade route between the south shore of Drowned Horse Lake and Kamloops. The Mountain trail was abandoned forever.

⇸ 2 ⇷

1828: GOVERNOR SIMPSON EXPLORES THE FRASER RIVER

I n 1828, two years after the journey described by William Connolly in the previous chapter, Governor George Simpson set off from Hudson Bay on a voyage of inspection of the territory west of the Rocky Mountains. His travelling companion, Archibald McDonald, kept the official journal, which began with these words:

> Saturday, 12th July—At one a.m. the crews of two "Light Canoes," consisting of nine men each, were in motion, carrying the provisions and baggage to the water side; and in a few minutes after, the Governor in Chief [Simpson],

The Peace River led the NWC men west to New Caledonia from the junction of the turbulent Rivière des Roches and the Slave. The only interruption was the twenty-mile-long Peace River Canyon, where the river forced its way through the Rocky Mountains.

Doctor [Richard] Hamlyn and myself, were accompanied down to our craft by fourteen commissioned gentlemen and about as many clerks. After something more than the usually cordial shake of the hand from all present, we embarked with three cheers under a salute of seven guns from the Garrison, and against a strong tide, were soon round the first point by the free use of the paddle and one of its accompanying "*voyageur*" airs.[1] (1)

On September 11 they reached the McLeod's Lake post via the Peace and Pack Rivers. From that post Simpson's party rode over the land portage to Fort St. James. At the top of the hill that overlooked Stuart's Lake, they changed into their best clothes in preparation for their arrival:

The day, as yet, being fine, the flag was put up; the piper [Colin Fraser] in full Highland costume; and every arrangement was made to arrive at Fort St. James in the most imposing manner we could, for the sake of the Indians.

Accordingly, when within about a thousand yards of the establishment, descending a gentle hill, a gun was fired, the bugle sounded, and soon after, the piper commenced the celebrated march of the clans—"Si coma leum cogadh na shea," ("Peace: or War, if you will it otherwise.") ... The guide, with the British ensign, led the van, followed by the band [the musicians]; then the Governor, on horseback, supported behind by Doctor Hamlyn and myself on our chargers, two deep; twenty men, with their burdens, next formed the line; then one loaded horse, and lastly, Mr. [William] McGillivray (with his wife and light infantry) closed the rear. During a brisk discharge of small arms and wall pieces from the Fort, Mr. [James] Douglas ... met us a short distance in advance, and in this order we made our *entrée* into the Capital of Western Caledonia. No sooner had we arrived, than the rain which threatened us in the morning, now fell in torrents. (24–25)

William Connolly, the gentleman in charge of Fort St. James, had taken the brigades out to Fort Vancouver and was expected to return shortly. As Simpson wrote a letter to be delivered to Connolly, Connolly's canoe appeared on the lake, and "in about twenty minutes, we had the infinite satisfaction of receiving Mr. Connolly on the beach, amidst a renewal of salutes from the Fort" (25). Simpson ordered clerk James Murray Yale back to Fort Alexandria, with instructions to send men to Kamloops to build a boat, or bateau, for Simpson's use. The governor had come west specifically to test the theory that the Thompson and Fraser Rivers might be used as a brigade route to the Pacific for the Kamloops and New Caledonia men. Hoping that the HBC men could take their furs out to Fort Langley on the lower Fraser and return with the trade goods, he took a two-pronged approach to the expedition:

George Simpson, Governor of the Hudson's Bay Company, was knighted in 1841, when he became Sir George Simpson. Artwork by Stephen Pearce, 1857.

> In order that I might be enabled to visit the Establishment of Kamloops, and descend Thompson's River, and at the same time obtain a particular report of that part of Frazers River which I should lose by striking across the country to Kamloops, it became necessary to divide ourselves into two parties at Alexandria; Mr. Yale, Clerk, with Fourteen Men in two canoes continuing the main stream, with instructions to wait for us at the Forks of Thompsons and Frazers Rivers, while myself with Chief Trader Archibald McDonald, Dr. Hamlyn, and Five Men, proceeded across Land on Horseback to Kamloops. (28–29)

Simpson and McDonald reached Kamloops on October 4. "Pipes played, and much firing on both sides," McDonald reported. "Much to our satisfaction, we find our boat is finished, and which was begun only six days ago" (34). Before he departed, the governor "harangued" the First Nations chiefs who had gathered to meet him, and they listened politely.

When Governor Simpson spoke to the First Nations men, haranguing them and demanding that they behave better, he was following a tradition originated by the First Nations and borrowed by the HBC men. At every gathering or feast, chiefs gave speeches that harangued their own people, and other important First Nations men responded with a speech of their own. Some Indigenous men were described by the HBC gentlemen as fine orators, mostly because they also, at times, harangued the fur traders. In fact, the tradition was so well known among the company's traders that at their Lachine parties, the head HBC gentleman harangued the attending gentlemen and all the employees, and everyone enjoyed the experience.

As a result of this tradition, long accepted by both cultures, the First Nations men understood what the governor was doing and listened attentively. They were entertained by the governor's harangue, and they liked him better for it. By haranguing the First Nations chiefs, the HBC governor was strengthening the company's connections to the local First Nations. By using the First Nations' style of making a speech, the HBC men built community and reduced conflict. They encouraged camaraderie with the First Nations so they would trade with them—a sales trick used by all professional salesmen to this day.

When the governor was satisfied with his harangue, his men put the boat into the water and "soon after, departed in *full puff*" (34). One of the three men in the boat was Jean-Baptiste Leolo, who would act as Simpson's guide on the dangerous Thompson River west of Kamloops Lake. McDonald described their journey down the Thompson River to the junction with the Fraser at Thlikum-cheen (Kumsheen):

> [When we reached the river we] ran a number of minor rapids before we got to *La Rivière Bonaparte* by one p.m. A little below passed a dangerous one, then three *dalles* which were perfectly smooth, and below which was *Rapide de la Grosse Roche*, which ought to have been taken on the left side, as we took in much water by running close to the rock on the right hand. This we ran at a quarter before two. In half an hour made Point Observation, or Wood Point, and in succession *Rapide Croche* [Crooked Rapid], and Long Rapid at quarter to four. To Coutaimine [Nicola] River Forks took us another half an hour. McDonald's Encampment at a quarter to five, and in fifteen minutes more, put ashore for the night ...
>
> Wednesday 8th. Off at six a.m. Three strong rapids to Nicumine [Nicoamen River]; ran all without examination by seven. Visited all the rest for about a mile which comprehended four principal ones: the second and last very dangerous indeed. In the latter we were nearly swamped, for in three swells we were full to the thafts [thwarts], and the danger was increased by the unavoidable necessity of running over a strong whirlpool while

the boat was in this unmanageable state. Left this place at eight, and in another hour, after running the worst places, arrived at the Grand Forks, where we were much gratified to find Mr. Yale and our people quite safe and well. This meeting is rendered still more interesting, from the circumstances of both parties descending rivers that were never ran before, and that were always considered next to impossible. (35)

The Black Canyon of the Thompson River, a few miles west of modern-day Ashcroft, B.C., during the construction of the Canadian Pacific Railway. Photograph by O.B. Buell, ca. 1886.

Contrary to McDonald's claim that the rivers had never been run before, Nor'Westers Simon Fraser and John Stuart had canoed most of the way down the Fraser to its mouth in 1808, then returned home to Fort St. James. It is true, however, that no HBC man had made the journey, and Simpson wanted to know what dangers his employees would face if he decided they should bring out their furs by this river. The two parties exchanged horror stories at Thlikum-cheen before continuing their journey down the Fraser.

McDonald's journal continues:

> We started at one p.m. The Governor took his own canoe with eight men. A gale of wind that commenced three days ago seemed to increase this afternoon, consequently our progress was slow and hazardous. Although none of the rapids from the Forks to this place [McDonald's Dalles] are bad, yet we found them dangerous, and did not perform the distance—4 miles below the Forks,—before five o'clock. The boat went down the *dalles*, but the canoes not daring to follow, [the boat] was brought up again on the line, and here we are for the night in a very bad encampment. The Indians hereabouts are about the usual number. Their salmon fishery must be over, for not one is there to be seen on their stages now. (35–36)

A birchbark canoe on a Canadian river, the paddlers hard at work while the passengers sit comfortably in the middle of the canoe.

"McDonald's Dalles" may refer to the rapids at Jackass Mountain. These same rapids gave Simon Fraser's men some trouble. They had descended the river in May, at the beginning of the summer freshets—high water resulting from the melting of the snow in the mountains—when the water ran swift and high between its banks and whirlpools formed. In October, when Simpson's party came down the Fraser, its waters were lower but the rapids more intense.

McDonald's journal continues:

> Thursday 9th [October]—Weather moderate. Off at six, when we could well see in the dalles. Governor embarked in the boat with me, and Mr. Yale took his place in the canoe. Were soon in a long rapid, with a small stream from the mountains on the right hand, at foot.
>
> Good run to Allitza [Nahatlatch?] River on the same side, which we passed at eight, leaving the other about half way. Strong whirlpools below, which forced Bernard to return and descend on the opposite side (the right). From this place, where we were detained three quarters of an hour, we had a good run over a current of great velocity to the Sandy River [Speyum Creek?], which we made about nine, and breakfasted. Gumming, and running *dalles* till twelve.
>
> This is a bad piece of navigation. Here also, we took on board Latzie, one of the Coutamine Chiefs. Five hundred yards lower down made use of our lines, and at the foot of the same cascade, on right hand, carried the canoes, and here were detained repairing, gumming, &c for two hours. The boat ran the portage part of the river, but required great skill and vigilance. Many Indians about us here, but they behaved well. The boat had a peep at the next place before the canoes came on. This place we call the Gate Dalles. Very good going down, but should a line be required to ascend, it will be a task of some difficulty to pass it on either side. First rapid of another nature at three: then a smooth piece of a few miles before we came to Mr. Yale's river, which has also a strong rapid at its mouth, and to get down, the guide was induced to land the passengers and two men out of each canoe. There was some delay before they could ford the river. (35)

Although it is impossible to know for sure, "Mr. Yale's River" might be Ainsley Creek. McDonald's journal continues:

> Left this place at four, and in twenty minutes arrived at the head of the fall. Examined it minutely. Boat undertook

to run right down mid-channel: did so, keeping rather in eddy to the right, and did not ship more than we had on one or two occasions already experienced. No passengers and only eight men were in the boat. The canoes crossed to the west side, and made a portage over a good sandy beach of about two hundred yards. Not an Indian there. After a detention of about three quarters of an hour, we again pushed on, and at a quarter past five, encamped in a small sandy bay on the west side, surrounded by detached rocks for fifty or sixty paces back, behind which, on both sides of the river rose mountains almost perpendicular, and of incredible height, well clothed in the lower part with Pine, Fir, and Cedar trees. A number of the natives soon gathered about us, and continued to arrive from below throughout the night, with large flambeaux [torches] to direct their steps. (36–37)

McDonald observed that the First Nations men who joined their party were quiet and polite. The HBC men gave them tobacco to smoke, and although they and the two First Nations men who accompanied the HBC party smoked until midnight, the visitors did not appear to be fond of HBC tobacco.

The next day McDonald wrote:

Our course to-day is about south. The river made no great bends, but owing to occasional delays, and being often in strong eddies and whirlpools, our distance cannot be estimated at more than fifty miles. At least half the distance, the river is deeply imbedded in the solid rock, and the other half is of bold rapids, with, however, plenty of water all over. The mountains in no part of this day's work, recede from the very edge of the water. (37)

At this point they were in the section of the river where the rock walls narrow, carrying them through two side-by-side canyons south of Scuzzy Creek: Hell's Gate and the curving Black Canyon. They likely set up their camp at the south end of the two canyons. McDonald's journal continues:

Friday 10th—The river in no part of this day's work was more than a hundred and twenty paces, and often not quite half that in width. In getting our boat and canoes in the water this morning, it was remarked that the river

had risen three feet during the night. The little rain we
had could not have been the cause of this. Started at broad
day-light, and in twenty-five minutes came to head of
Simpson's Falls [the Falls], where the river is choked up
by a most solid rock of about half an acre in extent [Lady
Franklin's Rock]. Examined it along the west shore, but
conceived the run on that side extremely dangerous, and
owing to the immense rocks all over, to carry was impossible. The East lead was then determined upon, crossed,
and run without landing on that side, by the Guide who
rushed on with his bark canoe, and a safe arrival below
was effected, but not without much risk in the whirlpools
against the enemy [the rocks] that hung over us. The boat
followed, but did not suffer by the eddies so much, as it
did by being swallowed into the swell of the Fall, out of
which the utmost power of twelve paddles could not
keep it. The second canoe having the advantage of being
behind, came on with greater precaution. A few hundred yards below this, we came to the next and last run,
which was steep but uniform. Then the river began evidently to assume a different form. The water was settled,
the beach flatter, and vegetation more profuse. (37–38)

The HBC men were now leaving the territory of the Nlaka'pamux of
the upper Fraser River and approaching the territory of the Tait (Yale First
Nations) and Stó:lō, who lived along the lower Fraser River. In his journal,
McDonald described the prominent hill that stood behind the Tait village:

At eight passed a large camp on right, which could only
have been abandoned a few weeks before. Behind it sprang
up a lofty, rocky Mountain in the shape of a cone, and
being the last on that side, we celebrated it by the name
of Sugar Loaf Mountain. Continued our descent till half-
past-nine, and landed for breakfast, which did not detain
us forty minutes, treating our people with some of the
taureau [beef] we had at Dunvegan. None of the small
rivers to the left attracted our particular notice.

At a quarter to two, passed the mouth of "Lilliwhit" [Har-
rison's] River, a stream of some size, as is indicated where

> Mr. F. Ermatinger arrived on its banks, a day's journey
> west of second Peselive [Lillooet] Lake in August, 1827, and
> as appears in his report to me on the subject, "Thomp-
> son's River Correspondence 1827–28." (37–38)

In 1827, Francis Ermatinger, then at Kamloops, had explored the lake
route to the Fraser River (the same route that Alexander Caulfield Anderson would follow in 1846—see Chapter 3). Although Ermatinger's arrival
at Fort Langley is not mentioned in the journals, McDonald's note indicates that Ermatinger did indeed make it all the way to Fort Langley, and
that McDonald had read Ermatinger's now-lost report.

McDonald's journal continues as his party descends the Fraser River
west of the mouth of Harrison's River:

> Another River [Chilliwack], half a league below, on
> opposite shore, which comes from the neighbourhood
> of Mount Baker, rich in beaver according to our Guide's
> account. At half-past three o'clock, MET THE TIDE FROM
> THE PACIFIC OCEAN. Work's river on right at five. Head
> of McMillan's Island at seven, and arrived at Fort Lang-
> ley precisely at eight, where we found Mr. [James]
> McMillan himself, Messrs. [Donald] Manson and [Fran-
> cis] Annance, and twenty men. (38)

At the end of this exciting river journey, Simpson decided that this
route could not be used by the HBC men to bring their furs to the Pacific:

> Frazers River, can no longer be thought of as a practica-
> ble communication with the interior; it was never wholly
> passed by water before, and in all probability never will
> again: the banks do not admit of Portages being made,
> and in many places it would be impossible to use the line,
> on account of the height of the projecting Rocks which
> afford no footing: and altho' we ran all the Rapids in
> safety, being perfectly light, and having three of the most
> skilful Bowsman in the country, whose skill however
> was of little avail at times, I should consider the passage
> down, to be certain Death, in nine attempts out of Ten.
> I shall therefore no longer talk of it as a navigable stream.[2]

From Fort Langley, Simpson continued his journey to Puget Sound and Fort Vancouver.[3] McDonald remained behind at Fort Langley. At this time Fort Langley stood on the south bank of the Fraser River, west of McMillan Island, and was described as being 135 feet by 120, with two good bastions and a four-foot-wide gallery around the inside of the palisades. In 1839 this fort was destroyed by fire and rebuilt a few miles upstream, where it was closer to its thriving farms. McDonald remained at the post until 1833, when Francis Heron took his place.

In the early days, change came slowly to the isolated Oregon Territory. By the 1840s, however, rumours about the discussions that were occurring between American politicians in Washington and the British government in London had begun to circulate among the HBC men. Newspapers that arrived with the London ships, which had left England nine months earlier, carried news that was already almost a year old. Reports from headquarters in Montreal were somewhat more reliable and recent, but the papers that came from the east every October with the incoming Columbia Express from York Factory, the HBC headquarters on Hudson Bay, were still at least six months old. But even the old news was worrying. The HBC gentlemen knew that change was coming and they would have to adapt—but it seemed so far away. How could these distant discussions affect them? No one knew the answer to that question.

✳ 3 ✳

MAY 1846:
EXPEDITION, KAMLOOPS TO FORT LANGLEY

I
n 1818, negotiations between the British and Americans had established a boundary line between the United States and British territory
as far west as the Rocky Mountains. For many years, the line through
Oregon Territory remained undetermined, and the territory was jointly
claimed by both Great Britain and the United States. The only residents
were the First Nations occupants and the HBC traders and employees, who
continued to operate as if the territory was British owned.

This could not last. The first Americans trickled west in the early 1840s,
shortly after Lieutenant Charles Wilkes returned from his visit to the
Columbia district with the United States Exploring Expedition. As a result
of Wilkes's glowing descriptions of Oregon, the British and American governments reopened negotiations. Most HBC traders were confident the
boundary line would follow Lewis and Clark's route to the Pacific, leaving
the territory north of the Columbia and Snake Rivers in British hands.

However, at Fort Vancouver Governor Simpson had listened to the views of members of
Wilkes's Exploring Expedition, and he was
not as confident as others in the HBC's ability
to maintain ownership of Oregon Territory.

Alexander Caulfield Anderson, then clerk-
in-charge at Fort Alexandria on the Fraser
River, thought the HBC should open a brigade
trail from New Caledonia to Fort Langley
on the lower Fraser River, just in case. In
spring 1845 he wrote to Governor Simpson
and offered his services for locating such a
trail.[1] The governor spoke to newly minted

Alexander Caulfield Anderson as
he was in the 1860s.

Chief Factor Peter Skene Ogden, who was slated to become one of three members of the new Board of Management at Fort Vancouver, alongside Chief Factors John McLoughlin and James Douglas.[2] When Ogden reached Fort Colvile on his journey west to Fort Vancouver, he wrote letters that advised the New Caledonia gentlemen of Simpson's instructions. Shortly before he had left Red River, Governor Simpson had suggested to Ogden that it was important "to ascertain if a communication with horses could be effected between Fort Alexandria and Langley." His letter went on to say that "as Mr. A.C. Anderson has volunteered his services ... I have to request he may be appointed."[3]

In 1846 the outgoing New Caledonia brigade left Fort St. James in mid-April and arrived at Fort Alexandria on May 2.[4] When it left Fort Alexandria, Anderson travelled with the brigade to Kamloops. At thirty years old, Anderson was confident in his ability to find a road to the coast. Unfortunately, he was also entirely unfamiliar with the country he had volunteered to find a path through. This was rugged country, and Anderson would be exploring for a brigade trail that would be used by hundreds of HBC pack horses, carrying furs to the coast and trade goods inland.

The finished trail would have to be ten feet wide for most of its course, and a path that might work for a man on foot would not necessarily be suitable for heavily laden pack horses. Although sturdy, the HBC horses were small: only seven hundred to a thousand pounds as a rule. They were also unshod, and sharp rocks on the trail bed could damage their hooves and cut their fetlocks. If the ground was soft, the passage of many horses would turn the trail bed into a quagmire. Because so much of the brigade's travel was done during the period of high water (freshets) due to snow melt, safe fords over creeks and rivers were essential. Gradient was also important, but a steep slope was acceptable if the hillside allowed for switchbacks. The horses needed good grass and water: the trail builders could sow timothy grass and white clover along the trail if the ground was good, but they could not manufacture streams. Building a brigade trail was a complex business, and Anderson would have to keep all these concerns in mind as he explored potential trails.

In many ways, however, this was a perfect job for the young Scottish gentleman who had joined the HBC fur trade looking for adventure. Anderson came from an agricultural background and had been sent north to Fort Alexandria to take charge of the important farming work that was done there in those years. He was an intelligent and thoughtful man who followed the slow-moving news. He was also ambitious: he looked around him and saw that no one was better able to explore for a new trail than himself. Fort St. James's Donald Manson, although still relatively young and vigorous, was tied to his job and would be taking the brigades out to Fort Vancouver that summer. Samuel Black, who had actively explored the Thompson River district, was now dead. John Tod, who had taken Black's place at Kamloops, was more than fifty years old and a far less active man than his predecessor. Anderson knew he was in better condition than any other gentleman in his territory, and more readily available. He also knew that if he was successful in finding a new trail, it might bring him a promotion—always a consideration.

On May 15, Anderson rode away from the Kamloops post with five men and N-poomsk, an "Indian from the Lakes." His journal begins with their journey along the south bank of Kamloops Lake:

> Friday, 15th May—Set out from Kamloops, having with me five men, viz. Edouard Montigny, J. Bte. Vautrin, Abraham Charbonneau, Theodore Lacourse, and William Davis. Left at ¾ p.m. [12:45] the New Caledonia & Thompson's River brigades still encamped there, and delayed by bad weather. At 6 ¾ encamped at the lower end of Kamloops Lake.[5]

They crossed Thompson's River with the aid of the Secwepemc people who lived at the end of the lake, and forded the Rivière du Défunt (Deadman River) with some difficulty because of high water. On arrival at Rivière de Bonaparte they found the riverbanks so inundated that they could not cross, so they set up camp eleven miles north of the usual ford. The next morning, they felled trees to make a bridge and crossed their goods, but it was not until late in the afternoon that they managed to cross the horses. They camped that night on Rivière à Chapeau (Hat Creek), and the next day rode through its picturesque valley towards a gap in the hills that took them into Marble Canyon, where "steep & lofty limestone crags bound the valley on either hand, diversified in spots by small waterfalls, swollen by the melting snows" (1–2).

Anderson's party reached the banks of the Fraser River at the mouth of Pavilion Creek, where there was a First Nations encampment called Le Pavillon, owing to the British flag having been conspicuously hoisted there. Downriver, at the Lower Fountain, Anderson viewed the twinned Pavilion and Fountain Ridges, which loomed twenty-five hundred feet above him, squeezing the Fraser into a narrow, twisting trench. His report

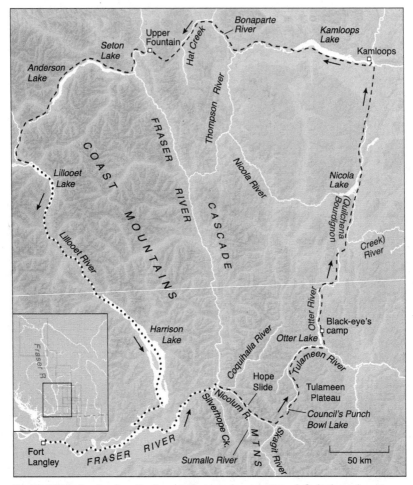

Map 11: 1846 Exploration from Kamloops to Fort Langley and return. A.C. Anderson's route through Setron, Anderson, and Harrison Lakes became the Harrison-Lillooet Trail in 1858, and his return journey over the Tulameen Plateau sparked the creation of the new brigade trail in 1849.

to the Board of Management, written on his arrival at Fort Langley, records his thoughts as he stared at the mountain that seemed to block his way:

> It was my object to discover, if possible, a horse com-
> munication, whereby the 1st lake conducting towards
> Harrison's River, whose immediate shores I had under-
> stood to be impracticable, might be avoided. I regret to
> state that I failed in doing so. A mountain upwards of
> 2,000 feet in height intervenes; at this season still thickly

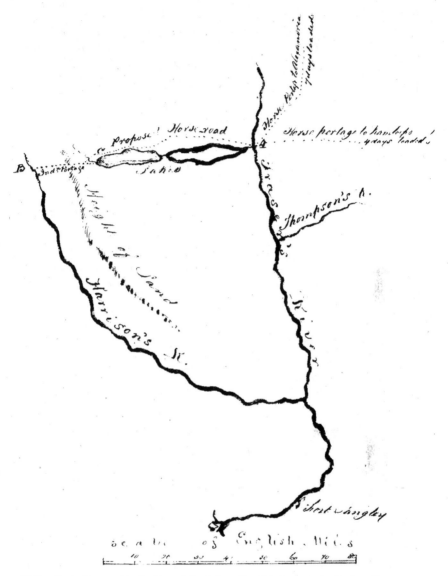

"A New Route Proposed for the Horse Brigade from New Caledonia via the Harrison River, 1845," by Alexander Caulfield Anderson.

covered with snow, and impassable save with snow-shoes. Indeed at a later period, after the snow should have disappeared, the passage of the tract in question, even if practicable for a single light horse or more, is quite unadapted for the passage of loaded horses.[6]

At Kamloops, Anderson had discussed with Tod the possibility of exploring what are now Seton and Anderson Lakes. In 1827, Francis Ermatinger had explored the same series of lakes and river all the way to Fort Langley. His suggested route was drawn on the working map for the Kamloops post, produced in 1839 by Samuel Black, who was in charge of the post at that time. Anderson's 1845 sketch map contains the same information that the Kamloops map showed, but neither had good information about the route and the lakes beyond a certain point, as Anderson's map makes clear.[7]

Anderson's first choice had been to walk down the east bank of the Fraser River, but it appeared to be blocked by the high mountain. Instead of wasting his energy on a route that would not work as a brigade trail for horses, Anderson paid some Secwepemc fishermen to transport his party across the river. From their landing place on the Fraser's west bank, Anderson and his men followed a footpath down its rocky banks to the mouth of Seton Creek, five miles distant. Unbeknownst to Anderson, Stó:lō Chief Pahallak (Pelek), who Fort Langley's James Murray Yale had sent upriver to guide Anderson past the canyons of the Fraser, waited at the mouth of Thompson's River.[8] By choosing the walkable west bank of the Fraser over the unfriendly terrain of the east bank, Anderson missed meeting Pahallak.

His party approached Seton River from the north and continued their journey along the north bank of Seton Lake, where he found that "precipitous rocks rising 1,000 to 1,500 feet in height ... preclude the possibility of all progress by land, save, perhaps, by scaling the craggy sides at some rare points less precipitous than the rest" (4–5). At the west end of the lake they walked across Seton Portage—the result of a series of landslides that tumbled down the steep hills and divided one long narrow lake into two. Once on the shores of the second lake, Anderson reported that the "mountains in this vicinity are lower than those that border the 1st lake, and the country altogether wears a more agreeable aspect" (7).

At the end of the lake later named for him, Anderson and his party began their portage over the height of land that separates Anderson Lake from the Lillooet River. They followed the course of a winding stream (Gates River) into today's Birkenhead River and continued to follow that larger river to a lake he called the Lillooet. Anderson's report to the Board of Management explains how he still considered this a possible, although difficult, route for the brigades:

> The chief impediments consist in the stoney nature of
> the ground, by which the hoofs of horses would be liable

to injury; in two or three rocky points which abut upon the river; in fallen timber at certain spots; and in several streams which it is necessary to cross. But the last three of these obstacles might, I consider, be overcome if found necessary, by rolling away boulders or filling up their interstices; by the free use of the axe; and by constructing bridges where necessary.[9]

At one of the villages these men encountered on their way down the Lillooet River, a nervous parent hid his child away in case of danger. Anthropologist Douglas Hudson tells the story of a modern-day Lil'wat man who remembered that his many-times-great-grandparent had been hidden because strangers were coming down the river. Hudson calculated the generations and realized the strangers might have been Anderson's party on their way down the Lillooet in 1846.[10] Anderson had no way of knowing of the hidden child, of course, but he described the Lil'wat people he found at the top end of Lillooet Lake:

> The natives whom I saw, amounting in all to about 50 men with women and children in proportion, were suffering for want of provisions, and were unable to supply us any. They ascribe the dearth to the state of the water, which impedes the usual fishing. The inhabitants are very miserably clad, and exhibit every symptom of abject poverty. They possess, however, some good cedar canoes, made after the model of those seen on the coast. After some parlaying I succeeded in hiring a couple of these, together with the necessary conductors. Embarked after 7 o'clock, and after proceeding three miles encamped on a low point at the entrance of a considerable lake [Lillooet Lake] trending off SE. (8–9)

They set off early the next morning, paddling down the fifteen-mile-long lake. In the evening they encamped at the head of a rapid, where it was necessary to portage the canoes. In his journal, Anderson noted:

> I find the river very different from what I expected. At this stage of the water it is a perfect torrent; and at a high stage (it is now at half-water) must afford a very precarious navigation. In fact, but for the expertness of our Indian boutes [bowsmen and steersmen] who are thoroughly

versed in the intricacies of the river, we should, I fear,
have had much difficulty in getting through. (9–10)

Anderson was impressed with the abilities of the Lil'wat canoemen,
who knew their river well and who took him and his men down in their
canoes with little apparent difficulty. For the most part, he and his party
were welcomed by the First Nations peoples who inhabited the areas near
the lakes above and the rivers he was now being guided down. When the
HBC men arrived in a village, they were often given gifts of food that were
so generous they could not be carried away. At Seton Lake a hundred
members of a village poured into Anderson's camp to shake the hands of
all the men who accompanied him: "Killing one with kindness," as Anderson said. The people at the end of Anderson Lake had shared their stories
with him: stories of magical beings called *transformers*, who had come many
years earlier to "transform" the First Nations people who lived in this
region into the people they had eventually become. Farther downriver,
the Lil'wat, although apparently starving, had willingly abandoned their
fishing and carried his party downriver in their fine canoes—a duty for
which they would be generously paid at Fort Langley. The HBC men were
vastly outnumbered by the First Nations inhabitants in this region, but at
no point were they threatened. Nevertheless, the danger was real. As
Anderson wrote, "One felt constantly as if seated on a powder magazine
which a spark might at any moment ignite."[11]

All of the First Nations peoples that Anderson met as he journeyed past
modern-day Seton and Anderson Lakes were people who were not
directly connected with the fur trade, nor was any HBC post close enough
that they could visit without travelling a great distance through what might
be considered enemy territory. Yet these people were not entirely discon-
nected from the HBC community. The N'Quatque and Stl'atl'imx peoples
who lived along those two lakes, and even some members of the Lil'wat
community, were familiar with the Lower Fountain, a historic First Nations
fishery and gathering place known to have been used by all nations for
hundreds of years. Here they would meet the Kamloops men who came
to trade for their fish.

And so, when Anderson and his men appeared among them, the
N'Quatque and Stl'atl'imx people, and the Lil'wats who lived farther to
the west, welcomed his party with gifts of food and transportation. The
company men by this time had become part of the First Nations' extended
community, and they already knew the fur traders and trusted them. The

fur traders, however, may not have felt safe among these First Nations communities, as these peoples were strangers to them. Because their party was so small, the company men might also have felt threatened by the large numbers of First Nations people who inhabited the villages along the lake-shore. With no community or trading connections that they knew of, this group of HBC men was uncomfortably aware of the threats that these people could have posed, yet nothing happened. The HBC men had come expecting conflict, but found none.

In the end, the journey down the tumultuous Lillooet River discouraged Anderson from considering this a possible brigade trail of any sort. In his report to Fort Vancouver he wrote about his change of mind. "I was, up to a certain period of my journey, truly convinced of the possibility of proceeding directly to Harrison's River, with horses." He had thought that boats could be used at the Fraser River end of the portage. It was not until he reached the Lillooet River that he changed his mind. "Far from finding the navigation of that stream so placid as I had been led by common report to expect," Anderson reported:

> I was disappointed to find a considerable portion of it greatly obstructed by rapids, and presenting obstacles of no inconsiderable nature ... I descended the river at half-water, and in that state the rapids were very violent, though not always dangerous. I do not consider that loaded boats could ascend the river in that state of the water; or if so at best, by very slow degrees; both from the violence of the current and the apparent impossibility, in many places, of poling or putting out the line.[12]

Having made the decision to not pursue this rough river as a possible brigade route, Anderson was eager to reach Fort Langley. His skilled canoe-men brought him quickly down the river to Harrison Lake and River (both named in 1827 in honour of then-deceased HBC director Benjamin Harrison). At 5:00 that night the party reached Fort Langley, where Anderson conferred with Chief Trader James Murray Yale. Yale had already informed Anderson of a possible route over the mountains to the Upper Similkameen (Tulameen) River, and Anderson prepared for a return by this trail.

JUNE 1846: FORT LANGLEY TO KAMLOOPS

When Anderson reached Fort Langley, he discovered that Yale's hand-picked Stó:lō guide, Pahallak, had not yet returned from Thompson's River. Yale found Anderson another guide, a Stó:lō man who was to show Anderson a road that would bring his party to the place the HBC called the Similkameen. Prior to leaving Kamloops earlier in May, Anderson had arranged for horses to be left for his use at the "Red Earth Fork," on the Similkameen River at modern-day Princeton.

James Murray Yale, chief trader in charge of Fort Langley, in 1880.

Four days after his arrival at Fort Langley, Anderson travelled up the Fraser with plans to follow a trail that crossed the Cascade Mountains on the east side of the river. His journal began with the words:

> Thursday 28th May—Fine weather. Set out from Fort Langley at 11 ¼ a.m., having a large canoe well manned. Part of the Langley men, who proceed some distance up the river to establish a salmon fishery, are to accompany as far as the spot where I leave the river, whence they will return with the canoe.[1]

After the party left Fort Langley, they spent the night near Smess (Sumas), a large shallow lake where many Stó:lō spent their summers. From there, Anderson's journal records his party's progress up the Fraser River:

> Friday 29th [May]—Set out at 3 ¼ a.m. Reached Lillooet Fork [Harrison River] in 4 hours. Under the combined

impulse of 13 paddles, our canoe makes good progress. The river is full of low poplar islands, and so far affords an excellent navigation for boats. Upon our right the hills are lofty and approach very close to the river. Such parts of their sides as have a Northern exposure are still covered with snow a great way down. (11–12)

At noon the next day the party arrived at the mouth of a river called Tlae-kullum (Silverhope Creek), which the Stó:lõ guide proposed to follow. A few hours later, Anderson reported the following:

After proceeding a few miles, and crossing the tail of a mountain ridge, very high and steep, a narrow valley (a continuation of the same), with precipitous sides opened to the view; and immediately afterwards, as we began to descend, large boulder rocks, quite impracticable for a horse road, impeded the narrow pathway. This decided me at once on retracing my steps, a decision which the direction in which the valley trends—far in the direction of Mt. Baker—helped not a little to confirm. (12)

As noted in Chapter 3, unshod horses cannot safely travel over stony roadbeds or tracks that are embedded with sharp rocks. Anderson's Stó:lõ guide would not have known that, even had he known the trail was to be used for horses. Had Anderson proceeded farther along this stony valley he would have turned east along the Skagit River and found a route that, excepting the rocks and swamps, might also have led him to his planned destination. But, as Anderson wrote:

True, by following up the defile in which we were now somewhat advanced, I might the sooner, perhaps, get through my journey, but it must necessarily be at the sacrifice of all useful issue. Thus I have determined to follow, at all risks, a defile having a much more likely appearance which attracted my attention this morning. It opens a few miles higher up than that of the Tlae-Kullum [Silverhope], and is called the Que-que-alla [Coquihalla]. Having retraced our steps for some distance, we encamped about three miles from our starting point of this afternoon. (12–13)

This map is found in the original of A.C. Anderson's "Journal of an Expedition under command of Alex C. Anderson of the Hudson's Bay Company, Return Journey, 1846."

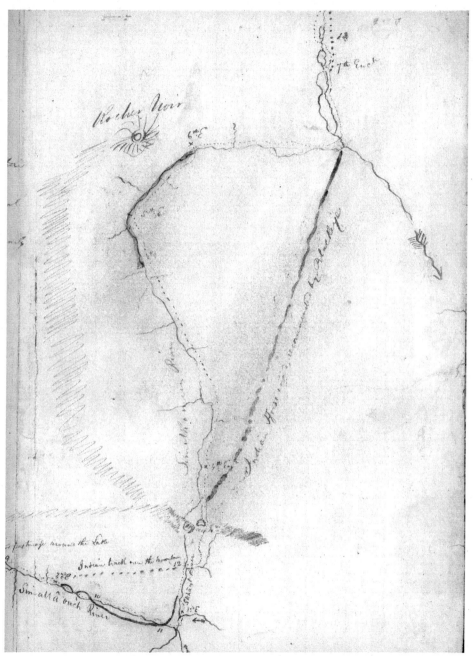

This section of A.C. Anderson's map shows the route of his climb up the south side of the
Tulameen Plateau from the Sumallo River, his crossing of the plateau to Otter Lake [Tulameen],
and where Anderson thought Black-eye's trail would lead him.

They breakfasted at the river mouth, where Anderson hired Stó:lõ canoemen to transport his party to the river his guide called the Que-que-alla. Anderson described the river as having "a broad valley, watered by a considerable stream, which we keep upon our right. Country favourable in this part. Pasture about the banks of the main river; wild pea [vetch], prele [horsetail] &c, in moderate sufficiency for the temporary sojourn of the brigades" (13).

There is a reason for every side note in his journal: grass was important, but vetch and horsetail would also provide good feed for the brigade horses. As Anderson walked up the river, he drew a map in his journal (see pages 60–61).[2] His journal continues:

> Burnt woods as we proceed. Two small lakes. At 12 ½ descend to the stream and cross. Good pasture here for a night or two, upon the gravelly expanse bordering the stream, which evidently at times inundates the whole. This, it appears, takes place only in the autumn or early spring, upon sudden flushes of rain or melted snow in the mountains. The water is rather high at present, but is confined within its ordinary channel, which it is said never to exceed during the summer season. A brigade would require to make a portage here at the present state of the water; but were it a little lower, might cross loaded with great ease. (13)

The HBC brigades would approach the Fraser River in the season of the freshets, when high water made crossing the streams difficult. Safe fords were essential. A little upriver the men found an excellent crossing place, "either for swimming or fording of horses—gravelly bottom with shelving banks" (13). Wisely, the men kept their feet dry by clambering across an "embarrass" or logjam of driftwood that seemed permanently "checked at a spot where the river is contracted into very narrow dimensions by steep rocky banks" (13). Anderson's journal continues:

> Having dined we crossed at 2 ½ p.m. & proceeded a short distance along the stream, downwards, then fell into one of its feeders, coming from E. by S, the width of which varies from 10 to 15 yards (N'Calaownm) [Nicolum Creek]. Cross on a tree and proceed along it. The opposite mountains which bound the valley approach very closely here,

and the Indian track (scarcely perceptible, by the way) is very bad; though with a good deal of labour it might be rendered available. But for a horse portage, it would be better not to cross at once, but to continue along the opposite side for a mile or two before crossing. The axe would, in this case, clear a passage; but by the present footway there are several rocky banks in the way. (13–14)

In 1859, Angus McDonald, then chief trader in charge of Fort Colvile, rode past the mouth of Nicolum Creek, which his companion described as flowing through "a large defile in the mountain range, bearing S.E. about 20 miles, and leading, as far as I could judge from that distance, through the main Cascade Range eastward."[3] This was the defile that Anderson's party now entered:

We reached the feeder [Nicolum Creek] in question at 3 ½ p.m. and stopped at our present encampment at 6 ½, having passed three hours in the piece of bad road alluded to. Of this interval, one hour elapsed while we were occupied in examining the vicinity, leaving two hours, during which our progress, as may be supposed, was very slow. Thus the extent of the bad road in question may be assumed to not exceed 4 to 5 miles at farthest. Labour alone is required to remove the impediment. (14–15)

The next morning they walked along the south bank of the river towards the east. "Country opens out a good deal & road good till 6 a.m., when we cross the river, here dwindled away to a mere trifle" (15). They climbed an easy hill and, following a mile or so along its summit, descended again to the stream. "The ground is soft, and with the hoe an inclined path might be easily made to facilitate the ascent" (15). They breakfasted at 8:30, probably on the banks of today's Eleven Mile Creek. Anderson's journal continues:

Set out again at 10.30. Strike off, leaving the little river on our left; ascend a small hill, cross a point of land & fall, at 11.20, upon a small lake [Outram Lake], whence the branch of the stream on which we breakfasted issues. This is the height of land between the streams falling respectively into Fraser's River & Southward parts of the Gulf of Georgia. Fine clear country—gigantic cedars with little or no underwood. Soft mossy ground (not wet and quaggy) with very few stones perceptible. (15)

In January 1965, 119 years after Anderson passed through the valley, the mountain that loomed above Outram Lake released an enormous landslide that buried the valley under seventy metres (230 feet) of rock and rubble. The massive Hope Slide, as it came to be known, displaced the lake's water and pushed it up the side of the opposite mountain, knocking down all the trees. Hearing the rumble of the massive fall, a Greyhound driver backed his bus out of the valley. Drivers who had passed through the valley a half hour earlier felt the tremble of the slide's impact. Four people were killed. Two are still buried deep under the mud and rocks.

Anderson's journal continues as he crosses the ridge east of Outram Lake:

> At 12 ½ fall on a stream issuing from a cut upon right— its course here N, bending round shortly and following a direction ESE. The Indians call it Simal-a-ouch, or Sim-all-a-ow [Sumallo], and say that it falls, as nearly as I can ascertain, somewhere in the vicinity of Bellingham Bay, but as I am little acquainted with that locality, I cannot identify it. I was at first inclined to set it down as the Scatchett [Skagit] River, and am still in doubt on the point. (15–16)

The Stó:lō guide's information was accurate: the Sumallo flows into the Skagit, which enters Puget Sound south of Bellingham Bay. The party walked over the point of land, in the middle of which they found "a lake, formed by the expansion of the stream" (16). Anderson noted the fine pasture for horses, but also commented on the slow progress of the party, "owing to the miserable traveling of our Indian assistants" (16). They recrossed the stream and found a road which, although good, was "impeded with fallen wood. But the Indians say that both these crossings may be avoided ... by following the left side, round the bend" (16). Anderson's journal continues:

> Fell in at the last crossing with an Indian from the Forks of Thompson River, who is hunting beavers in this neighbourhood. As he appears to possess a knowledge of the country superior to our other pseudo-guides (who are miserably at a loss), I have engaged him under the promise of some Ammunition & Tobacco, to accompany us

for a day or two. This portion of the country is very little frequented. As far as the lake just mentioned a narrow hunting path appears at intervals; but beyond it nothing of the kind. (16)

Anderson's new guide (apparently a Nlaka'pamux from Thlikum-cheen) led the party down the left bank of the Sumallo, where Anderson noted that "the axe is required here" (16). Once again he complained about the slow progress of the group, "owing to the dilatoriness of our Indians, who are miserable walkers" (16). He was tired and in pain, having to do "a great deal of extra walking in the worst parts, in order to determine the practicability of doubtful passages" (17), which was particularly hard work in the sultry weather. "Unfortunately for my efficiency," he went on, "I this evening find myself suffering considerably from stiffness of my right leg, arising from varicose veins—an evil contracted some years back, and which threatens to be attended with painful if not altogether alarming, results" (17).

Anderson appears to be furious with the Stó:lō men, who could not walk as fast or as far as the HBC men. He was also fully aware that the entire success of this journey had devolved upon him. He probably now understood how mountainous and impassible this country was.

It was also possible, if not probable, that more than exhaustion and fear of failure prompted him to write these peevish notes in his private journals. Like all men of his time, he had his prejudices, which were based on his unfamiliarity with the coastal tribes, who differed markedly from those he had worked with in the interior. Like many HBC men (and like the Royal Engineers, who came to British Columbia after 1858), he had been drawn to the company because of the writings of James Fenimore Cooper, who penned novels like *The Last of the Mohicans* that described First Nations warriors as noble savages. At Fort Alexandria he had worked with the Dakelh, who he had come to respect for their ingenuity. The post was also visited by the Secwepemc—horsemen who resembled the romantic Indian that Cooper had written of. The First Nations on the coast differed considerably from these horsemen, who, "nerves and sinews braced by exercise and minds comparatively enabled by frequent excitement, live constantly amid war and the chase."[4]

The Stó:lō people were connected to Fort Langley and did not often trade at the inland posts; nor, generally speaking, did they trap and trade furs—something that confounded the HBC gentlemen from the interior. From James Murray Yale, Anderson knew that the Stó:lō could generally be trusted. Slavery was rampant among the Stó:lõ people (as it was every-where on the northwest coast), and that practice probably coloured Anderson's opinion of his guides. Nor were the Stó:lõ capable horsemen, and although we do not know if Anderson's guides understood they were looking for a horse trail, Anderson certainly doubted their ability to find a trail that horses could travel over in safety. To Anderson, the Stó:lõ appeared very much less active than the Lil'wats, and also less capable than the Dakelh and Secwepemc men who formed his own HBC community. He did not fully trust these "lazy, fish-eating" strangers, and without trust, he and his men guarded against possible treachery and conflict.

But the Stó:lõ had strengths and abilities he had yet to recognize. Although the Stó:lõ were used to hunting in these mountains, they were primarily canoemen and fishermen who did not roam far from their rivers unless they were hunting deer or mountain sheep. They also spent time in these mountains collecting a type of flint now called Hozomeen chert, which they used for tool making. Because of their searches for both game and flints, the Stó:lõ were familiar with the territory they had chosen to explore, but they appeared not to have explored the plateau itself. Anderson later met a First Nations man named Black-eye, who explained that "there was a reluctance on the part of the Fraser's River Indians to our opening a road in this direction, from a dread of its affording facilities of the Similkameen to make war upon them."[5] Yet today there are stories of the Stó:lõ being gifted meat by a mysterious hunter called Yo:a'la, who came from the other side of the mountains. It is even suggested that this hunter might have been Black-eye.[6]

Anderson's journal continues:

> Tuesday 2nd June—Set out at 4 a.m. Breakfast at 7 ¾,
> 4 to 5 miles. Country up to this point a good deal
> obstructed with fallen wood. There are two rocky points
> abutting on the river, which may be avoided by making
> a circuit. The axe would be required here. (17)

They continued their journey up the Sumallo riverbank, finding a few obstacles in their path but none that could not be overcome. At 3:00 p.m. they reached the fork in the river where they were to leave the Sumallo:

> Encamp early, say 6 p.m., owing to the fatigue, or laziness,
> of our Indians. The men [the HBC employees] hold out
> well in comparison. Personally I am suffering much from

my leg, which is swelled and irritated. We are encamped
a little more than a mile from the forks of the Simallaouch,
upon one of its feeders coming from N by E. At this point
it is divided into two branches, one, the principal, from
the East; the other, which is much smaller, from N by E.
The Eastern fork is that which our former guides intended
to follow; the other is recommended by the Thlikum-
cheen whom we met yesterday; and as it is said to be
preferable in all respects, we are to follow it. (17–18)

From their camping place, they set out early and breakfasted at the spot
where the trail ascended the mountain that rose to their left. "It is said to
be very short, and must evidently be so," Anderson wrote, "but it at present is thickly covered with snow; and the ascent appears, moreover, to be
too steep for horses to go up with loads. A beautiful Rhododendron, with
splendid crimson flowers now in bloom, abounds in this vicinity" (18).

The party had reached Rhododendron Flats in what is now Manning
Park—one of the few places in British Columbia where the California
rhododendron grows wild. These evergreen shrubs grow in thickets, each
plant standing six to twelve feet tall with branches that stretch towards the
sunlight. Unlike other rhododendron, the California rhododendron grows
under trees, in forests of Douglas fir, cedar, or ponderosa pine. The plant
blooms spectacularly in early June, and Anderson picked a blossom and
preserved it in his Latin Bible.[7]

The HBC men began the climb up the hill, reaching the summit of the
mountain ridge at noon. "The ascent is very gentle," Anderson said, "and
perfectly clear of impediment throughout the greater part; frequent fires
having destroyed the timber that heretofore encumbered the ground"
(18–19). At the top of the hill there were a few snowdrifts, but Anderson
was not concerned about what he would find on the north side of the
mountain ridge. His journal continues:

> But alas! On reaching the summit a dreary prospect met
> the view. The whole surface of the valley, as well as of
> the confining mountains, was white with accumulated
> snow. The difference is of course ascribable to the rela-
> tive positions of the opposite side; that by which we
> ascended has a southern exposure, lying open, conse-
> quently, to the full influence of the sun's rays, aided by
> the southern winds, and vice versa.

> There is a small lake here bearing a marvellous similitude, in some respects, to the 'Committee's Punch Bowl' in the Rocky Mountains. It is still covered with ice, save in one small spot, where through the limpid water, the bottom is seen shelving off, apparently to an immense depth. Our Indian assistants turn back hence, according to agreement; save three who wish to visit their relations in the Nicontamene country. We have no one who knows anything of the country beyond this point. The water must guide us. (19)

Anderson named the lake Council's Punch Bowl, and his party rested on its shores. In a map drawn more than ten years later, Anderson indicated the position of "Anderson's Tree," which stood southeast of the lake. This was, in all likelihood, a "lobstick," or maypole tree: a bushy-topped pine or cedar tree lopped of many of its branches and bearing a flat surface on which the man it honoured carved his name. Making a maypole tree to honour a man or a special occasion was a long-standing tradition among the voyageurs, and like all voyageur traditions, it followed the fur traders across the Rocky Mountains. In 1847, Paul Kane described the making of a lobstick to honour him as he waited at Boat Encampment (an important fur trade encampment; now a historic site buried beneath Kinbasket Lake) for the incoming Columbia Express.[8] Anderson's Tree, created one year earlier, likely honoured the fact that Anderson's group of explorers had reached a height of land that no other HBC man had yet seen.

Anderson's journal continues:

> Left height of land at 2.20, and after walking 3 hours through a country presenting every facility for a horse road, save the depth of snow, we encamped on the right bank of the descending stream, which I take for granted is one of the tributaries of the Similkameen [Tulameen River]. The whole country is still thickly covered with snow; but we have found a clear spot among the Cypress [Lodgepole pine] to encamp upon, and are very comfortable. The depth of snow hereabout is from 3 to 4 feet in general. About the height of land, as nearly as I could judge, it varied from 10 to 12 feet on the levels. Fortunately it was sufficiently compact to support us; and, except for an occasional plunge leg deep, we did not sink

beyond our shoe tops [moccasins]. Nearer our encampment the snow was softer, and the difficulty of walking
became proportionately enhanced. (19–20)

Overall, Anderson was not too alarmed by the deep snow. "Up to this
spot, snow only excepted, I see no insuperable obstacles to a horse road,"
he wrote. "It would of course be practicable only at a later season, when
the disappearance of the snow, and the low waters (natural concomitants)
would have removed the chief natural impediments. All the Indians I have
met with concur in their statement, that the snow is usually all disappeared
at the Poire [service-berry] season—that is, from the beginning to the
middle of July" (20).

The party set out early in the morning the next day and found that the
freezing temperatures had formed a crust on the snow that enabled the
men to walk across its slippery surface. They crossed several small streams
that flowed into the main river and made their way along what they considered a good road. At noon the "defile began to contract, and we have
since been traveling through an abominable country, impracticable for
horses" (20). But there was good news too:

> We saw the track of 3 persons about noon. The Indians
> are quite at a loss as to our position, knowing nothing of
> the country, and puzzling themselves and the Interpreter
> (Montigny) with fifty silly conjectures, sometimes sup-
> posing themselves upon a fork of the branch of the
> Thompson River that falls in near its junction with Fra-
> ser's River [Nicoamen River]. In fact, all of them seem
> to be much dispirited, but as I feel pretty secure, from
> the course which the river seems to follow (apparently
> bending round eastward in advance of us), that we are
> upon the right stream, so I have no anxiety on the sub-
> ject. We saw & heard siffleur ["whistler"] marmots today
> and yesterday, but have killed none. One of the men
> [Charbonneau] got lost today, and I had to ascend the
> side of a mountain to find him, which I at length did by
> falling upon and following up his track. (20–21)

The "siffleur" marmots are large groundhogs or ground squirrels that
live in colonies on the high mountain ridges of the Tulameen Plateau, where
they can hide away in the rocks. Their whistles alert others of danger. First

Nations men hunted them for their soft, rich skins, from which they made warm robes. In the late summer the marmots grew especially fat, providing a delicious meal for anyone who could trap them.

Anderson's journal continues:

> Friday 5th June—Continue as before. The river bends round very gradually towards East, receiving several tributaries of some magnitude from left side; others of inferior consideration upon that on which we are traveling. Upon most of these we find drift trees to serve our purpose; but have occasionally (the waters being high) to fell a tree for a bridge. About 10 a.m. the country began to open out a little; and a few scattered Red Firs [ponderosa pine] appeared—an encouraging indication that we are approaching the level country. (21)

The river they were following was the Tulameen River, which flowed across the top of the Tulameen Plateau and down its northern edge, eventually joining the Similkameen at Red Earth Fork (Princeton). Anderson's party had walked the east bank but soon hoped to cross the stream, "both because the country appeared more favorable for walking; and because we were fearful from the increasing magnitude of the stream, of experiencing great difficulty to cross lower down, as we must necessarily do eventually" (21). His men spent three hours felling large trees to make a bridge, but were forced to abandon their plans when the water flowed over the tree trunks, making the bridge too dangerous to use. But all was not lost:

> A few miles lower down, however, to our great satisfaction [we] found a stoppage of drift trees in a rapid, when the river is about 30 yards in breadth. Fearful of its being soon swept off, we placed hurriedly an extra tree or two to connect the sides more firmly; and taking off our shoes to avoid slipping in the wet drift wood, succeeding in our object. Altogether our bridge was a tremulous and marvellously unsteady affair; and my mind was relieved of no small degree of anxiety when I saw the whole party safely across. The old proverb tells us to 'bless the bridge which carries us safe over,' and I say not do less than this, our friend in need, however dubious its pretension to security.

> What with the delay thus occasioned, and the rugged nature
> of the country, our progress today has been very small—
> perhaps 10 miles or so. But the fatigue of the day has
> been great, and the weakest of our men are low. (21–22)

The river now curled to the east, and the men followed its course around the curve, breakfasting on a feeder that flowed in from the north. They felled a tree to cross the stream and discovered "vestiges of horses at this place. After breakfast found a beaten road and soon fell in with the recent tracks of horses. A fine open country before us—Red Firs, with little or no underwood" (22). His journal continues:

> Proceed six miles and meet two Indians, who proved to
> be old Black-eye, the Similkameen, and his son-in-law,
> on their way to visit their deer snares. It appearing that
> we are about 20 miles from the Red Earth Fork, the
> appointed rendezvous, the old man sent his son-in-law
> on horse-back to have our horses brought to us; promis-
> ing to guide us by a shorter and better road to fall upon
> the track to Kamloops. This, as the river shortly makes a
> great stretch South-eastward, I can readily credit, and
> therefore willingly accede to. (22–23)

Anderson had not previously met Black-eye, but he seemed to be aware of who he was. This Upper Similkameen chief was well received at the Kamloops post, and John Tod had probably told Anderson to look for Black-eye's help. For the HBC men of the day, the more familiar road would have been the Zouchameen Road that led north from Red Earth Forks through a wide fault, brushing past Gulliford Lake on its way to Quilchena Creek. Now Anderson viewed the course of the Tulameen as it turned towards the south and Red Earth Fork, and he thought that Black-eye's trail might be a better road to Kamloops. The HBC men walked north towards Black-eye's lodge, following a stream to Otter Lake, where they set up camp. "Our provisions are exhausted," Anderson wrote, "but the old man supplies us with a few fresh carp, which though nowise tempt-ing at another time, are very acceptable now" (23).

Before he left Black-eye's camp, Anderson talked with the Similka-meen man:

> Black-eye (who it appears was trusted implicitly in these
> points by the late Mr. [Samuel] Black [of Kamloops]) informs

me that the horse road to the height of land strikes straight across the bend of the river, and falls beyond our encampment of the 3rd inst. [Council's Punch Bowl]. He states that it is a wide and good road, with plenty of pasturage at the proper season; and that but for the depth of the snow, we could not have missed seeing it after crossing the height of land. It is of course very short as compared with the long and painful circuit made by us. He says they never go with their horses in that direction beyond the spot where we fell in with their tracks this morning. The road mentioned by Black-eye is that by which all, or most, of the Indians of the neighbourhood proceed every summer (in July) to the height of land with their horses, to hunt Siffleurs and gather roots; a journey of two days with their loaded horses. He expresses his willingness to guide us through it at the proper season; but like the rest of the country in that vicinity, it is impossible at present owing to the snow. This of course renders it futile for me to think of visiting it now, which, under other circumstances, I should have wished to do; as by determining the practicability of the passage in question (should the fact of the Indian road passing it not sufficiently do so) the only part of the communication which I have deemed impassable, would be satisfactorily avoided. (23–24)

Anderson spoke to Black-eye through his interpreter, Edouard Montigny. On the map in his journal, he indicated the route of the "Indian horse road recommended by Black-eye," which led directly from Campement des Femmes (where the stream that flowed out of Otter Lake joined the Tulameen River) to the lake Anderson had called the Council's Punch Bowl. He presumed that Black-eye's trail descended the south side of the plateau to the place where the California rhododendron bloomed. It did not, but it would be three years before Anderson realized this. His journal continues:

Sunday 7th June—Rainy. Our horses reach us at 5 p.m. They had been waiting at the rendezvous two days. Though late, we made a start and went about 3 miles to the end of a second lake of smaller dimensions [Frembd Lake], communicating with the first. We have received a supply of salmon by the horses, sufficient, with economy, to take us to Kamloops. Course N by W. (24)

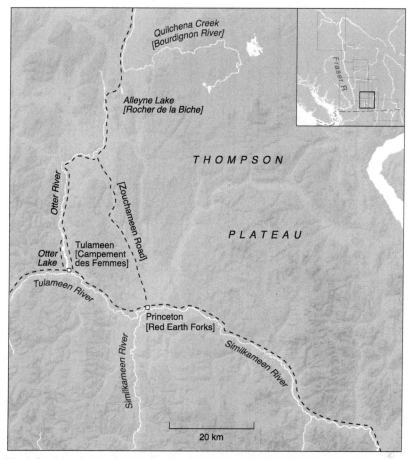

Map 9: Similkameen River north to Bourdignon River (Quilchena Creek). The Indigenous road Black-eye showed Anderson in 1846 led the HBC men up Otter River to Quilchena Creek and Nicola Lake, and in 1849 it became the route to and from Campement des Femmes for the HBC brigades.

On the next day the men set out at 4:00 a.m., walking along Otter Creek and passing a third small lake, now named Thynne ("thin") Lake. There they left the stream and walked across country, "through a fine country till we fall on the Zouchameen Road a little above the Rocher de la Biche" (24), which might be Mount Pike. His journal continues:

> Proceed along it about 10 miles Westward of N, then
> 5 miles NNE to encampment on McDonald or Bourdi-
> gnon's River [Quilchena Creek], a stream falling into Lac
> de Nicholas [Nicola Lake]. Our road today has lain, for
> the greater part of the distance, through a charming coun-
> try. Beautiful swelling hills, covered with rich verdure,

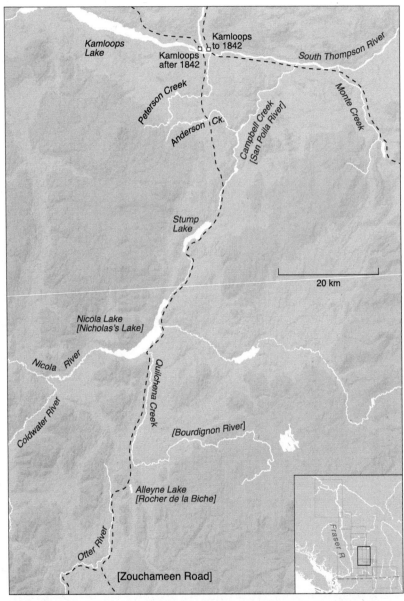

Map 10: Rocher de la Biche north to Kamloops. Once beyond Rocher de la Biche [Doe Elk Rocks/Mtn.], the HBC men followed Quilchena Creek to the Nicola Valley, then rode over the range of hills to Kamloops.

and studded at rare intervals with ornamental clumps of the Red Fir [ponderosa pine] and the aspen. This is the chief characteristic of the scenery; in some directions as far as the eye can reach. (24–25)

The next morning a missing horse delayed them until 5:00 a.m. They followed Bourdignon's River northward to Nicola Lake, where they continued along the lakeshore to another ford "over a stream coming in from a South Easterly direction [Nicola River]" (25).

Anderson's journal continues:

The water was too high for us to cross loaded, so we carried the baggage over upon a tree and drove the horses across light. Breakfasted here. This is a much frequented summer fishery of the Nicontamenes. Many of them are set out on their return towards Thompson's River to gather roots and prepare for the salmon fishery. Those who remain supplied us liberally with fresh carp. (25)

At 10:00 a.m. they set out on their way to Kamloops, and at 1:00 p.m. reached Sans Poila River, now Campbell Creek. There they rested the hard-working horses, "whose feet are very sore—they having been constantly on the march since spring" (25). From Campbell Creek they set out for Kamloops, reaching the post at 6:30 p.m.:

Thus we reach the point whence we set out in 26 days, including the day of our departure, 10 of which (including one of detention by high water) were occupied on the downward journey, 3 at Fort Langley, and 13 (including a day of detention waiting for the horses to reach us, and the greater part of another lost near Tlae-kullum [Silverhope Creek]) on the way back. (26)

Anderson reached Fort Alexandria on June 13, leaving plenty of time to prepare for the return of the New Caledonia brigades.[9]

———

Over the winter, the members of the Board of Management reconsidered their position on Anderson's suggested trail over the Tulameen Plateau. In January 1847, Ogden wrote to commend Anderson on the work he had done, but asked him to explore a new route in the summer.

Ogden's letter read:

> Recent information received by Chief Factor Douglas a
> short time since induces us to hope that a route can be
> opened from Langley to Thompson's River even more
> favorable than the one you returned by. The great objec-
> tion to it appears solely to arise from the depth of snow
> that the Brigade might be liable to meet with and while
> there is a prospect of another route being found prefer-
> able we feel most anxious to ascertain if it be, so ere we
> decide on commencing operations we consider it highly
> expedient that it should be explored.[10]

Montrose McGillivray, Métis son of Simon McGillivray of the NWC,
delivered the letter from Ogden and stayed at Fort Alexandria to accompany Anderson on the 1847 expedition.

⭈ 5 ⭇

MAY 1847: KAMLOOPS TO FORT LANGLEY

On April 23, 1847, Chief Trader Donald Manson left Fort St. James with his outgoing brigade, arriving at Fort Alexandria eight days later. Manson had arrived in the Columbia district in 1825, and in 1844 was assigned the charge of the New Caledonia district when Chief Factor Peter Skene Ogden left the territory. It would have been natural for him to expect to be promoted to chief factor, like all others who had come before him; the promotion, however, did not take place. Now forty years old, he was a giant of a man—tall, muscular, and active. While there was no apparent animosity between Manson and Anderson in 1847, Manson was a violent and hot-tempered man who did not get along with his own employees. Nor did he easily get along with many of the HBC gentlemen he worked with.

An HBC bateau in front of Fort St. James. These flat-bottomed boats resembled the York boats used on the Saskatchewan River but also differed from them.

Normally Anderson would have remained at Fort Alexandria for the summer. On May 7, however, he reported that "the Brigades set out yesterday; I follow today, having been appointed to conduct an expedition to Fort Langley during the summer."[1] On this occasion, he probably rode out with Manson, who may have allowed the brigade to travel ahead on its own.

On his arrival at Kamloops, Anderson was astonished to learn that the boundary line had been drawn along the forty-ninth parallel all the way to the Strait of Juan de Fuca. This made it more likely that at some point in the future the HBC men would be cut off from their Columbia River route to Fort Vancouver. The pressure on Anderson to find an alternative route intensified.

On May 19, Anderson's party set out from Kamloops on its second expedition to Fort Langley, leaving Manson readying his brigades for the journey to the HBC's Columbia River headquarters via the well-established Okanagan trail. Anderson's journal begins with his departure from Kamloops:

> At 10 a.m. set out from Kamloops, striking towards Lac de Nicholas. At 5 p.m. (having delayed to refresh the horses during the interval) we reached the first brook running towards Lac de Nicholas, where we encamped. The party consists of 5 individuals in addition to myself, named—Montrose McGillivray, Edouard Montigny, Theodore Lacourse, Michel Fallardeau, and Joe Desautel. I met with an untoward accident this afternoon which nigh put an end to my explorations for the nonce. My horse stumbled & rolled completely over, I narrowly escaping a broken leg. Fortunately, though painful, the injury is less severe than I first feared.[2]

They camped at the west end of Nicola Lake, "where I had appointed to meet Black-eye, from whom I hope to get some information in regard to the country we are to pass through. He is not yet arrived" (77). The next day, Anderson's party "pursued the usual road followed by our trading parties on their way to the forks" (77).

The "forks" Anderson referred to was the "Grand Fork," or Thlikumcheen (Kumsheen), where Thompson River flowed into the Fraser. Several maps show the shortcut he planned to take: the trail forded the Nicola River west of Nicola Lake and crossed the valley to an apparent gap in the hills that would bring them to the mouth of the Nicoamen. On their arrival at the ford, however, they found the river so deep that they could not cross. As a result, they were forced to follow the rugged east bank of the Nicola River north, "to the mouth of the stream where we expect to find canoes" (77). Anderson noted that:

> as far as the ford in question the road is passably good, but below it, as far as our present encampment the contrary, quite unsuited, indeed, for the passage of many loaded horses ... The country rugged with volcanic rock, wormwood, the cactus known as the Crapaud Vert [Brittle Pricklypear], and Rattlesnakes, characterize the lower land. (77–78)

Indigenous people sitting on a rock with the Thompson River and Spence's Bridge in the background. Photograph by Charles Gentile, 1865.

The HBC men travelled over a rocky road to reach Thlikumcheenâ, or the Petite Forks, at 6.30 a.m.[3] There they breakfasted, sending their horses back to Kamloops with the First Nations man who had accompanied them for that purpose. "Cross the South branch [Nicola River] at its junction with Thompson's River, in a canoe, set out on foot, & after proceeding 16 or 17 miles along the left bank of Thompson's River encamp on a hill close by Nicaomeen. Road hilly but practicable with loaded horses. Very warm, but refreshing breeze" (78).

Anderson's camp was near the Nicoamen River, which drops in a spectacular waterfall down the side of its namesake plateau into the hole it has carved into the rock over the years. From that turbulent pool it is but a short tumble into the rapids-filled Thompson River. Five miles west of the junction of the Thompson and Nicoamen was the Grand Fork, or Thlikum-cheen.

The next morning, another sultry day, Anderson set off on foot down the south bank of Thompson's River. After crossing the Nicoamen on a fallen tree, he reached the fork at 10:45, finding the "river much impeded with rapids, which are said to be worse at a lower state of water" (78).

It was at the Grand Fork, Anderson said, that "the Sierra Nevada or Cascade Range absolutely terminates."[4] The mountain range that appears to break at the mouth of the Thompson River is a series of mountains without an apparent collective name, but which includes Mount Lytton and Kanaka Mountain. Samuel Black, chief trader at Kamloops, had explored a section of country south of the mouth of Thompson's River in the late 1830s. He noted that there were "Terrible Mountains all over Hereabouts."[5] It would not be an easy task to locate a good horse road through or around this mountainous country, but it was Anderson's job to do so.

At Thlikum-cheen, where the Thompson flowed into the muddy Fraser, Pahallak, the Stó:lō chief that Chief Trader Yale of Fort Langley had engaged to guide Anderson for the second time, made his appearance, "accompanied by a large concourse of Indians of every age and sex" (78):

> A general handshaking took place. Before our little arrangements were completed part of the day had elapsed and at the earnest entreaty of the Indians I consented to encamp here. They are on their good behaviour and show every external desire to conciliate, but they are a scampish looking set of vagabonds; nor does their ordinary conduct, I believe, at all belie their looks; and though there is little to be apprehended from them under present circumstances, we are, of course, on our guard ...

> Thompson's River at its junction with the Fraser is restricted within rocky shores to a width of 50–60 yards, flowing smoothly, evidently to a great depth. Its shores above this place consist chiefly of limestone & granite rocks & are very rugged. (78)

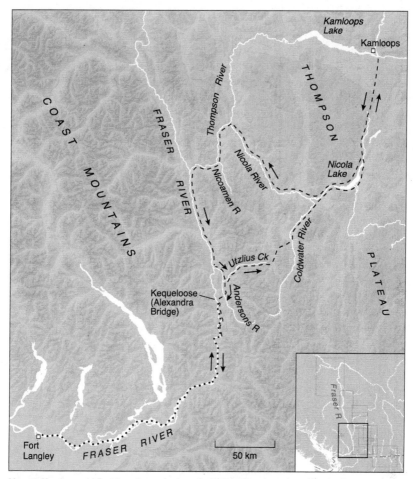

Map 12: Kamloops to Fort Langley and return. In 1847 Anderson explored Fraser River to modern-day Boston Bar, then climbed over Lake Mountain and made his way to Fort Langley. On his return, his party walked up the hill behind Boston Bar, and returned home via the Nicola Valley and Kamloops.

Early in the morning the HBC party started their walk down the banks of the Fraser River, accompanied by their First Nations guides. After enjoying an early breakfast, they crossed an "impetuous" stream that flowed into the Fraser from the east. They had reached Siska Creek, where they encountered the first of many primitive bridges built by the First Nations. Anderson's journal read:

> Owing to the height of the water, we did not cross at the usual ford, but on a tree higher up. To regain the road it is necessary to scale the edge of a precipice which is effected

with the aid of a long withe of plane, fixed there permanently by the natives for the purpose. (78)

The "withe of plane" was a pole or large branch, one end of which rested on the broken rocks of the narrow trail, while the other end might have been suspended from the overhanging cliffs with deer-hide ropes. The First Nations guides crossed their flimsy bridges with confidence, but the HBC men clutched the rock face and inched their way across, knowing that one false step would cause the poles to sway out and dump the traveller into the stream below.

On this occasion, the HBC men regained the banks of the Fraser River with relative ease. "Four miles further on a stream falls in on the opposite side, 3 miles below which we dined: a little beyond a village called Skaoose, said to enjoy a good sturgeon fishery" (78). Skaoose probably stood just south of Falls Creek.

Anderson's journal continues:

> 4 ½ miles further to a stream called Lzaehoose [Nowhokan Creek], 15 yards wide. From the forks to this place the mean course is about South by East. Hence to Squâ-zoum as pointed out to me, S.E. by S, 4 ½ miles further a stream called Kapthe [Inkitsaph]; thence 3 miles to camp at 6.20 p.m., making a total by my computation of 28 ½ miles. (78)

Anderson mentions "Squâ-zoum as pointed out to me." One of Anderson's companions on this journey, unidentified until later, was Black-eye's son, who must have joined the HBC party after Anderson had noted his father's absence at the meeting place on Nicola Lake. By the time the party reached today's Nowhokan Creek, Black-eye's son had told Anderson of a newly opened trail that led up the hills behind the village of Squâ-zoum, still some distance downriver.

So far, Anderson was disappointed in this journey down the banks of the Fraser River. "My report of the country we have passed through must, I regret, be unfavorable," he wrote (78). His journal continues:

> In the vicinity of the village called Skaoose is a succession of rocky hills, some of which are avoidable by making a circuit, while others appear to offer no such alternative. And though I do not condemn these passages as <u>impassable</u> with horses, in the strict acceptation of that term,

I decidedly think them quite impracticable for a loaded brigade, or loaded horses, however limited in number, or indeed for anything beyond possibly a light horse or so. These rocky passages extend for a long distance, nor did all my enquiries of Pahallak or others, satisfy me that any means of obviating the difficulty exist. (78–79)

Another problem he noted was the roughness of the path which was "studded with pebbles and sharp projecting fragments of volcanic rock" (79), which would damage the horses' feet. However, the Nlaka'pamux who lived along this section of the Fraser River seemed friendly, something they were not always known to be:

We have fallen in with a good many Indians today who receive us with clamorous vociferations of welcome, expressed in a peculiar and amusing style of oratory. We are now encamped near a populous village, one & all, I believe, fairly wearied out. A day's march among the arid hills of Fraser's River, with the thermometer between 80 & 90° in the shade, is a trying matter, however willing the spirit. (79)

"Fraser Canyon, British Columbia, 1887. Below North End." Likely North Bend is meant, as the town was founded in early 1880s as a CPR town. Photograph by Edward H. Phillips, ca. 1900.

Early the next morning, the party started their walk down the river-bank, crossing the River Tse-wamnia (Ainsley Creek) at its embouchure in canoes they borrowed from the Nlaka'pamux. At 11:00 a.m. they crossed a stream called Tummuhl (Stoyama Creek), "near which is a village containing 120 inhabitants of all ages. Part of these are busily engaged erecting a stockade enclosure, as security against enemies" (79). The HBC men mistrusted these First Nations communities because they were always at war with each other and had little interest in, or connection to, the fur trade.

The next village they came to was Squâ-zoum, "a populous village of Indians. The immediate banks of the river are clearly wooded with cedar, pines, and the plane tree; behind the hills rise somewhat abruptly and are in parts free from timber, affording good & abundant pasture" (79). On their arrival at Squâ-zoum, the entire party set off to explore what Anderson called "the horse road to the Similkameen country" (79). This newly opened horse trail followed the Squâ-zoum (Anderson) River and today's Utzlius Creek up the hills behind the village. Anderson was pleased to report that:

> the feasibility of a horse communication with Squâ-zoum is established more successfully than I at first anticipated, having always understood that no practicable passage for horses existed down the hill to the river side. Such indeed appears to have been the case by the road once followed. It is only recently that the Similkameens have examined the country, and opened a new road, which the height of the hill alone excepted, is unexceptionable in its facilities of ascent or descent. Thus far on our route since leaving the Similkameen road, the country is favorable, but I defer special observations until hereafter.
>
> P.S. There is abundance of fine pasture about Squâ-zoum. The land is level near the immediate banks of the river. Ascending the hills the herbage is very luxuriant, and the surface of the ground bedecked with larkspur, the red flowering vetch, and the flaunting glories of the dwarf Sunflower, presents an agreeable contrast to the arid declivities through which our way has hitherto lain in many parts. (80)

Anderson noted that the country at the top of the hill was familiar to his guide Montigny, "who has passed through it with horses several times"

(80). Michel Ogden, son of Peter Skene Ogden, had also passed through it, and Anderson wrote that "their united testimony goes to represent it as favorable for our purpose, after the bestowal of some labour upon it. I am thus relieved from the necessity of examining the path in question personally until my return, when I shall be able to do so more effectually, meanwhile devoting all our endeavours to connect this point with the country about the falls" (80)—the falls being the strong set of rapids south of Hell's Gate and Black Canyons, which Archibald McDonald had named "Simpson's Falls" for Governor George Simpson in 1828 (see Chapter 2).

Having established there was a possible trail to the Nicola Valley by the Squâ-zoum River, Anderson now had to discover whether there was a route south from Squâ-zoum, past the rapids of the canyons. Pahallak suggested that a trail over Lake Mountain, immediately south of the Squâ-zoum River, was feasible.

The next morning they set off at 3:00 a.m., crossing Utzlius Creek about a mile from the encampment, ascending a hill, and following along its brow. Anderson was told that from this spot it was possible to rejoin "the present horse road considerably above where we diverged from it, so as to materially shorten the distance" (80). They breakfasted beside the east branch of the Squâ-zoum (East Anderson) River, and then crossed it on a fallen tree:

> It is impetuous & stony. At the present state of water it would be difficult, if not impossible, to cross horses, without constructing a bridge. Breadth of stream about 40 ft. Pass over the interjacent tongue of land & reach the Southern branch of the stream [Anderson River]. These 2 branches unite a little below. Lost a good part of the day in making a bridge at the second branch, and in examining the neighbourhood. (81)

The exploring party crossed today's East Anderson River and then followed it upstream for a few miles before beginning their clamber up the side of Lake Mountain. Anderson reported that "the ascent is tedious, but by making the road deviously, the inconveniences of the hill may be easily overcome" (81). What he meant is that the HBC men would build switchbacks up the rocky slope, making the hill easier for the horses to climb.

Anderson's journal continues:

> Upon the top of the mountain is an even surface free from underwood extending a couple of miles, when by diverging

a little to the right, Fraser's River is again seen winding below. Mr. McGillivray being taken unwell, we abandoned the intention of proceeding down to the river, & we are camped upon the brow of the mountain. Around us are a few patches of snow.

I struck off the road to take a bird's eye view of a rapid which obstructs the navigation near this spot & which is said not to be practicable at this season. Judging from the agitated appearance of the stream as seen from our elevated position, this rapid is a succession of dangerous whirlpools, apparently unnavigable, and I am informed unavoidable by portage. It resembles some of the Columbia rapids in the dalle-like formation of the banks, and there seemed to me to be little facility for putting out the line. But the Indians say that it loses its dangerous character at a lower state of the water. (81)

Far below his viewpoint atop the mountain, all the water that flowed down the Fraser River pushed its way through narrow, curving Hell's Gate and Black Canyons. At their narrowest point, the canyons were only 110 feet wide. In passing through the two canyons in 1828, Governor Simpson described riverbanks that "erected themselves into perpendicular Mountains of Rock from the water's edge."[6] Anderson stood on the top of those same mountains, looking down at the thundering river below. The freshets began at the end of April and reached their height in the middle of June.[7] At its height, the surge of water piled up until the river was as much as 60 feet deeper than it had been in March.[8] No one could come safely down this river and through these canyons in summertime, when the water was so high.

In the morning the party set off on foot down the south side of Lake Mountain, following the First Nations footpath through the heavy forest. It took them two hours of "slow travelling" to reach the village of Kequeloose on the river, although Anderson believed "the track may be easily improved and by making an occasional circuit a good horse road may be constructed" (81).

Kequeloose was the southernmost Secwepemc village and stood just north of the place where the first Alexandra Bridge was constructed twenty years later. From Kequeloose, Pahallak led the HBC party down the east bank of the Fraser until they stood across the river from the Nlaka'pamux village at Spuzzum Creek:

The water flows rapidly down the river in this impressive view of the Fraser River Canyon. Photograph by Edward H. Phillips, ca. 1900.

From Kequeloose it took us 2 ½ hours to reach Spuzzum, the ferry proposed by Pahallak, a distance of about 6 miles. The country is very rough & much labour with many painful circuits would be necessary to complete a road anywise practicable for horses. There is a village upon the right [west] bank of the river, at the mouth of a stream [Spuzzum Creek] issuing from the direction of Lillooet Mountains. Procured a canoe & after some delay succeeded in crossing. At this season both the nature of the banks and the strength of the water preclude the practicability of a horse ferry upon a large scale, nor is there any spot near suitable for this purpose. (82)

In a later letter to Governor Simpson, Anderson indicated his skepticism of Pahallak's plan to swim horses across the Fraser River at Spuzzum Creek:

From the character of the informants [the Stó:lō] who are quite ignorant of the powers of the horse, I was from the first not sanguine of success, and the result justified my anticipations. I was reluctantly compelled to condemn the proposed scheme unconditionally. By the plan laid out it was necessary to cross Fraser's River with the horses a few miles above the Falls: a hard condition under any circumstances, and in such a locality, where to swim horses is almost an impossibility, presenting obstacles next to insurmountable with our means.[9]

If it was impossible to swim horses across the river, the animals must remain at some place that offered good feed, and the furs must be delivered to Fort Langley by boat. The upriver journey must also be possible, as the HBC men would have to carry their trade goods by boat to the place where they left the horses.

First, Anderson had to discover whether it was possible to travel to Fort Langley through the rapid-filled section of the river the HBC men called the Falls. "The information I had recently received from the Indians induced me to hope that means of overcoming the obstacles, by portage & otherwise, might possibly be devised" (82). He sent McGillivray down-river by the land track marked on Pahallak's sketch, "while with Montigny & some Indians I proceeded in a canoe by the river" (82). In a little more than half an hour the canoe party reached the head of the Falls. McGillivray did not arrive until several hours later, "reporting very unfavorably on the road. We are now encamped upon a rocky eminence about 2/3rds of the distance down the rapids" (82).

Anderson now faced a descent of the toughest part of the Fraser, at a season of high water when even First Nations travellers did not use the river. In his letter to Simpson, he wrote that for three miles the river rushed "between rocky precipices, towering in parts to a height of 600 feet or more. From these lofty escarpments, however, enormous fragments have toppled down, which, protruding on the stream, present a perpendicular, and apparently unbroken, front of solid rock."[10] In his journal, Anderson wrote that "these rapids extend at the present stage of water, with intervals of navigable space, for a distance of about 3 miles, confined in some parts between lofty walls of rock" (82). He also noticed that on both sides of the river were "numerous scaffolds upon which the natives suspend their salmon to dry, at the proper season" (83).

Anderson thought that the first stage of the rapid might be run loaded, as it seemed free from danger. Ascent, however, would be much more difficult. "But in either direction there is every facility on the right hand side for carrying both boats & cargo by the portage, 630 paces in length, used by the natives for the purpose" (82). The second stage, a couple of hundred yards down the river, appeared relatively easy. "The third stage is formed by a rocky island in the middle of the river, where a portage over a rocky point upon the right shore is again quite practicable" (83). (The rocky island was later named for Lady Franklin.) "Below this we are encamped," Anderson noted (83).

On the next morning they resumed their journey "as soon as daylight enabled us to thread our way among the broken rocks" (83). A little downriver from their encampment they faced another rapid, which they bypassed by portaging over a rocky point on the river's east bank. "This is the lowest Rapid of the series, save one which is unworthy of our notice," Anderson said. "I have no hesitation in pronouncing my opinion that they are far from presenting an insurmountable obstacle to our progress, even at the present high state of water" (83).

Once they were past the rapids, "the pathway led along a dangerous causeway of cedar boards connecting the several projecting points of a precipice" (83). Once again on terra firma, the men waded across a stream and walked into the first palisaded village of the Tait people. "Here we breakfasted," Anderson said, "being supplied by the inhabitants with excellent fresh salmon and well preserved potatoes of fine quality" (84). Anderson hired canoes from the Tait residents, and he and his party reached Fort Langley at seven o'clock that evening. "At the present high stage of the water, the current is very swift in the middle of the stream" (84).

On his way down the Fraser, Anderson encountered many different First Nations, the three major ones being the Nlaka'pamux (Couteaux); the Secwepemc (Atnah), who had a single village, Kequeloose, on this section of the Fraser; and the Tait (Yale First Nation), whose village was where Fort Yale was built in 1848. The Nlaka'pamux lived in palisaded villages up and down the banks of the Fraser from Spuzzum to the junction of the Thompson River and along the Thompson itself, and were related to the Secwepemc, who lived on the Fraser north of Thlikum-cheen.

The Secwepemc at Kequeloose were closely related to those who lived in the Nicola Valley, as the Coldwater River and the trail over the plateau had always been used by this First Nations group as a route to the Fraser River fisheries. Anderson had not yet met many members of the communities that lived below the barrier of Simpson's Falls, although his guide, Pahallak, was one. Pahallak, however, lived closer to Fort Langley than the Tait, who resided in the extreme south end of the Fraser Canyon.

Of all these First Nations people now present, only the Secwepemc, and some Nlaka'pamux who lived along the Thompson River and in other places closer to the Kamloops post, were connected to the fur trade and as a result were considered part of the HBC community. Both the more isolated Nlaka'pamux, most of whose communities lined the rugged banks of the Fraser, and the Tait were entirely independent of the HBC's fur trade. To the HBC men these First Nations people were warlike strangers; people to be wary of and not entirely trusted. "Poor, naked, and numerous," Anderson wrote of the Nlaka'pamux along the Fraser, "the habitual treachery and vindictiveness of their character are fostered by the ceaseless feuds which they entertain with all around. Nearly every family has a minor vendetta of its own to prosecute."[11] Of the Tait, he wrote, "Cowardly and treacherous to a degree, these Indians possess all the vices of the coast tribes, while exhibiting none of the redeeming qualities of the interior nations."[12]

Paradoxically, Anderson did not witness the treachery he wrote of; in fact, he experienced the opposite. "I was received among these people with the kindest demonstrations, certainly at the time sincere," he wrote. "Man, woman and child at every village brought a trifling present of welcome, whether of fish, wild fruits, or other local production."[13] So even though he wrote that "Everything was *coleur de rose* on these occasions," the stories Anderson carried with him, told to him by members of other HBC communities, made him aware that, at any moment, everything could go disastrously wrong.[14]

Only three First Nations men came down to Fort Langley: presumably Black-eye's son and his two companions. It is likely that the Stó:lō guides dropped out of the expedition as they passed their home villages. At the fort, Yale offered Anderson the use of some of his employees to help him return upriver, but Anderson refused. He decided "on returning as I came, trusting to hire Indians to assist my men (of whom I had three only available for labour) in my subsequent operations. After a delay of three days, we set out; having procured one of the larger sized North West canoes, which I resolved, if possible, to take up to the Falls, thereby to set the question of practicability at rest."[15]

6

JUNE 1847:
EXPLORATION, FORT LANGLEY TO KAMLOOPS

After a three-day rest at Fort Langley, Anderson and his men began their journey up Fraser River to Kequeloose. His plan was to follow the trail over Lake Mountain, up the hillside via Utzlius Creek, to the Coldwater River, and finally to Kamloops. The original journal has been lost, but Anderson's updated personal copy still exists:

> June 1 [1847]—Left Fort Langley at 8.50 a.m. and at 7 p.m. camped a couple of miles below the fishery. Very sultry. Our party consists of the same individuals as on the way down. In addition to the canoe hired below the Falls, which is manned by part of our Indians, we have a large N.W. Coast canoe which we took up last year. The first will be left with its owner below the Falls. The second it is my wish to take as far as Kequeloose, the spot where I propose the horse portage to commence, thus to afford evidence that the navigation is available so far.[1]

The next day it rained heavily, and they encamped across the river from Pahallak's village.[2] On June 3 they travelled through rain and camped early at the foot of the rapids close to the Tait village they had passed through on their way downriver. "The water has fallen a good deal since we passed" (85). It appears that the level of the water in the Fraser River, which was normally at its highest in mid-June, was already subsiding.

Anderson's journal continues:

> June 4—Rainy. Commenced ascending the Rapids, cross to the eddy at the foot, make a short portage and re-embark. This portage is over a rocky point. There is a low defile

passing behind on which is a good Indian track, but it is considerably longer. This rapid is occasioned by a rocky island in mid-channel [Lady Franklin's Rock]. At a lower stage of water it might be easily navigated. At present, light boats, might, I conceive, be taken up with a line, or at most require to be transported for a short distance at the worst part. A series of eddies conducts to a second portage upon the same side (right ascending). It is 700 paces in length & very favorable in its nature. Carried our canoe here, or rather dragged it, for the overhanging branches prevented our carrying. (85)

As he made his way upriver, Anderson noted the heavily treed banks of the Fraser River. "The country, from the mouth of Frazer's River up to the Falls, is thickly wooded, mountainous, and impassible, so to speak, for man or beast. The river becomes more contracted above Fort Hope. Above the Falls, as far as Squâ-zoum, the character of the country continues to resemble the same distance below. At Squâ-zoum, however, as already noticed, a change takes place, and the evidences of a drier climate begin to appear."[3]

The men paddled across the river to its east bank and breakfasted at the foot of a rapid formed by an isolated rock that lay near what Anderson called "left shore." The HBC tradition of naming a riverbank "left" or "right" based on the bank that was on the trader's left or right side as he descended the river, meant that, in this case, the rocky islet was close to the east bank of the Fraser River.

The heavily forested shoreline with its thick underbrush created difficulties for the party all the way to Anderson's River. From the rapid, the First Nations men proposed to cross the river "in order to ascend with the line on the opposite side" (86). Anderson noted that:

all went very well, when, after almost every obstacle except the last rapid had been surmounted, an untoward accident occurred. The line, which was composed of several lengths of half-worn cod line (none other being procurable at Fort Langley), notwithstanding that we had doubled it as a precaution, suddenly broke, owing to the canoe taking a sheer out while the steersman was disembarked. An Indian, the bowman, was alone in the canoe. It was swept downwards with rapidity, in spite of the lad's

exertions to propel it to shore. Fortunately, after running
some of the worst of the rapids, he succeeded in getting
into an eddy, the canoe half full of water. (86)

"This untimely mishap greatly disheartened the Indians," wrote Anderson, "and at first some of the near relations became a good deal excited,
taking their arms [trade guns] apparently disposed for evil." But once they
saw their family member was safely ashore at the bottom of the rapids,
Anderson and Montigny were able to calm them down. "After some par-
lay & a smoke the Indians consent to assist us as before" (86). But no one
was willing to trust the rotten lines, so the canoe was transported upriver
by land to their encampment at the head of the Falls. In his private letter
to Governor Simpson, Anderson gave a little more detail of the real danger
that this accident created: "Under the impression that their relative had
gone to the bottom, the natives around showed symptoms of great excitement, and I was for a while suspicious of an attack. But the cloud blew over,
and having restored their good humor we continued our labours."[4]

On June 5 Anderson settled with the First Nations men before setting out
once more on his upriver journey. They reached Spuzzum at 7:00 a.m., and
the village of Kequeloose at 11:00. "Secure the canoe in the woods, being in
charge of Pahallak, and set out on the proposed horse portage at 1.40" (86):

> Having distributed the axes we made the road where
> necessary as we proceeded, & encamped on the summit of
> the hill at 6 p.m. An old man with his followers, to whom
> I lent an axe for the purpose on the way down, has, during
> our absence, rendered good service in tracing and clear-
> ing the road from Kequeloose up to this spot. (86–87)

Anderson later reported to Governor Simpson that, at Kequeloose, he
"hired a score of Indians, and supplying part of them with axes, ... set out
to open the track at once. Thus we proceeded in the direction of the
Similkameen [Nicola] valley, making a road 10 feet wide and quite free of
underwood, until we struck upon the beaten track."[5] In his journal Anderson wrote of the willingness of the First Nations men to work on the trail:

> Today, not being decided as to the line [path] to be adopted
> we merely chipped the road, the Indians undertaking to
> finish it, under the superintendence of Pahallak. Having
> had proof of their willingness & capacity in this line, I
> have no hesitation in confiding the matter to them, more

especially as the distance to be cut is short, the chief portion lying over bare hills. Our horses are not yet arrived,
they ought to have reached this spot to-day, according to
my appointment. (87)

However, not all the First Nations men were happy. "This morning at
the encampment a scampish fellow from a village below the Forks, began
playing pranks *à la mode sauvage*" (87). Anderson continues:

> The scamp in question seized one of the men's guns &
> attempted to pull off the gun cover. Discovering, how-
> ever, his action, Montigny and myself advanced to prevent
> him; Mr. McGillivray with the others standing aloof, in
> readiness to repel any treachery on the part of the rest,
> would they have shown symptoms of interference.
>
> They, however, betrayed no signs of sympathy. The chief
> actor in the scene upon being grappled with, evinced evi-
> dent marks of trepidation, and after a momentary hesitation
> yielded up the gun. I afterwards spoke to the Indians in plain
> terms, enquiring once for all whether we were to look
> upon them as enemies or friends in order that we might
> regulate our conduct accordingly, and whether I was to
> judge their disposition in general, from that manifested by
> the individual in question. They all denied in strong terms
> having any desire to side with him, condemning his con-
> duct, and loading him with long winded objurgations
> with all the energy of their cacophonous dialect. (87–88)

On this occasion, Anderson's harangue was successful in achieving his
goal of turning the other First Nations men against the rogue who threatened the safety of the HBC party. But there were still hazards and the HBC
men remained on guard, waiting for trouble.

On the morning of June 9, Anderson settled with the First Nations who
had built the road, paying them with "ammunition, knives, &c." (88). He
also loaned three axes to the chief of Squâ-zoum, an axe and a hoe to the
Spuzzum chief, and one hoe and three axes to Pahallak. All of these tools
were loaned "for the purpose of making further improvements where necessary in the road, for which they are to be compensated upon our passage in
the spring" (88). Then, as the HBC men set out from their encampment, the
Nlaka'pamux scamp who had troubled them the day before began again:

This morning after all the party had set out from the encampment, as I was bringing up the rear with the interpreter, our friend of yesterday, who had been sitting during the morning moodily aside, ensconced himself behind a tree and cocked his gun. Montigny and myself advanced upon him to ascertain what his intentions might be. Seeing his gun cocked, I took off the cover of my own gun as a precautionary measure, and then directed Montigny to examine that of the Indian, to see if it was primed. The fellow got quite confused, and suffered Montigny to take the gun out of his hand. Eventually the affair assumed rather a ludicrous aspect, since the arm proved to be neither primed nor loaded. The fellow's sole object seems to have been to make a demonstration, either with a view to intimidating us, or to have something to boast of among his comrades. None of the other Indians, I may here remark, interfered; and I state the occurrence as not being irrelevant to the object of this journal. (88)

That night the HBC party encamped at the height of land. On June 10 Anderson reported that all further risk of collision with the First Nations was at an end. The Nlaka'pamux and Stó:lõ men had returned to their villages, and none but their guides from Kamloops were with or near his party. In a letter written to Montrose McGillivray, a copy of which is found in his journal, Anderson gives the names of the First Nations men who were so trusted by the HBC men:

Meanwhile you will employ the men in cutting the road, beginning from the first ford we passed today. The Indian guides now here will point out to you the line it will be necessary to follow, in order to avoid this, and the other fords, which are very great impediments to the present track. Any other improvements I refer entirely to your good judgement, guided by the Indians in question:

Fallardeau, Lacourse, and Desautel remain with you. Also Nicholas' Nephew, Black-eye's son, and Laronetumteun —the last as interpreter. With best wishes, &c, Alex C. Anderson, HBC. (90)

Anderson knew the man he called Tsilaxitsa as a young man, but in later years, Chillihetsa became the legendary head chief of the Okanagan Nation. Artist unknown.

As mentioned, Black-eye's son had joined Anderson's party sometime after Anderson left the west end of Nicola Lake on their way down the river. It appears that his close relative, who Anderson described as "Nicholas' [N'Kuala's] Nephew," accompanied him. N'Kuala had many nephews, but the man the HBC men usually called his nephew was Tsilaxitsa. Thirty years later, in 1877, Anderson, then Dominion representative of the Indian Reserve Commission, mentioned the now-powerful Okanagan chief Tsilaxitsa, whom he had known as a young man: "Sela-heetza, the Chief of the Okinagans, who when a young man travelled with me a good deal..."[6] It appears that both Black-eye's son and Tsilaxitsa accompanied Anderson down the Fraser River to Squâ-zoum and Fort Langley, and both were with him on his return journey to Kamloops.

These two young First Nations men were not only closely related to each other but also direct relations of two well-known First Nations chiefs connected to the Kamloops post: N'Kuala, the grand chief of the Okanagans (whose story is told in Chapter 1), and Black-eye, the Upper Similkameen chief who Anderson met on the Tulameen River in June 1846. As a result of their connections to these two trusted chiefs, both strong friends of the HBC at Kamloops, these two young men were also accepted as trusted members of the HBC community. They acted as informants, guides, and independent contractors for HBC exploration parties; they also had strong connections with the First Nations around them, and their presence in Anderson's party likely helped to prevent conflict with the Nlaka'pamux and Tait, who were relative strangers to the HBC. As we see from Anderson's letter, Tsilaxitsa and Black-eye's son also worked in the HBC brigades. In later years, when the new brigade trail crossed over the Tulameen Plateau, it is likely that Tsilaxitsa and Black-eye's son acted as its guides, taking N'Kuala's position at the head of the brigades.

His letter written, Anderson left Montrose McGillivray with his road-building party and rode on to Kamloops, which he reached on June 11 "after an absence of 24 days, including those of departure & arrival" (90).

After Anderson's exploration party had left Kamloops in May, the New Caledonia brigades also departed from Kamloops and arrived at Fort Vancouver in late June, when James Douglas reported that the Columbia River "did not rise so much as expected this year."[7] After the men had returned to Kamloops, John Tod wrote that "a great scarcity of Salmon was apprehended throughout Thompson's River and New Caledonia districts, from the uncommon low state of the water in all the Rivers."[8] These reports indicate that when Anderson made his way down the Fraser River canyon in May 1847, he travelled it at the season of high water, but in a year when the water was unusually low. On the Columbia River it was generally accepted that lower waters increased the intensity of the rapids, while higher water levels encouraged the formation of whirlpools. In summer 1848, when Anderson again travelled this section of the Fraser, he would notice a marked difference in the behaviour of the river.

Chief Factor James Douglas was made Governor of the Colony of Vancouver's Island in 1851, and in 1858 he became Governor of the Colony of British Columbia. He was knighted in 1864, after his retirement from the HBC. Photograph by Stephen Allen Spencer in 1876.

Anderson's report on his 1847 exploration arrived at Fort Vancouver in September. In the fall, John Work and James Douglas travelled to Fort Langley to become familiar with Anderson's proposed route. While James Murray Yale travelled upriver with James Douglas (accompanied by Douglas's private secretary, William Sinclair, Jr.), Work remained behind at Fort Langley. In a letter to Governor Simpson, Douglas reported that he "proceeded with an Indian Canoe up Fraser's River to the Saumeena Village [Spuzzum], where the horse road to Fort Kamloops falls upon the river, about 100 miles beyond Fort Langley."[9] Douglas was horrified by the ferocity of the rapids. The two HBC gentlemen spent several days examining the chain of rapids known as the Falls, and came away with the opinion that "they will be found exceedingly dangerous at every season, and absolutely impassible in the summer freshets when the River is full, and attains a level of 40 feet above the low water mark in Autumn."[10] At high water, the rapids stretched from side to side of the narrow canyon, where the river appeared to push its way through the mountain barrier, and extended all the way from the Tait village (Yale) north to the village at

Spuzzum Creek, a distance of thirteen miles with few intervals of smooth water. "It is impossible to conceive anything more formidable or imposing than is to be found without that dangerous defile," Douglas said, "which cannot, for one moment, be thought of as a practicable water communication for the transport of valuable property."[11]

Douglas proposed to avoid that perilous section of the river by continuing the horse road an additional thirteen miles, from the lower end of the rapids to the Spuzzum village. "The extension of the horse road must be carried through the mountains," Douglas wrote, "in a narrow winding defile on the north [west] side of Fraser's River ... Though neither smooth nor level, it is practicable, and when the timber is cleared away will make a much better road than we expected to find in so rugged a section of country."[12]

In December, Yale also reported to Simpson on this excursion up the Fraser River:

> I should not presume to say a word on the subject of Mr. Douglas's travels in this quarter were it not that he may omit to say that before he reached the head of the falls he was convinced that Fraser's River was not quite the placid Stream he before seemed to imagine, but he however believed the route to be perfectly practicable by crossing the river and passing through an opening that now bears his name.[13]

Douglas was at Fort Langley in early November. On November 10 Yale "sent off a party of six men with the Interpreter, Ovid Allard,"[14] to build a house and store at the foot of the Falls, and to open a new horse trail by what they now called Douglas's Portage. Douglas and Yale disagreed on when the new trail could be opened. At times they planned for an 1849 completion; on other occasions they spoke of the brigades coming out by the new road in 1848. From Fort Alexandria, Anderson expressed his concern at the changes that Douglas was making to the trail he had explored in 1847. He had recommended that Columbia boats be used on this stretch of river. Although they carried less weight than the Fraser River bateaux, they were lighter and easier to portage. In his letter to Governor Simpson (now Sir George Simpson, as he had been knighted in 1841), Anderson also expressed his concern about Douglas's plan to bring the horses down to the newly constructed Fort Yale, proposing that they cross the river in scows: "But you have descended Fraser's River, Sir

George, and I leave you to imagine the difficulties of ferrying from 2 to 3 hundred horses, in scows, over such a stream as it is in that part, and in the face of the numerous hordes of ragamuffins that infest its banks. I merely hint at this objection, leaving untouched the question of scaling the precipices, or of finding pasture for horses amid those rugged environs."[15]

Although Douglas had spent some time in the New Caledonia district, he had seen only the upper reaches of the Fraser River between Forts George and Alexandria. In 1846, James Murray Yale (who also descended the Fraser River with Governor Simpson) was chief trader in charge of Fort Langley. As a result of his journey down the Fraser with Simpson, Yale knew the river better than any other man in this territory. He understood how the water levels in the river changed with the season, and he knew the dangers of its freshets. As the man in charge of Fort Langley, Yale was also aware of the thousands of First Nations fishermen who swarmed the riverbanks when the salmon came upriver.

Douglas thought he knew better, however, and did not listen. Later HBC men commented on Douglas's lack of geographical knowledge, saying, "His confidence in his knowledge of localities is only exceeded by his deficiency on that Point."[16] Future events would prove them correct.

Unbeknownst to the men in New Caledonia and on the Fraser River, developments out of HBC control that were occurring in American territory meant that a new trail was needed for the brigades, which usually travelled to Fort Vancouver. The Old Brigade Trail was abandoned, and Anderson's trail was now the only one that led to the coast. Although unfinished and untested, this was the trail the HBC men were forced to travel to Fort Langley the next year.

❖ 7 ❖
1847:
FORT VANCOUVER AND WAIILATPU MISSION

From its early days, the HBC's Fort Vancouver was the most important community west of the Rocky Mountains, the centre of civilization for all the non–First Nations people who lived and worked in the Columbia district. When first constructed in the 1820s, the fort stood 318 feet square. By 1836 it had doubled in size, and in the 1840s its employees extended the palisades by another hundred feet. The chief factor's residence was an impressive one-storey building with two old-fashioned muzzle-loading cannons prominently displayed on its front steps. The Fort Vancouver stores stocked British goods of all sorts, and the missionaries who came to the Columbia described it as the "New York of the Pacific."

The first outsiders in the Columbia district were the American or European missionaries who, against the advice of the HBC gentlemen, established their missions among the Indigenous peoples on both sides of the Cascade Mountains. The Wesleyans, under Reverend Jason Lee, were sent to the Columbia by the American Methodist Mission Board and established missions in the Willamette Valley, at The Dalles, and near Fort Nisqually (Tacoma, WA). The Presbyterians, also from the eastern United States, confidently established themselves among the First Nations east of the Cascades: Henry Spalding built Lapwai Mission among the Nez Percés; Dr. Marcus Whitman established Waiilatpu among the Cayuse, twenty-five miles east of Fort Nez Percés; and Cushing Eells and Elkanah Walker built their Tshimakain mission near now-abandoned Spokane House. The Roman Catholics arrived last of all, and a few of these unstoppable missionaries penetrated New Caledonia as far north as the HBC's northern headquarters at Fort St. James, on Stuart's Lake, in north central British Columbia.

In 1842 a few American citizens travelled over the Oregon Trail to settle in the Willamette Valley. Two years later almost three hundred wagons travelled west from St. Louis, in what was then Louisiana Territory; by autumn 1847, more than three thousand Americans had settled in the Willamette Valley. With the arrival of these immigrants, gradual but significant changes took place in Oregon Territory.

As mentioned in Chapter 3, everyone in the territory was aware that the British and American governments were negotiating the placement of the international boundary line west of the Rocky Mountains. The ship HMS *Modeste* remained at anchor off Fort Vancouver in support of the British position. In July 1846, the USS *Shark* arrived in the river. Her captain had been sent to obtain information about the territory and to encourage the American settlers with her presence. In their report to the HBC governor, the members of the Board of Management noted that "before the arrival of the *Shark* the Americans with very few exceptions were settled in the Wallamette [Willamette]." Like many HBC men, the Americans believed the boundary of the United States would follow the Columbia River to its mouth. For this reason, "they never showed much inclination to take lands on the North side" of the Columbia River, where "the Country from being densely wooded is by no means so attractive or favorable for settlement as the beautiful plains of the Wallamette."[1]

Fort Vancouver, as it was painted by Henry James Warre in the fall of 1845.

Two English spies, Lieutenants Henry James Warre, a British army officer, and Mervin Vavasour, a Royal Engineer, disguised themselves as travellers and arrived on the river with Peter Skene Ogden in fall 1845. Over the winter of 1845–46 they examined the country and discussed the situation with Lieutenant William Peel from the British ship HMS *America*, who was also visiting the Columbia. Even while they were in the Columbia district and at Fort Victoria, Warre and Vavasour advised British residents that the "the United States would never accept of any Boundary short of 49°, and that this settlement of Fort Vancouver and all the Country south of that line would certainly become United States property."[2] Although the HBC men blamed Warre and Vavasour for submitting the reports that changed the course of the boundary settlement, it is more likely that the British government rewrote its draft treaty based on information received from Lieutenant Peel, who reached London before Warre and Vavasour's report.

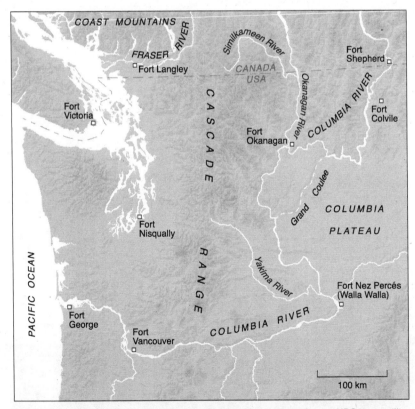

Map 8: Oregon Territory to Fort Okanagan and Similkameen. In the 1850s, nine HBC posts still remained on the Columbia and lower Fraser Rivers, and on Vancouver's Island. Forts Okanagan, Nez Percés, Fort George, and Spokane House (not shown) were the oldest posts in the region and were built by either the Pacific Fur Co. or the North West Company before 1821.

The Oregon Treaty was signed on July 15, 1846, although the official news did not reach the district until the arrival of the Columbia Express (the incoming York Factory Express) at Fort Vancouver in December. The wording of the treaty delighted the Americans and disappointed the HBC men. Instead of following the Columbia River south past Fort Vancouver, the boundary line cut across country, following the forty-ninth parallel to the Strait of Juan de Fuca and west to the Pacific Ocean. Under the new treaty, the HBC retained its possessory rights over land and property until such time as the United States purchased it from them. HBC men were allowed to travel through the territory as they always had done, and they could continue their trade with the First Nations. But the company now had to pay duties on all items imported from Great Britain, a tax of sorts imposed by the American government.

Although many Americans respected the company and understood what the treaty actually said, others had been raised to think of Great Britain as the enemy. The more aggressive Americans squatted on HBC property and tore down the company's fences, using them to build their houses. Others questioned the right of the HBC to trade with First Nations, and many became more assertive and demanding of their supposed rights, questioning the presence of any and all HBC men in the territory. As the HBC gentlemen reported:

> This opinion resting on the authority of a person in whom they had confidence, [the captain of the USS *Shark*], and falling in with their own prepossessions on the subject, produced an [immediate] effect in the settlement, which put the whole host of Yankee speculators and depredators in motion, all rushing towards Vancouver to be in time for a snatch at the loaves and fishes, not a morsel of which was to be left for us, the rightful owners, as they made no secret of their intention to take possession of [illegible word] and of land in this neighbourhood, in defiance of any rights thereto, on the part of the Hudson's Bay Company.[3]

Long before the boundary line was decided, however, the HBC had made changes outside the Columbia district. Governor Simpson's original idea was that Fort Langley could become the HBC's headquarters on the coast, but his journey down the Fraser River in 1828 (see Chapter 2) convinced him that would not work. Acknowledging the need to move HBC headquarters north of the Columbia River, the governor recommended that new headquarters be constructed on Vancouver's Island. James Douglas investigated a waterway on the south end of Vancouver's Island in summer 1842, declaring it the perfect place for a new post. Fort Victoria, which was constructed one year later, would play an important role in the HBC's history, but for now, and for a few years in the future, Fort Vancouver remained the most important Pacific coast post.

By 1847, more trouble was brewing in the Columbia district. The missionaries at the Waiilatpu Mission were experiencing some difficulties with the Cayuse Indians, who were proud and independent traders. The HBC men were always careful to pay for whatever they received from the Cayuse, but Dr. Marcus Whitman took a different tack. On their arrival, the missionaries promised to pay rent for the lands they occupied, but they did not follow through. The Cayuse considered Whitman stingy, and Whitman called the Cayuse savages, heathens, and beggars. Many HBC men warned Whitman that his treatment of the Cayuse was creating a potentially dangerous situation, but Whitman ignored that uncomfortable fact.

Whitman understood that his mission was failing, and he changed its focus to the Americans who made their way west over the Oregon Trail. The newcomers often suffered from dysentery, but in 1847 it appeared they had also brought measles with them. In March 1848, the HBC gentleman at Fort Vancouver reported that the "highly contagious disease has since extended its ravages over the whole country from Fort Hall [Idaho] to Nisqually [Tacoma] and destroyed about one-tenth of the Indian population."[4] As Ogden and Douglas reported to Governor Simpson:

> That appalling circumstance, and the well-known fact that the disease was contracted from the immigrants, excited a strong prejudice in the minds of the Indians, who believe that the Americans are resolved to destroy them. Such feelings took so strong a hold on the minds of the "Cayouse" that in a fit of desperation, they attacked the American mission at Waiilatpu, near Walla Walla, and murdered Dr. Whitman, his accomplished Lady, and 11 other American citizens, with the most heartless and revolting barbarity. Intelligence of that fatal disaster arrived here five days posterior to the event, through a messenger dispatched from Walla Walla [Fort Nez Percés] by Mr. McBean.[5]

This is a Columbia boat, a wooden canoe used only on the Columbia River. Watercolour by Henry James Warre, 1846.

The gentlemen at Fort Vancouver had little warning of the attack on the missionaries. In November 1847, the Columbia Express from York Factory arrived at Fort Nez Percés to a traditional seven-gun salute. Thomas Lowe, leader of the Express that year, reported: "Here we found the Measles very prevalent, the Indians were dying in great numbers."[6] When his Express reached The Dalles, where normally dozens of First Nations men helped the Express-men across the portage, Lowe's employees "succeeded in getting the boats and pieces across with our eight men & only about a dozen Indians, most of them being sick."[7]

The dysentery might have come into the territory via the Oregon Trail, but the measles actually came north with a First Nations trading party under Walla Walla chief Peu-peu-mox-mox, who in January 1846 travelled to California on a cattle-trading expedition. At Sutter's Fort, on the Sacramento River, his party was exposed to the measles. As they began their journey home in spring, the deadly virus spread through their camp and sickened many. Peu-peu-mox-mox's son rode home ahead of the trading party, and the virus travelled north with him. Soon sickness was everywhere, and by September many First Nations people had died of the virulent mix of measles and dysentery.

The Cayuse who lived near the Waiilatpu Mission were particularly hard hit, and two hundred men died over the first few months. Although Whitman was a medical doctor, he appeared to be unaware that he might be spreading the contagious disease among the Cayuse. He continued to visit the village to treat the sick, and the mortality among the Cayuse people increased rather than diminished.

The Cayuse had no immunity to the disease, and no understanding of how contagious measles was and how quickly it could kill. However, they could see the results of Whitman's treatments, and they came to believe he was poisoning them. Living among them was a mixed-blood Creole from the eastern states, a troublemaker who whispered in Cayuse ears that Whitman plotted to take their lands by killing off the Nation. The stories appeared to be true, and the Cayuse set a trap for Whitman. According to William McBean of Fort Nez Percés, they asked Whitman to treat three boys. Two were sick, "but the third party [was] only feigning illness, and ... the three were corpses the next morning."[8]

Not long after, on a bleak and cold Monday morning, two Americans butchered a cow in the mission-yard, while three Cayuse watched silently. Two Cayuse knocked on the kitchen door of the mission-house, asking Whitman for medicines. When Whitman returned with the medicines they had requested, one man talked to him about the deaths in the village, while the second stepped behind him and buried his pipe tomahawk in Whitman's skull. They shot a young man lying sick in the kitchen, and as the gunshot rang through the mission-yard, the other three Cayuse attacked the Americans who were butchering the cow. Eleven or more men were killed in the attack. One man hid his family under floorboards in the blacksmith shop and later made a complete escape. A carpenter evaded the attackers entirely, attacking an innocent Cayuse on the riverbank, robbing him of his gun, and running off.

There was a long pause in the attack while the Cayuse encouraged Mrs. Whitman to leave the mission-house. The names of two students were called out; they were the sons of Donald Manson, chief trader in charge of Fort St. James a thousand miles to the north. Scrappy seventeen-year-old John Manson told the Cayuse that if anything happened to him or his brother, the full force of the Hudson's Bay Company would come down on their heads. The Cayuse knew this, and they removed the boys to the safety of Nicholas Finlay's residence.[9]

The Cayuse killed Mrs. Whitman as she was carried from the house. She was the only woman to die; others were taken hostage and removed to the Cayuse villages where they were raped by their captors.

The carpenter reached Fort Nez Percés with the first news of the massacre, and Finlay later arrived there with the Manson brothers, carrying a letter from one brave woman who had listed the names of eleven people she thought had died. William McBean sent interpreter Edouard Beauchemin to the mission-house to confirm what had happened. Outnumbered by the Cayuse but relatively safe because he was a member of the HBC community, Beauchemin could do nothing. He saw the bodies and checked that the women still in the mission-house were okay before returning to Fort Nez Percés to report to William McBean.

McBean then sent Beauchemin downriver to Fort Vancouver with a letter for the Board of Management. Chief Factor Peter Skene Ogden wrote, "On the evening of the 6th of December we were seated around our cheerful fireside ... when a loud knocking at the door attracted the attention of all present."[10] Thomas Lowe reported that Beauchemin "arrived from Walla Walla with the surprising intelligence that Dr. Whitman and his lady, besides 9 other Americans, have been massacred by the Cayuse Indians at Waiilatpu."[11]

The next day Ogden headed up the Columbia River to negotiate for the release of the American women held hostage. Lowe's journal records:

> In consequence of the massacre at Waiilatpu Mr. Ogden started for Walla Walla later this afternoon with a boat and 16 men, taking Mr. [John] Charles along with him. Mr. McBean writes that the Fort is threatened by the Indians, but this is not supposed to be the case, and the principal object of Mr. Ogden's trip is to rescue the surviving women and children and to prevent further outrage.[12]

Ogden's boat pulled onto the beach in front of Fort Nez Percés on December 12. The chief factor summoned the Cayuse to a meeting but refused to bargain. Instead he told them that the HBC would not help them against the Americans who were coming to punish them; he could not prevent a war. However, he offered to pay for the American women they held.

To the strongly independent Cayuse, Chief Factor Peter Skene Ogden represented the HBC community in all its power: a community that the Cayuse had long trusted and to which they felt closely connected. That did not mean, however, that these strong-minded Cayuse chiefs would agree to part with the women they had taken by force, and who they now felt they owned. Ogden understood the difficulties of dealing with these forceful First Nations men, and he knew he stood a good chance of failure. He faced their rejection and turned it aside. Over the days and weeks that followed, he gradually convinced the Cayuse that they must negotiate with him. Ogden's strength of character, and the trust the Cayuse

Peter Skene Ogden, painted by John Mix Stanley at Fort Vancouver in 1847.

had in him and in the company, carried the negotiations, and eventually, in return for shirts, blankets, guns, and tobacco, he purchased the American women from them.

It was a long negotiation, Ogden said, with many lengthy and tedious conferences. "Many an anxious hour was endured," the Board of Management reported, "but fortunately, attended with every success and equally so without compromising either Party—rather a difficult card to play. The Indians appeared most anxious to remain on terms of friendship with us."[13]

On December 29 the Cayuse rode into the fort with their hostages, and the ransom was paid out the next day. In a letter written before he left the post, Ogden explained some of the difficulties he had faced:

> Since that period [I] have been employed in rescuing the captives and have succeeded in securing all that were taken prisoners and shall now take my departure for Fort Vancouver. In effecting this humane object I have endured many an anxious time and for the last two nights have not closed my eyes, but thanks to the Almighty I have succeeded. During the captivity of the prisoners they have suffered every indignity but fortunately now all are provided with food. I have been enabled to effect this object without compromising myself or others.[14]

On January 8, 1848, Ogden reached Fort Vancouver "with 3 boats, bringing all the women and children who survived the massacre at Waiilatpu, as also the whole of those at Mr. Spalding's Station [Lapwai], amounting in all to 61 souls."[15] Two days later he delivered the Americans to Oregon City, and returned to Fort Vancouver on January 17. Lowe recorded that "on his way up he was saluted both at Portland and Oregon City."[16]

While Ogden led his heavily armed voyageurs up the river, Chief Factor James Douglas remained behind to tell the Oregon Territory legislature what had happened and to control the situation around Fort Vancouver. From the beginning, Ogden and Douglas maintained "a rigid neutrality in the hostilities that cannot fail to grow out of that detestable murder;

therefore though we expended every effort to relieve the distressed we positively objected to assist in punishing the Indians, a duty which belongs to the United States Government."[17]

The Americans were more than eager to punish the Cayuse. The Legislative Assembly of the Provisional Government of Oregon Territory was in session when news of the massacre reached Oregon City. Its legislators authorized the enlistment of a regiment of five hundred volunteer soldiers to go into the interior. In short order, the district east of the Cascade Mountains became a war zone.

As a result of the chaos on the lower Columbia River, the HBC gentlemen were forced to make difficult choices. Every June the New Caledonia brigades had delivered their furs to Fort Vancouver via the Columbia River, returning with their trade goods. Although the First Nations had always treated the HBC men with respect, in 1848 there was war the entire length of the river. The Board of Management told James Yale, possibly as early as December, that he must begin work on the new trail, as it would be used the following summer. In March the board wrote:

> We trust these measures have been carried into effect with all the energy possible as we have ordered the Brigades of Thompson's River, New Caledonia, and Fort Colvile with their returns to Fort Langley—and you may therefore expect them about the first week in June next, and the Outfits of these Districts are now forwarded by the Brig *Mary Dare* with an assortment of Goods to [quiet] the officers and men ...

> The Brigades are directed to meet at Fort Kamloops on the 15th of May and they will probably reach the Saumeena village [Spuzzum] about the 25th following, the boats from Langley with a supply of provisions for the men and officers must therefore be at the new Fort [Yale] on or before that date. We think that three of the large bateaux will suffice to bring everything down from Douglas' Portage, it being expensive to send them up, and you will probably find it a difficult matter to man them—Four bateaux, at least, will be required for the return of the interior parties, but you will of course have more ready if wanted for the upward transport.[18]

The Fort Colvile men had always brought their furs out by boat down the Columbia River. This year, however, they were to join the New Caledonia brigades at Kamloops and come out on the new, untested trail. Henry Newsham Peers was one of nine men sent upriver to Fort Colvile with the outgoing York Factory Express to Hudson Bay. Peers was there to help the Fort Colvile men, who had little experience with pack horses. Chief Factor John Lee Lewes, who was leaving the territory, had delayed his furlough and remained at Fort Colvile for the summer. Because Lewes was there, Anderson, newly assigned to take charge of the post, did not go to Fort Colvile immediately. Instead, he was "disposable for the summer trip to Fort Langley with the Brigade."[19] In later years he described the conjunction of events:

> Debarred for the time from our usual access to the sea by the Columbia River, through the war that existed between the American Government and the Indians—known locally as the Cayuse wars—we were compelled, in 1848, to force our way to the Coast by the line of the Fraser in order to import the annual supplies for the interior. Fortunately, as if by prophetic anticipation, routes in this direction had been explored during the summers of 1846 and 1847. By one of these, striking the Fraser at the point above Yale where the Alexandra Bridge now spans the river, we succeeded in penetrating to the depot at Fort Langley— and thenceforward, at first by this route and subsequently by the way of Hope and the valley of the Similkameen, the transport continued to be performed.[20]

But in the spring of 1848, the die was cast, and no one knew what the future would hold.

8

1848 BRIGADES: ANDERSON'S RIVER TRAIL

At the northern headquarters of Fort St. James, on Stuart's Lake, the cold winter finally ended and the men prepared to leave for Fort Vancouver. Douglas's instructions to come out to Fort Langley by the new trail may not have reached them at the time of departure, as the post journal reported on Saturday, April 22: "Today after breakfast Messrs. Manson and [Ferdinand] McKenzie took their departure for Vancouver with the returns of Stuart's Lake, McLeod's Lake, Connolly Lake, Fraser's Lake and Babine, number of packs amounting to 58 packs and 3 Kegs Castoreum."[1]

The Fort St. James men reached Fort Alexandria in late April, and on May 5 the brigades began their journey to Kamloops. In the meantime, the Fort Colvile men undertook the unfamiliar task of loading their furs on pack horses and making their way to Kamloops. Together the combined brigades would continue over the mountains to the Fraser River by way of Anderson's newly explored trail. Anderson described the outgoing brigades:

> Our party consisted of the three "brigades" of New Caledonia, Thompson's River, and [Fort] Colvile. We had about 400 horses (many of them unbroken) and in all about 50 men. Mr. Donald Manson, of New Caledonia, as senior officer, was in general charge. I as head of the Colvile District (to which I had been recently appointed by Governor in council) was second, and there were several other officers in company.[2]

Anderson worried about some of the changes that Douglas had made for the new brigade trail. One of Anderson's suggestions to Governor Simpson had been that the HBC build a post at Kequeloose, where they would leave the horses. Instead, Douglas instructed the men to build a storehouse (Simon's House) at the north end of Douglas's Portage, at the place where the HBC men were to swim or ferry the horses across the Fraser River. Although Anderson considered the route between Kamloops and Kequeloose feasible, he suspected that the six-mile-long trail down the east bank of the Fraser south of Kequeloose would be difficult for the horses. And so it proved. On their return to Kamloops in August, Anderson reported that "from the traverse [at Spuzzum] to Kequeloose the tract (about 6 miles in length) characterized by me in my reports as practicable only through much labour and many painful circuits, is very bad and dangerous. It is in this part that our chief loss of horses by maiming occurred, both in outgoing and incoming. There likewise property was lost by falling down into the river from the precipices."[3]

When they reached the end of that bad road, the men looked across the Fraser at the Saumeena village on the little flat at Spuzzum Creek. It was late May, and it worried them to see how the river flowed past them, roaring under the influence of the high, rushing waters of the freshets.

Another of Anderson's suggestions had been the adoption of the Columbia boats, to be built at Fort Langley. However, Douglas (who was probably unaware of Anderson's suggestions) proposed that different boats be built. Samuel Robertson, a boat builder from Fort Vancouver, was sent north to Fort Langley, where he constructed both bateaux and river boats, or scows, which were taken up to be used at the traverse at Spuzzum.[4] In his later report to Governor Simpson, Anderson stated that "the scheme of employing scows, as had been proposed, and the craft in consequence provided for that purpose, proved, I need scarcely say, entirely futile."[5] The scows were not the Columbia boats Anderson had recommended to Governor Simpson, nor were they well built or designed for this ferocious river, causing the loss of some of the HBC's valuable horses.

Governor Simpson's son, George Stewart Simpson, was one of the nine men who had been sent up the Columbia River from Fort Vancouver to help the Fort Colvile men bring their furs out to Fort Langley. He reported to his father: "The Brigades started from this place [Kamloops] on the 1st June and arrived our destination [Fort Langley] on the 14th with no obstacles worth relating, indeed the opinion of all seemed to be favourable in respect to the road."[6] Never having travelled in a brigade before, he may not have noticed the difficulties of the trail, but Anderson did. "It is needless to enumerate the difficulties which we had to encounter and surmount," Anderson wrote. "Suffice it to say that we continued to reach Fort Yale, which had meanwhile been established, with our packs, and thence ran down speedily to Langley."[7]

Artist Henry James Warre painted Fort Victoria as he saw it in late 1845.

A few days after his arrival at Fort Langley with the first boats, Anderson delivered the outgoing letters and reports to the gentlemen at Fort Victoria via the Fort Langley canoe. The Fort Victoria journals reported on his arrival:

> Thursday June 15. Early this morning Mr. C.T. [Chief Trader] Anderson with a party of 20 men arrived from Ft. Langley, two of whom are to remain at this place and six are to proceed to Vancouver by the [schooner] Cadboro late in the evening ...
>
> Monday June 19. About 9 am Mr. C.T. Anderson left this for Langley, previous to his departure one of his men deserted.[8]

The men who stayed at Fort Victoria in order to return to Fort Vancouver by sea would not be available to help the brigades on their return journey across the mountains, but no gentleman appeared to consider this important. The Fort Vancouver gentlemen reported to the secretary of the London Committee that all was well. "I am happy to inform you that the [outcoming] Inland brigade under the charge of Chief Trader Manson assisted by Chief Trader Anderson arrived safely at Fort Langley on the 8th of June," Ogden and Douglas reported from Fort Vancouver. The brigades then left Fort Langley "on the 15th July to return to their respective districts. This trail has decided in a satisfactory manner the practicability of the new route to the interior, and makes us in a great measure independent of the former route by the Columbia River." [9]

The New Caledonia brigades remained at Fort Langley for five weeks. One reason for their delay might be based on a suggestion that Anderson made to Governor Simpson in February. He had proposed to delay the departure of the brigade from Kamloops for a month so that the turbulence of the water would be less and the navigation of the Fraser River easier. He considered that the horses' condition might be improved by a later start, and he also suggested "the timing of the Brigade's arrival and departure from Langley with the ascent of the salmon." [10] However, the real reason for the long delay at Fort Langley may be contained in a letter from the Board of Management to James Murray Yale, in which he was informed that the barque *Vancouver* was wrecked on the bar of the Columbia River. "The noble ship with the whole of the valuable cargo on board, consisting of our supplies from England for the year 1849, having alike perished in the remorseless deep, through this lamentable disaster," Ogden and Douglas wrote to Yale. "In consequence of that misfortune you must expect a reduction in your supplies for this and next year, particularly in the article of woollens, and you will see the necessity of making a frugal expenditure of the present stock of goods at Fort Langley, in order to reserve the means of carrying on the fur trade until we can replace our loss." [11]

The *Vancouver* had already delivered trade goods to Fort Victoria, but goods intended for the interior posts were always sent to Fort Vancouver, and as the ship had left London long before the HBC men could instruct the London Committee to deliver the interior goods to Fort Victoria, it was indeed likely they were lost in the wreck. Douglas made a hurried trading journey to the Sandwich Islands (Hawaii) to replace as many of the trade goods as he could.

Whatever the reason for the delay, the men from the interior—and especially those from New Caledonia—made their stay at the post a difficult one for the gentlemen. Yale described the tumultuous time, when desertions became the order of the day. "The disorderly state of a portion of the men of the interior has become if not alarming, distressing," Yale wrote. "This motley set of renegades scruple not in the least to threaten on any trifling pretence and without a shadow of real provocation to desert their employers and thus keep the Gentlemen in constant perplexity of mind." [12]

At last the first four boats headed up the Fraser River, one carrying Anderson as passenger. Like the three accompanying boats, and the seven boats under Manson and Peers, Anderson's boat carried supplies for the winter trade: forty-seven pieces weighing ninety pounds each. An incomplete list includes twelve bales of trade goods, four bales of ironworks such as shovels, a bundle of sundry goods, five rolls of tobacco, and thirteen bags of ball and shot. In addition to trade goods, they carried provisions: "90 pounds of fresh beef, 100 pounds fresh pork, 90 pounds fine biscuit (sea biscuits), 100 pounds of flour." Each boat was equipped with similar supplies, and all also carried essential equipment such as a large square-headed axe, a cooking kettle, and a boat line.[13]

"Hitherto, bateaux of about three tons burthen have been employed by the Hudson's Bay Company for transport below the Falls," Anderson wrote, "a slow method when the water is high, as the ascent can then be effected only by warping along shore with the aid of Indian canoes to pass the lines. By this tedious process, an ascent was made during the freshet of 1848, to the foot of the Falls, in eight days; under ordinary circumstances, it would occupy five."[14]

Donald Manson and Henry Peers followed a few days later. Peers's journal read:

> Started from Fort Langley on the 17th July with 5 Batteaux and two river Boats manned by Indians, all deeply laden; (4 Batteaux loads having been taken up before in charge of Mr. Anderson). The water was low for the season but still we had much trouble in warping up, along the steep and bushy banks, precluding the possibility of poling, and the current too swift to use the oar. The water not being at more than half its height our portage was made, and we reached Fort Yale on the 24th (8 days).[15]

The HBC men were surprised by the presence of thousands of First Nations fishermen who now occupied the many fishing stages along the riverbanks. This was the most dangerous part of their upriver journey: the passage of the HBC boats rattled the fishermen and interfered with their all-important fishing. Manson later informed the Fort Vancouver gentlemen that "the hosts of barbarians who are congregated on Fraser's River at that season and among whom we have recently passed, under circumstances where neither courage, prudence nor precaution could avail to resist surprise or guard against treachery, is more than sufficient to deter us from again attempting that route."[16] In April 1849, Anderson reported to Governor Simpson that "after witnessing the immense concourse of Indians who assemble there in the Salmon season, as I did last year [in 1848], I should consider it highly imprudent to risk valuable cargoes again within their reach. Novelty alone, I suspect, was our protection last summer, for nothing would have been easier than for those bands of daring and unscrupulous ragamuffins, to have molested us in such wise as entirely to preclude our passage."[17]

When Manson and Peers arrived at Fort Yale, they found that Anderson had already ridden over Douglas's Portage with the first load of goods. Anderson described the portage as running "from the upper Teet [Tait] village, below the Falls, to Spuz-zum, above the Falls, the lowest village of the Saw-mee-nas, or Couteaux [Nlaka'pamux]. It is much longer, but not so rough as the passage of the river bank, which is for some distance extremely broken."[18]

Peers and Manson remained at Fort Yale nine days, "during which time half the goods were being carried over the river portage by 80 Indians in three or 4 trips under the superintendence of Messrs. Anderson & [George Stewart] Simpson." The remainder of the goods were sent across Douglas's Portage on horses that had eaten down the grass "from the length of time they had been at the place" and were "reduced to a very feeble state" (1). At the portage's north end, the trade goods were stored in Simon's House, the new storehouse that had been built that spring on the banks of Spuzzum Creek.

Peers and Manson left Fort Yale on August 2 with thirty horses that were carrying the last of the goods over the trail. "We got on very well on the portage," Peers recorded, "with the exception of a couple of horses falling in the ascent of the big hill & some little confusion in a swampy part of the road rendered worse than its original state by the frequent passing & repassing of horses." The trail climbed a gentle although rocky slope as far as Douglas's River (Sawmill Creek), "where there is a steep descent of about 700 feet to a bridge & a somewhat steeper tho' shorter ascent on the opposite side of this ravine." Once the horses had clambered up that steep hill, however, it was level ground until within a mile of Simon's House "where the road descends pretty gradually to that place." It took the two men three hours to make the crossing, and they encamped on the banks of the Fraser, where they remained three days, "crossing Baggage & horses etc. etc." (1).

Peers makes no mention of deserters, but Yale reported that "four deserted at the falls, two of whom however were recruits from this place."[19] Along with the eight or nine men sent home to Fort Vancouver and the

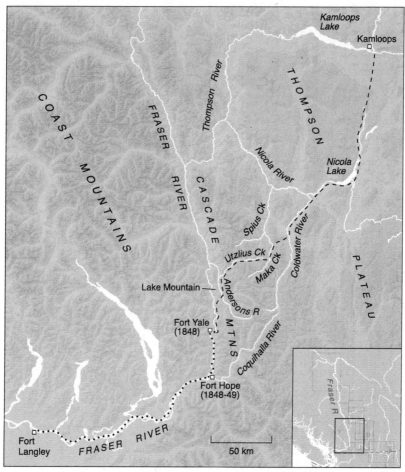

Map 13: 1848 Brigade Trail. In 1848 the gentlemen of the HBC brigades rejected this new trail after travelling over it once. As a result, Fort Yale was abandoned, and Fort Hope constructed over the winter of 1848–49.

man who deserted at Fort Victoria, these brigades were travelling over this rough trail with at least thirteen fewer men than they had come out with. The situation would only become worse.

From Simon's House, the HBC men crossed their goods in the scows. Anderson later reported, "We drowned some horses in crossing Fraser's River, though only a certain number of the strongest were risked, necessarily, in that formidable traverse."[20] He also found that the river had behaved differently than it had in 1847. "I saw them [the rapids] at a lower stage of the freshets last summer [1848], & found the difficulties greater than the year before [1847] when the water was higher." It holds true that lower water in the Fraser made the rapids more intense. However, Anderson said, "I had calculated on an opposite effect."[21]

Peers continued his journal as he and Manson made their way up the east bank of the Fraser River over the rough six-mile trail to Kequeloose. "Started on the 6th [August] at 3 p.m. with some 500 & upwards pieces of goods in 15 Brigades, each Brigade having 18 & some a greater number of horses to 2 men" (1). In a brigade, the normal number of horses assigned to two mounted men was about seven; in this brigade, each pair of men was in charge of as many as eighteen horses. Because of the shortage of horses, moreover, all but the gentlemen were on foot. It was an impossible task, and disaster could be the only result.

That night they encamped at the foot of Lake Mountain, with "many of the Brigades only arriving when pitch dark & consequently great confusion from horses straying with their loads and so forth" (1). Some exhausted horses fell down a steep hill near the encampment, one horse was killed, and "a bale was swept off in the river before it could be seized" (1). Peers's journal continues the next morning, with alarming news:

> 7th August—Rainy weather. This morning Jacob Ballenden was found dead near the encampment with his gun discharged, shot thro' the heart; it is supposed he committed suicide. The day was spent in collecting strayed horses with their loads and all found but 6 pieces and another horse killed. A war party of the Chute Indians against those of Anderson's River passed the camp and created some little alarm. Weather cold & showery, interred the deceased, Père [John] Nobili saying the funeral Service— nothing I may say here for the horses to feed on. (1)

Manson's later report gives more details of Ballenden's apparent suicide. His body was found a half mile from the camp, "shot through the heart, his Gun lying by his side & discharged."[22] Ballenden was a Fort Colvile employee, so Anderson and several men from that post carried his body into camp. They had found no signs that Ballenden had been attacked and murdered, and stated as their opinion "that the poor unfortunate man must have put an end to his own existence."[23]

The next stage of their journey took men and pack horses up the big hill to the top of Lake Mountain and down the steep cliffs on its north side to Anderson's River. Anderson later described the trail, which avoided today's Hell's Gate and Black Canyons:

The banks of the river immediately above this [Keque-
loose] are very rugged; consequently the trail ascends the
height (some two thousand feet or more), crosses it, and
descends upon Anderson's River, at the forks of which
two bridges were formerly in existence.[24]

Without giving many details of the difficulties the voyageurs experienced, Peers's journal records the scramble over Lake Mountain and the
continuation of their march up the long hill beyond, on their way to the
height of land by Utzlius Creek. "Started about 12 o'clock and encamped
at the Bridges, Anderson's River. Some of the rear Brigades got on very
badly & 80 pieces were found deficient" (2). They remained at this encampment until the lost packs were brought in, "all of which were rendered but
2 Bales. Mr. Simpson went back with Indians this evening to look for
them ... Fine weather. Very little for the horses to eat" (2).

The brigades set off the next afternoon, following the bed of Anderson's River upwards "a few hundred yards and thence ascended a steep hill
which brought us to a sort of prairie where most of the horses passed the
summer" (2). Men and horses continued the climb up the hill, following
Utzlius Creek, until they reached a rough corral, which Peers described as
"a small patch of thinly wooded ground in which had been constructed a
miserable horse-park. Two or three of the rear brigades arrived when quite
dark and many horses necessarily strayed away before they could be freed
from their loads, passing the night with the rest in the woods under a
heavy thunder storm with little or nothing to eat" (2). The next day was
no better than the previous one:

> 11th August. The horses were collected and driven to the
> park for an early start tomorrow morning; the poor animals
> of course much reduced from this constant want of food
> and the hard labour they had already undergone in the ups
> & downs of such a rugged & mountainous tract of country.
> —The pieces all but two or three were recovered after much
> searching and order was again restored. The Indians who had
> been employed for the last four days in searching for &
> bringing lost goods to the camp were paid off and seemed
> satisfied altho' there is some doubt as to their honesty. (2)

Twenty-five packs were lost on this journey from Fort Yale. Some had
fallen in the river, where they were unrecoverable. There may have been

some dishonesty among the First Nations men who were helping the HBC recover their goods, but certainly not a great deal. Many of these helpers were Nlaka'pamux men who lived far from an HBC post and had little connection with the fur trade and less interest in their goods. They also had their fisheries to attend to. And yet it seems they laboured hard and unselfishly, helping the HBC men reach the top of the hill in safety.

The brigades were a new experience for these Nlaka'pamux men, who now worked to ensure the HBC men reached Kamloops in safety. Although they had worked on clearing and marking the trail up the hillside in 1847, they would not have known what it was for. It appears that in 1848, they willingly became a part of the HBC community; that they felt a connection with the HBC gentleman they had only met and worked for a year or two earlier. Any thought of conflict was put aside, both by the anxious HBC men, and by the First Nations themselves, as the Nlaka'pamux helped the HBC brigades make their way up the hill to the Nicola Valley. It may have been the uniqueness of the situation that interested the Nlaka'pamux; it may also have been a human need to help someone who was in a desperate situation. Peers's journal continues:

> 12th August. Fine morning; started at midday and continued our journey along the source of Anderson's River [Utzlius Creek]; the road winding along the side of steep rugged hills and thick woods, the horses' feet suffering very much from the former. (2)

They had hoped to reach the height of land before nightfall, "but from the jaded state of our animals and the general confusion among the rear brigades we were obliged to encamp in the woods about five miles from the above-mentioned point." Again, many pieces were lost on the road, and three brigades overnighted on the hill, "night having overtaken them before they could reach the camp" (2).

On August 13 Anderson and Simpson loaded the strongest horses and proceeded to the height of land, while Manson and Peers remained behind "to await the brigades & pieces which had been left behind, and towards evening had recovered all except six bags of salt, two bags of ball and two rolls of Tobacco" (2–3). Anderson sent back some of the horses that, by previous arrangement, had been waiting for them at the top of the hill. Manson and Peers reached the height of land about 2:00 p.m., where there was "a swampy piece of open ground and comparatively speaking pretty good feeding at this season" (3). By the next day the horses had recovered some of their strength, as Peers reported that "the early part of today was devoted to catching and loading our horses, about which some time was wasted and we started at midday" (3). Their route that day took them over "stony barren hills and into the valley of 'La Rivière des Grimaces' [Maka Creek] where we encamped. Four Bales were lost this day" (3).

On August 15 Peers remained behind with those brigades whose horses were so weakened by starvation they could not travel far. They set up camp only four miles from where they had started that morning. Still, when he wrote his journal entries for that day, Peers seemed quite cheerful. "Good feeding. Fine weather. Here we may consider ourselves out of difficulty, the country being more open" (3).

The next day, August 16, Peers's brigades joined Manson's and Anderson's. They were moving very slowly: a day's hitching carried them a mere eight miles, little more than half the distance they normally covered. Within two days they made it to Nicola Lake, and on the evening of the third camped at the lake's east end. Another eight miles brought them to Stump Lake, and ten miles more brought them all the way to the Kamloops post.

Peers's report of twenty-seven horses lost referred only to the journey from Fort Yale to Kamloops. Governor Simpson remarked that seventy

The Coldwater River led the HBC men from the height of land above the Fraser River all the way to the Nicola Valley. Watercolour by Henry F. Tasker-Taylor, n.d.

horses in all were lost in this brigade, "together with 25 pieces of merchandise, either lost or stolen by the Indians."[25] Peers's journal entries continue with the men sorting the goods at Kamloops, while the gentlemen crossed the river to the fort, where they had their meeting. They discussed and disagreed about every section of the trail. Anderson disliked Douglas's Portage, but he considered the road over the height of land feasible. "There is nothing in it at all either as regards the tract or the pasture to be considered of a serious nature for fat horses and proper men to drive them."[26] Manson thought Douglas's Portage was possible, "were it not for the crossing of the horses [at the traverse], which will always be attended with great risk in the summer when the water is always high."[27] However, as much as he approved of Douglas's Portage, Manson disapproved of the climb up the hill to the Coldwater River. "We have now tested its advantages and disadvantages thoroughly, and I have no hesitation in declaring it as being utterly impracticable for a large Brigade such as ours," Manson stated. "The rugged rocky mountainous & thickly wooded country which lies between Frasers River and the Plains, say a distance of about 45 miles and which took the Brigade ten days to pass, seven of which the horses were entirely without food, is in my opinion sufficient in itself to condemn this Route."[28]

John Tod had not seen any part of the trail and reported only on the heated discussions between Manson and Anderson. "The reports of the two gentlemen who conducted the transport of last summer ... are so much at variance in regard to the state of the road, that it is impossible for me, who has not seen it, to form a correct opinion of it."[29] Although he agreed one must guard against the Nlaka'pamux's lack of loyalty to the HBC, he thought their dread of the First Nations fishermen was overdone. "But last summer," he reported to Governor Simpson, the Nlaka'pamux and Stó:lō peoples "were intrusted with large quantities of property to take over the portage, without anyone looking after them, yet none of it was missing—and they frequently assisted in seeking & finding that which had been lost."[30]

One result of the gentlemen's contentious meeting was that Henry Peers was ordered to explore Black-eye's suggested shortcut to Anderson's 1846 route over the Tulameen Plateau. Edouard Montigny would guide Peers to Black-eye's camp, and both men would accompany Black-eye over the mountain to Fort Langley.

Various reports to Governor Simpson explained much of what had happened that summer. Yale suggested that the brigades could have left Fort Langley at an earlier date. "Unfortunately the measures adopted for their return, instead of diverting probable difficulties, tended in a high degree to augment them," he wrote. "For several reasons, and that of time and facility to the Natives to assemble on the [river], the greatest error seems to have been their prolonged stay here."[31] His letter also explains that the horses used on Douglas's Portage were not immediately sent back to their grazing ground on the east bank of the river, but were left in the portage where there was little feed for them. More than that: "200 extra horses were brought from Kamloops to Fraser River 25 days or a month too soon to share in the very scanty means the place afforded for the 100 that were already there, and thus [when they returned] the whole band [was] found in a more or less weak state."[32] It is clear that the month-long stay at Fort Langley had not been planned before the brigades left Kamloops.

George Stewart Simpson also gave a good description of the state of the horses in his personal letter to his father, Governor Simpson. "On our return owing to the length of time we were detained at Langley the poor Horses were in such a miserable condition, that when they were brought to carry the goods they were literally skin and bone," he wrote. "Had it not been for the friendly feeling of the Indians towards us one half of the property would never have reached this."[33] But his letter also stated that although the brigades had arrived at Kamloops sixteen pieces short, most of those missing pieces had since been recovered.

From Kamloops, the brigades returned to their home posts. On August 15, the New Caledonia brigades reached Fort Alexandria, where Donald McLean was in charge. After crossing the baggage and gumming the boats, the Fort St. James men began their journey north on August 21.[34] As they made their way upriver, a First Nations man who stood on the bluffs (Quesnel) that overlooked the river shot the boute, Alexis Belanger, through his body. Belanger was immediately taken downriver for medical attention at Fort Alexandria, where he died. At Fort St. James, Peter Ogden, who was unaware of what had happened, waited for the delayed Brigade. It reached Fort St. James a month later than usual, on October 11.[35] The New Caledonia voyageurs returned home fighting mad. Many of the men whose contracts were expiring at the end of May said they would not be renewing their engagements. Donald Manson reported that "a bad feeling towards the service has arose among them in consequence … of the misery they underwent on the last summers' voyage, and being obliged to walk on foot almost all the way inland, from the great scarcity of horses, a thing they never were required to do before."[36]

In the meantime, at Kamloops, preparations were underway for the exploration of the new route to the Fraser River by what Anderson had called "Black-eye's trail." Black-eye was a familiar friend to the HBC men, and Samuel Black, an earlier HBC trader, had always enjoyed a good relationship with the Upper Similkameen chief. In the seven years that John Tod had been in charge of Kamloops, he too had developed a good working relationship with Black-eye. It is not known whether Tod asked Black-eye to explore for a new trail, but it seems unlikely that he would do so. However, Anderson states that Pahallak had been asked by Chief Trader Yale to explore a part of the country "during the summer while hunting,"[37] so it is possible that Tod made the same request of Black-eye.

It appears that by the time Anderson was ready to set out on his second expedition in 1847, Black-eye's son and his close relative Tsilaxitsa had explored and opened a new section of trail, suitable for horses, that could replace a First Nations footpath that led down to the Fraser River. In his journal, Anderson stated that the Similkameens had only recently opened the new road, and that it replaced an older trail that horses could not travel.[38] The willingness to do physically hard work, such as hacking trails through the brush, indicates that both these First Nations men had a strong commitment to the interests of the Hudson's Bay Company, and that they trusted the HBC men to reward them for their work. They were a part of the HBC community, strongly committed to the HBC's success in the territory.

Unfortunately, in spite of all the work these men put into the trail, it failed. But that made no difference to the relationships they had already established with the HBC men. When Peers and Montigny arrived at their camp, asking that Black-eye take them over his hunting trail to Fort Langley, the Similkameen man was more than willing to help once again.

It was Black-eye's son who guided Peers and Montigny over the plateau to the headwaters of Sowaqua Creek. As he rode over the mountain, Peers saw that "the snow had but lately disappeared in some parts and the grass was very short, every indication of a very late spring."[39]

The First Nations trail led Peers to the Coquihalla River and, eventually, to the Fraser River. He passed through Forts Langley and Victoria, then hurried down to Puget Sound to deliver his letter to Douglas at Fort Vancouver. By chance, he met Douglas on the Cowlitz Portage and returned with him to Fort Victoria. From Peers, Douglas heard of the safe arrival of the brigades at Kamloops and forwarded his report to the London Committee:

> We have lately received intelligence of the arrival of the
> brigade at Thompson's River on its return to the interior
> having unfortunately lost twenty seven horses and 14 pieces

of goods by various accidents on the way. Chief Trader
Manson complains much of the road between Fraser's River
and the Plains, a distance of 45 miles which he represents
as dreadfully severe upon the horses, in consequence of steep
hills and stony ground which fag and wear out their feet.
He also complains of the Indians, and being of opinion
that the route will have in consequence to be abandoned.
He dispatched Mr. Peers from Thompson's River to examine another route to Fort Langley—a service which the
latter successfully executed. The report Mr. Peers gives of
the country he examined is favourable enough as to ground,
there being no very steep or fatiguing hills, and the ascent
of the mountains being gradual on both sides, but he was
informed by his Indian Guides that the snow is very deep
in the winter and that the mountains are, from that cause,
impassable with horses until the beginning of July. The
same difficulty is found on every route we have yet examined except the one by the Falls of Fraser's River opened
last year, which avoids the range of mountains that bars
every other avenue to the interior.[40]

In the last days of October, Douglas travelled to Fort Langley, leaving
instructions with Yale in person and by letter, as was usual. "We have determined on carrying Mr. Manson's views as soon as possible into effect," Douglas
wrote, "by employing Mr. Peers during the approaching winter and spring
in opening the road he lately explored."[41] Peers's map indicated that the trail
passed through the valleys of the Coquihalla River and Sowaqua Creek,
and, crossing over the height of land, reached the banks of the Tulameen.
"For the executing of that important service you will have Mr. Peers and ten
men, who are to be dispatched as soon as the necessary arrangements can be
made, to select a convenient spot [near] the mouth of the Quequealla for a
small establishment to be surrounded with stockades."[42] Douglas instructed
Peers to construct a dwelling house and two stores, but more important than
the fort itself was the trail. "The road is after all the main object and we trust
it will be completely opened by the time the snow is sufficiently melted next
summer to permit the passage of the Brigade, which will probably occur
about the beginning of the month of July."[43]

It was already November. Even in a normal year, snow can fall on the
mountains in October. Henry Peers built Fort Hope over the winter, but

he got little work done on the trail. The winter of 1848–1849 brought in deep, heavy snows that blanketed the mountains and buried the entire district. At Fort Colvile, sixty cattle and fifty horses perished. At Fort Alexandria, 150 horses died, and those that survived were thin from lack of food. The hard winter so depleted the stock of horses at Kamloops and Fort Alexandria that John Tod feared there were not enough animals to supply the brigade. George Stewart Simpson reported to his father on the massive loss of livestock at Kamloops. "You may feel some curiosity about the severity of Winter, which was the most severe ever experienced by the oldest inhabitant, the Winter of '46 was nothing to be compared to it," young Simpson wrote. "Our livestock have suffered severely, out of a band of 400 horses which we had in the fall only 150 now remains, and those in a wretched state, a general starvation has proved in our neighbourhood and many Natives starved to death, and a miserable trade made in consequence on so much so that I fear the Fur trade will scarcely cover servants wages."[44]

Even at Fort Langley, the deep snow killed almost all the cattle; a few head were saved by Stó:lō people who gathered rushes for them to eat.[45] The Fraser River froze solid, and on one occasion Henry Peers skated downriver from Fort Hope to Fort Langley.[46] As late as March 1849, Yale reported that the Fraser "was firmly taken with Ice on the 19th December [1848] and still remains so. The depth of snow was, and is still great, about the fort, and more is falling."[47]

"Hudson's Bay Company's Fort Hope marked by a flagpole." Artist unknown, drawn from a photograph by David Withrow.

⇸ 9 ⇷

1849 BRIGADES: THE FORT HOPE TRAIL

On January 24, 1848, a millwright employed at John Sutter's Sacramento River post spotted a glittering rock in the bed of the stream and uncovered the nugget that set off the massive California gold rush. Seven months later, news of the rush reached Oregon Territory. In a letter to a friend, Peter Skene Ogden wrote:

> It was in the latter end of August [1848] the first tidings reached us that a Gold mine had been discovered in the Interior of California, and in September it was truly confirmed and a rush took place, for in less than a week two thousand of our Population started abandoning large fields of Wheat ready for the sickle and others again leaving them in stacks for the benefit of their cattle. Rely on it, Gold has a charm about it that is irresistible ... It is said in October already had five thousand Men reached the Mines and truly a Golden harvest have they reaped, at least all those who have returned, I say rich for they average two thousand dollars each, this for Men who before they started were not owners of two shirts and this collected in fifteen days labour was well repaying them. This so far is the bright side—the dark side you shall also have. In two Months one hundred and fifty lost their lives by murder and fever and many were robbed of all they had collected.[1]

In the early months of 1849, the men in distant New Caledonia still knew nothing of the gold excitement. The brigades left Fort St. James on April 26, and the Fort Alexandria journal reported the brigade boats' arrival on May 6. A few days later, Donald McLean, now in charge at Fort Alexandria, described the rocky beginnings of the journey to Kamloops:

Thursday 10th [May]. Donald Manson Esquire accompanied by Mr. F[erdinand] McKenzie with the outgoing Brigade have crossed the River, Bags and Baggage.

Friday 11th. Mr. Manson and Brigade could not start, there not being a sufficient number of Horses, and he is under the necessity of taking all the farming horses together with the horses belonging to individuals who remain inland.

Saturday 12th. The Brigade started, every animal young and old being under loads and some of them look more like living skeletons of the Animals, than like anything fit for work. Donald Manson, Chief Trader, will certainly have his own share of troubles.[2]

There is no record of the HBC gentlemen arranging to meet at Kamloops on a specific date, and the New Caledonia brigades waited several weeks before the Colvile brigades made their appearance in the latter part of May. According to Yale, his Fort Langley men "went up the old road [Anderson's River] to repair it, and to meet the Brigade which was expected to be near, but they were found lolling away the time at Kamloops."[3]

Once again the Brigades travelled out to Fort Yale by the Anderson's River trail, passing through the mountainous country that Anderson had explored in 1847. As they reached Kequeloose, they saw that the grave of Jacob Ballenden, who had committed suicide the previous year, had been decorated with "a large cedar statue, of Indian workmanship, and a small enclosure."[4] Once at Fort Yale, Manson brought men and boats all the way downriver to Fort Langley. In doing this, James Murray Yale reported in his letter below, Manson caused many of his own problems.

The Langley party, who were desired to resume their work on the new route after their return with the Brigade to Fort Hope [from Fort Yale], were brought down here [to Fort Langley], and then did Mr. Manson subject himself to the sad necessity [of] disencumbering the track of some of its obstruction but which he might have got performed without any inconvenience some 15 or 25 days earlier. Considerable has been done to the road since.[5]

Before he left Kamloops, Manson arranged that Jean-Baptiste Leolo and ten First Nations men should come over the mountain by Peers's new route. Leolo was to work on clearing the road "until he reached a point in the mountains called Campement du Chevreuil [Deer Encampment]."[6] Either at Kamloops or Fort Yale, Manson asked Anderson to undertake the work of clearing the new trail from Fort Hope to Campement du Chevreuil. He was disappointed in Anderson's response:

> Mr. Anderson, however, declined undertaking this duty
> unless I would furnish Mr. Peers to accompany him, and
> then not before he had previously visited Langley. By this
> arrangement much time was lost and we were at Langley
> at [least] ten days as he proceeded on this important duty.[7]

Other than these few reports, there is little information about the outward journey. Douglas must have heard about the long delay at Kamloops, but he made no mention of it in a letter to Simpson in September 1849:

> The Brigades from New Caledonia and the other Inland
> Districts arrived safely at Fort Langley with the annual collec-
> tion of furs on the 10th day of July and left that place on
> their return with the respective Outfits on the 25th fol-
> lowing. They came out by the road opened last year [1848];
> but have returned by a different route, now first tried,
> which branches off from Fraser's River about 60 miles
> beyond Fort Langley, and rejoins the former road about
> one day's march on the [south] side of Thompson's River.

The men were in a good mood this year; as Douglas further reported: "They were proceeding in high spirits towards their several destinations."[8]

There is no record of the events of their return journey over the mountain via Fort Hope. The only information comes from the letters that the gentlemen wrote from Forts Victoria and Vancouver, and the reports written in spring 1850 to Governor Simpson by the gentlemen at the interior posts. At first the news was good. Then, in September, Peter Skene Ogden wrote to Governor Simpson with worrying news:

> My last account from Langley states the Interior Brigade
> left that place on the 25th July, the men in high spirits
> and not one desertion had taken place, but since my
> report I learn that after their departure from Langley

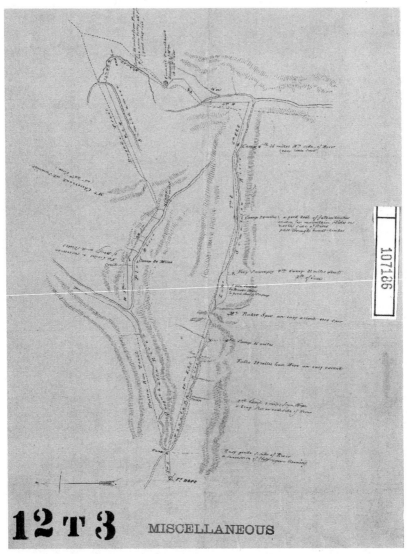

Sketch of the mountainous part of the brigade trail, Fort Hope to Horseguard Encampment. Artist unknown, ca. 1849.

Messrs. Manson and Anderson had disagreed as to the return route and the Brigade had divided. I do hope and trust this may not prove correct as from the numerous tribes of Indians [illegible] who were the principal cause of all their troubles last year, and not the road, they may be weakening their forces [and] have some serious trouble to escape without loss of life or property.[9]

Douglas confirmed the argument in February 1850 in a report to Governor Simpson: "Manson and Anderson do not pull well together, they came to high words last summer at Fort Hope, and I believe, parted in anger. I have not been able to discover the cause of the quarrel, as they make no allusion to it in their letters, but I must deeply regret the occurrence on account of its baneful influence on the servants."[10] Nor did Anderson tell the gentlemen at Forts Vancouver and Victoria what had caused the disagreement, and they worried over the incident for some time. The best information on its cause comes from Donald Manson's 1850 report to the governor. On his way up the river in July, Manson had followed Anderson, hoping that when he reached Fort Hope he would find Anderson's men at work on the road. In his letter, Manson wrote:

> You may readily therefore imagine my disappointment when on the way up with the boats I received a note from Mr. Anderson informing me that he had just returned from Campement du Chevreuil and that, from many causes it would be quite impossible to clear that road for the incoming brigade that season, and that he had seen nothing of Lolo [Leolo] or his party, and [I] therefore had no alternative, and consequently passed Fort Hope and proceeded to Fort Yale, where I had made several arrangements for [crossing] the portage, when to my surprise Lolo came up from below and informed me that he had come out to Fort Hope with and by Mr. Peers' route and that if I attempted the route of the former year [1848], I would lose my horses, as the [majority] of these animals was in such a worn out state that it would be quite impossible for them to pass and repass again through such a stony and rugged country.[11]

When Anderson set off from Fort Hope, he may have expected the new trail to follow his 1846 path up the Nicolum and Sumallo River valleys. Instead, Montigny, who knew the course of the new trail, guided him up the Coquihalla River to Peers's Creek, where the trail mounted the steep ridge that soon became known as Manson's Mountain. Anderson might have ridden as far as Campement du Chevreuil and returned to Fort Hope to prepare his men for the journey. If Donald Manson and Alexander Anderson argued at Fort Hope, as Douglas claimed, it can only have happened when Manson returned from Fort Yale and found Anderson still at Fort Hope. Manson's report continues, without mention of the argument:

On receiving Lolo's report I immediately re-embarked
the property and returned with everything to Fort Hope,
arriving there in the evening, and on the following morning I [trusted?] myself with twenty good axemen and Lolo
as guide. Our labour commenced I may say immediately
and the men worked well and cheerfully, indeed I never
saw men work better and you may have some idea of the
quality of work the poor fellows performed when I tell
you it took fifteen days to finish the work from Fort
Hope to Campement du Chevreuil, a distance of almost
25 miles. The season being so far advanced I could not
afford time to do this work as it ought to have been done,
but still we succeeded in making it passable and got through
with the brigades with much less trouble and loss than was
exercised in the last years route.[12]

Anderson's brigades reached Fort Colvile on September 7, eighteen days
after leaving Fort Hope. A week later he wrote to Governor Simpson that
"everything with the exception of some little inconvenience arising from
the scarcity of horses, proceeded in a very satisfactory manner." He added
that he had "subsequently to our separation received a note from Mr. Manson, stating that he had safely passed the Mountains with his Brigades. Our
experience of this season leads us to hope that, after matters shall have been
reduced to a more regular train than at present, the route now in process
of improvement or some modification of it, will prove extremely eligible
for the import of our interior supplies."[13]

A later, more detailed report to the Governor and Council regarding
his journey from Fort Hope may explain why Anderson refused to stay
behind to help Manson clear the trail:

Owing to the delays incurred in opening the road, I was
unable to leave Fort Hope ... before the 20th August.
On the 7th September my brigade reached Colvile,
with the Outfit in good order. The scarcity of horses
had constrained me to leave some pieces behind at Fort
Hope, which I afterwards procured by sending a small
party in quest of them. They effected the trip easily in
17 days; reaching Colvile, on their return, on the 12th
October.[14]

In 1849 the Fort Colvile brigades did not return to their home post via Kamloops. Instead, from Campement des Femmes, they followed the Tulameen River southward to the junction of the Similkameen. They then rode through the Similkameen River valley eastward to Osoyoos Lake, where the trail joined the old HBC trail to Fort Colvile. Although he had probably not travelled this road before, Anderson had almost certainly seen it marked on the Kamloops maps. Various other fur traders had also ridden through the valley; the HBC was no stranger to the Lower Similkameen people, who might already have been connected to the Kamloops post by trade.

Bringing a large brigade through the lower valley for the first time, however, might be inviting conflict with the Lower Similkameens, who were not members of Black-eye's Upper Similkameen community. It is likely that Black-eye's son and Tsilaxitsa convinced Anderson that they could guide the Fort Colvile brigades safely through the valley, over the trail that had been explored and mapped by the HBC gentlemen at Kamloops but rarely used. These two First Nations men, who were strongly connected both to the HBC community and to nearby First Nations communities, were known to be friends with the Lower Similkameens, who would trust them and allow the brigades to travel their valley in safety.

It is also possible, however, that in spring 1849, Anderson had already made the decision to bring out his Fort Colvile brigades by the Similkameen River valley and the Tulameen Plateau, and that Manson's angry letter from Kamloops forced him to change his plans, making him late in arriving at Kamloops and delaying Manson's brigades. If so, this was the first sign that Anderson was intentionally attempting to break away from Manson's control.

But it is also interesting to note that if Anderson had taken his brigades out over the Tulameen Plateau, he would have led them down the south side of the plateau to Rhododendron Flats, possibly creating a trail that would have worked better for the HBC men over the next few years. But this did not happen, and that trail never became the solution to the HBC's brigade trail problems.

From Fort Colvile, where he was stationed as Anderson's clerk, George Stewart Simpson reported to his father, the governor, on the brigade's passage over the new trail:

> I am happy to inform you that Mr. Peers' new Route to
> Langley has been tried last summer, and found to answer

very well, the fact of the Colvile and Thompson's River men having made two trips without any mishap is, I should think, a sufficient proof that the road is practicable.[15]

On September 3, Donald McLean of Fort Alexandria heard that the New Caledonia brigade was approaching Kamloops on its return from Fort Langley. To his surprise, however, his first visitor came downriver from the north. On September 15, Eden Colvile arrived at the post. Colvile was Governor Simpson's newly appointed deputy governor, and he was making a tour of inspection of the HBC's territory west of the Rocky Mountains. For his journey to Kamloops, Colvile took seventeen of the Fort Alexandria horses. His report to Governor Simpson stated:

> I made out pretty well on the whole, though I experienced much difficulty in getting horses to bring me on from Alexandria to Thompson's River & thence to Langley. Some measures must be taken for increasing the stock of horses, for I believe that many of those that were employed in bringing in the New Caledonia outfit this year are so galled & done up that they will not live through the winter. They appear to have no men in that district fit to act as horse keeper, & the numbers of horses is greater than the men can properly attend to, so that they are galled by their loads more awfully.[16]

A Royal Engineer who saw the HBC horses as they arrived at Forts Colvile and Hope in the 1860s was critical of the gear they used and wrote a good description of it and the damage it did to the pack horses:

> First, a sheep or goat's skin, or a piece of buffalo "robe," failing either of the former, called an "apichimo," is placed on its back, with the fur or hair next to that of the horse, and is intended to prevent galling; next the pack-saddle is put on. This miserable affair with its two little pillows or pads, tied into the cross-trees of woodwork, is girthed with a narrow strap of hide, which often, from the swaying of the load, cuts a regular gash into the poor animal's belly. Next a bale is hung on either side, and the two are loosely fastened together underneath the horse by a strap of raw hide. This completes the operation of packing, and the horse is set free, to await the general start ... The

horses, as I saw them at Fort Hope, and as I have repeat-
edly observed them at Colville on the return of the Brigade,
were nearly every one of them galled badly on their backs,
cut under the bellies in consequence of the sawing motion
of the girth, as well as being terribly chafed with the crup-
pers. [A crupper is a leather strap that is attached to one
side of the pack saddle, passes under the horse's tail, and
is then attached to the other side of the pack saddle to
prevent the load from sliding forward].[17]

Donald Manson's brigades straggled into Fort Alexandria on September 23, four days after Colvile had left the post. "Got all the baggage
crossed and gave out several of the Servants orders,"[18] McLean wrote. On
September 26:

About 9 o'clock Mr. Donald Manson Esquire accompa-
nied by Mr. Montrose McGillivray and Mr. F[erdinand]
McKenzie and 30 men started for Stuart's Lake in 5 Boats.
I am left but with 2 men and no Interpreter, Baptiste
Lapierre having gone to Stuart's Lake to take the place of
the deceased Waccan dit Boucher [Jean-Baptiste Bouche],
Marrineau busy trading salmon, Vautrin gathering up the
horses in order to see how many we have.[19]

On his return to Fort St. James, Manson praised the new trail, although
he suggested it still needed much work:

I am happy to inform you that the route explored by
Mr. Peers in the Fall of 1848 is in many respects much
better than Mr. Anderson's of the former year, still there
remains a great deal of work to be done on it before it is
made a suitable road for our interior transport, and to do
this properly an active officer with at least twenty men
would be required; the Autumn would be the best season to do this work, & I trust it may soon be commenced.
I think that twenty men, well conducted, would accomplish all that can be done in one month. I myself with
twenty men employed fifteen days at this work last
summer, & would have then finished the job but the
lateness of the season would not admit of my doing so.
There are many difficulties in this route as well as in that

of Mr. Anderson's but there can be no doubt it is infinitely
preferable to the latter in every respect:—the greatest
impediment in this route is the snow, which lies until a
very late period upon two of the principal mountain
Heights, indeed from what I saw last summer, I do not
think that the route will be possible for Horses before the
beginning of August, the thickly wooded portion of this
road is, an extent of about 25 miles, pasture is by no means
abundant on this part of the route, still a little was found
every night sufficient to keep the poor animals in working condition. I regret, however, to say that we lost several
of our best Horses from having eaten a poisonous weed
which grows in great abundance on the mountain Heights.[20]

The poisonous weed that Manson mentions appears to have been
Indian hellebore (*Veratrum viride* Aiton), a member of the lily family that is
toxic to horses.

In the same report, Manson gave more information about the loss of
horses during the winter of 1848–49 and its effect on the brigade and the
trade in New Caledonia:

The report which reached you last summer, of our having lost many of our Horses from the great depth of snow
last winter [1848–49] was quite correct, not less than 150
New Caledonia horses perished during that winter, and
I understand much difficulty was experienced in producing the few who were traded at Walla Walla to replace
them, & those few were of the most inferior description,
quite unfit for the transport of property through such a
mountainous country as we have now to travel through,
& many of them were unavoidably lost there in consequence, as I had from the scarcity of these Animals, to
make them carry as long as they could do so, or otherwise leave the property on the route. All our old good
Horses got through the journey pretty well, & if we are
furnished with a sufficient number of good animals &
some attention paid to other improvements which I have
suggested to the Board of Management, there will be
few or no obstacles to impede the progress of a brigade
in another year. From the scarcity of horses last summer

I was under the necessity of leaving 55 pieces of Outfit
in Depot at Langley & Fort Hope, and which arrangement has caused considerable inconvenience all over the
district throughout the last winter.[21]

In the meantime, Eden Colvile continued his journey south to Fort
Victoria. Of his travels through New Caledonia to Fort Langley, he wrote:

In the summer of 1849 I proceeded by the Athabasca
and Peace River to New Caledonia, and descended the
upper part of Fraser's River to Alexandria (below which
point the navigation becomes dangerous down to Fort
Hope)—crossed from Alexandria to Thompson's River
on horseback, a journey of five days, through a country
mostly prairie but with some hills, and thence, still on
horseback, a further journey of six days to Fort Hope on
Fraser's River, from which place I descended the lower
part of Fraser's River a distance of 60 miles, to Fort
Langley, which may be considered the sea port.

The only difficulties to be found on this route are a range
of wooded hills that lie between the Similkameen [Tula-
meen] River and Fort Hope. I crossed them with loaded
pack horses in three days, although the road had only
been opened that season. It was through some of the
heaviest timbered land I ever saw. I measured one tree
that was forty-two feet in circumference, and the avoid-
ance of such trees as had fallen across the road necessarily
consumed much time.[22]

Chief Trader Paul Fraser travelled to Fort Hope with Eden Colvile.
Brash and overconfident, as he would always prove to be, Fraser had good
things to say about the new Fort Hope trail. "The new road from Thompson's River to Fort Hope we found much better than reports anticipated,"
Fraser wrote. "The fact is things in this country are always made much
worse than they really are ... I am of [the] opinion, however, so soon as
the fallen timber is removed off the road and the hills arranged, that it will
become an Easy route for Horses."[23]

On his arrival at Fort Victoria, Colvile reported to the London Committee on his journey across the Tulameen Plateau by the new brigade trail
to Fort Hope:

I left Thompson's River at 10 am on the 1st October with five loaded horses, the men being on foot, as it was impossible to collect a sufficient number of horses to mount them. For three days we passed through a fine open prairie country, where we met with no hills of any consequence, & which affords an abundant supply of good grass for the horses. At 9 am on 4 October we breakfasted at the Horseguard where the plain country ends & the thickwoods commence.[24]

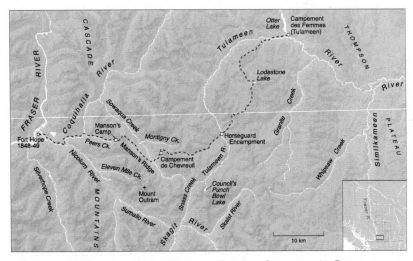

Map 14: The HBC Brigade Trail. The HBC Brigade Trail, from Campement des Femmes at Tulameen, to Peers Creek and the Coquihalla River near Fort Hope. From Fort Hope the HBC men enjoyed the short down-river journey to Fort Langley.

At this time the HBC horseguard was at Campement des Femmes, where modern-day Tulameen stands. They waded across the river at its ford, which was a few hundred yards east of Campement des Femmes, or the Women's Camp. (Today the river can only be crossed when the water is low.) Ahead of them lay the heavily wooded heights of the Tulameen Plateau. Colvile's report continues as he climbs the hill:

> I then crossed a hill of considerable height [Jackson Mountain], descending on a branch of the River Similk-ameen & following the valley of this small stream for some miles. It runs between high hills along the side of which the road is carried, & I think this part of the road is susceptible of some improvement, by passing along the bank of the river,

crossing & recrossing the stream when requisite instead of
continually ascending & descending the hills.[25]

Colvile is describing Collins Gulch and the creek that ran down
through it from the top of the Tulameen Plateau. At the upper end of the
gulch the HBC men would be four or five miles from the Tulameen River,
and ahead of them lay Blakeburn Creek and its tributaries, part of the
Arrastra Creek system, which joined the Tulameen near modern-day
Coalmont. Colvile's report continues:

> At nine o'clock the following morning we breakfasted
> on the main stream of the Similkameen River [Blake-
> burn Creek]. After remaining a couple of hours to refresh
> the horses, we commenced the ascent of the first range
> of Mountains & encamped on the top of the hill [Lode-
> stone Mountain] about 5 p.m. As we were going up hill
> nearly the whole time this mountain must be very high.[26]

They probably camped at Lodestone Lake. At this place, the HBC men
were 5,971 feet above sea level and almost 3,000 feet above Campement
des Femmes, at the base of the hill. More than one hundred years later,
some brigade trail explorers described Lodestone Lake as a gem, about four
hundred yards long and home to "immense mosquitoes." Between Lodestone Lake and Podunk Creek were the "western high reaches of Lodestone [Mountain]," and the country they travelled through was "easy open
timbered country leading westward and downward into the Tulameen
river basin." These modern-day explorers found that "much of the trail
was along a steep slope across heavy brush country and over soggy moss-
covered streams—slipping and sliding, the journey had to be held up often
to allow the slow to catch up."[27]

Colvile's record continues with his party's descent of Lodestone Mountain and the climb up the hill to Campement de Chevreuil:

> The following morning we again descended to a branch
> of the Simil-kameen [Podunk Creek, atop the plateau],
> & followed the valley for some miles; we, on leaving
> this, again climbed a hill of considerable elevation to the
> Campement de Chevreuil.[28]

At the Campement du Chevreuil, they were more than five thousand
feet above sea level. Colvile's record continues with his three-thousand-foot

descent of the face of the mountain by a zigzag trail into the Sowaqua
Creek valley:

> From this place to Fort Hope, a distance of nearly thirty
> miles, there is no grass to be found for the horses & I
> started at 6 am hoping to reach the Fort. Soon after leav-
> ing the Campement de Chevreuil the road descends to
> the Sa, anqua [Sowaqua] River, & at the bottom of this
> hill the chief difficulty of this route first presents itself, viz
> the "boue biers" or to use the American phrase "Mud
> holes," which are very numerous, of great depth, & exceed-
> ingly fatiguing to loaded horses. These swamps are found
> at intervals, between the hill just mentioned & the top
> of another & the last considerable elevation which we
> reached about 2 pm.[29]

The bogs were in the Sowaqua Creek valley, and Colvile's "last considerable elevation" was the steep climb through Fool's Pass to the top of
what the HBC men called "Manson's Mountain"—actually a rugged ridge
that reached out from Mount Outram and separated the Sowaqua Creek
valley from that of Peers Creek. The trail that led down the Peers Creek
valley zigzagged across the creek a number of times while losing two thousand feet in altitude.

Colvile's letter continues:

> The next morning we crossed & recrossed the Quaqui-
> alla [Coquihalla] River & arrived at the Fort at 10 am.
> We thus made out the journey in seven days with horses
> that were quite unfit for the work, but which necessity
> compelled us to make use of. Of this, three days journey
> was through a fine prairie country, & of the remainder of
> the road, only two days journey was through any thing
> very distressing to the horses.[30]

On his arrival at Fort Victoria, Colvile suggested some important
improvements be made to the trail, including "the sowing of a sufficient
quantity of timothy & white clover," both at the grass-starved encampments atop the plateau and at Fort Hope. He thought men should be sent
ahead of the brigade to cut the fallen timber, "as it is very fatiguing to the
loaded horses to be continually stepping over these fallen trees." Then he
said that ditches should be cut to drain the swamps along Sowaqua Creek,

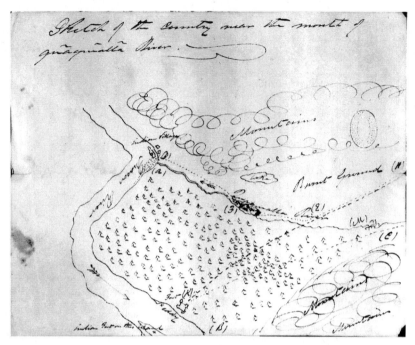

"Sketch of the Country near the mouth of the Coquihalla river, post 1849." Artist unknown.

with logs and brush laid down to create a good footing for the horses. Douglas agreed with Colvile, who further reported that "these operations have already commenced."[31]

Governor Simpson expressed his delight that the new trail appeared to be a good, workable road. Not all was well, however. The chief factors worried about the ability of the pack horses to travel over the new trail early in the spring, when snow lay deep on the ground. They were also aware that having the brigades come out by the Anderson's River trail and return by the Tulameen Plateau trail (as it seems they had intended) meant that the Fort Langley men must maintain two mountain trails. Douglas instructed the gentlemen at the interior posts that they should use the new trail coming out to Fort Hope as well as going in. "The hills are not so steep and severe upon the horses, as those on Anderson's road," Douglas advised Governor Simpson, "but the snow lies at least seven weeks longer in spring and we have yet to ascertain if horses can force a passage at the early season the Brigades must necessarily come through. If the snow is compact enough to support horses, or can be made so by sending people ahead on snowshoes in the heat of the day, the difficulty will vanish."[32]

The disagreements between Anderson and Manson were a worrisome problem, but these two men were not the only HBC gentlemen who did not get along. Ogden and Douglas were also often at odds: although Ogden was the superior member of the Board of Management, Douglas was overly ambitious and resisted his authority. Douglas was also by far the pricklier of the two men. Ogden got along with everyone else. Evidence of this was given by another HBC man, Francis Ermatinger, who had worked in the Columbia for years and who knew both Ogden and Douglas. His opinions on the cause of staffing difficulties in the district were reported by Eden Colvile:

> I found Ermatinger, as you warned, full of jaw. He says that the reason of the clerks at [Fort] Vancouver giving notice of retirement is not from a wish to go to the "[gold] diggin's," but from disgust at the way they are treated by the Chief there, meaning, I suppose, Douglas, but I could get no particulars out [of] him [Ermatinger] & I should judge from his manner that he is somewhat loose in his assertions.[33]

As well, Chief Traders John Tod and Donald Manson loathed each other and had for years. Manson argued with Tod, who was his senior in the district (although Manson was in charge of the larger district); Tod called Manson a "ramping highlander." Anderson, now a chief trader in charge of his own important territory, expressed his desire to be free from Manson. Ogden told Simpson that "Anderson . . . requests not to be under Manson's control, but such an arrangement could never occur, the Very reverse. Manson as Senior Officer must be the Chief Leader."[34] Tensions between Manson and Anderson were so bad that before the brigades came out to Fort Langley in 1850, Ogden told Governor Simpson that "Mr. Chief Factor Douglas will be there [at Fort Langley] to direct affairs— although strange it may appear to you, and I regret to state it, without a conductor the Gentlemen are not competent to conduct their own affairs, trifling as they are, and a separation is absolutely necessary as Pugilistic affairs between the two leaders is not exactly the proper mode of conducting Brigades in the presence of the Company's servants."[35]

In 1849, it became evident that not all was well within the HBC community, as conflicts between the gentlemen became more violent and the previously friendly connections were damaged, if not broken forever. Douglas himself decided:

The Brigades will probably travel to Fort Langley this year [1850] in separate detachments, at least we have written Manson to make the best of his way out with the New Caledonia and Thompson's River people should it appear, as last year, that the Colvile party do not reach Kamloops in time to join them. It will be much more convenient to travel in separate divisions, and there will be less hurry and confusion at the Depot. The Fort Hope road is perfectly safe, there being no Indians to give the slightest cause of uneasiness.[36]

From his headquarters in Lachine, Simpson complained about the large number of horses needed for the New Caledonia brigades. Still, it appeared that everyone thought this new trail was rapidly becoming a functional trail, one that would be the solution to many of their problems with the Americans. Nevertheless, it was not perfect. There was still a good deal of work to be done to make it the easy road to the Pacific that the HBC needed.

⇢ 10 ⇠
1850 BRIGADES: THE BRIGADE HORSES

In late May 1850 the Fort St. James men cut poles and carved oars in preparation for their journey down the Fraser River. The post journal entry for May 30 reports: "Early this morning got the boat loaded and about 9 o'clock this morning Mr. C.T. Manson took his departure with 4 boats, manned [by] 28 men, cargo 63 packs of furs & 3 Kegs Castoreum, with Leather for Alexandria and Fort George."[1] At Fort Alexandria, McLean sent axemen ahead to clear the road to Kamloops, and the Fort St. James men hauled their boats into the now-empty hayshed for the summer. On May 13, Leolo rode in with seventeen Kamloops horses, and the brigades soon departed.

From Fort Colvile, Anderson brought two of his children out to Fort Langley with the brigades in order to enroll them at the Fort Victoria school. Ten-year-old James wrote of his journey to Fort Victoria many years later: "Our route on the occasion of which I write was up the Kettle River which debouches into the Columbia at the point we crossed the latter, thence across country to the Similkameen which was followed up to the Coast Range."[2]

The trail led west up the Kettle River valley, where it followed Rock Creek around the southern edge of today's Anarchist Mountain. They crossed Osoyoos Lake on its esker and rode up the Old Brigade Trail northward to today's Richter's Pass.[3] As A.C. Anderson explained:

> As the lower part of that river [Similkameen], where it breaks into the Okinagan Valley, is very rugged, it is advisable to ascend the Okinagan some miles, and along the lakes, by the main road towards Kamloops. A trail then branches off, as by the sketch, and ascends the hills towards the Similk-a-meen. After proceeding some distance, there is a small lake, affording a good encampment (called in

the map "Crow Encampment.") Continuing thence, the trail falls on the Similk-a-meen above the obstacles referred to. The valley of the Similk-a-meen abounds in good pasture. Except during the freshets, the stream is readily fordable; and the trail accordingly is made to cross it frequently at such seasons, whereby several hills and some stony places are avoided. During the freshets, the left bank [descending] is followed without interruption.[4]

James Anderson's description of his father's Fort Colvile brigade continues:

Preceding everyone else, the gentleman in charge rides; his duty was to keep the track and should anything occur by which the trail becomes impassible or hostile natives appearing, to halt the brigade in time. Next is a superior servant whose duty it is to keep up communication between the officer in charge and the brigade ... Then follow the pack animals conveying the necessary impedimenta in the shape of tents, provisions, bedding etc; then the first detachment of what was known as the brigade consisting of a certain number of pack horses attended by two men and then the second and possibly a third detachment. The finding of a suitable camp where water and fodder were obtainable often entailed a long wearisome day's journey over arid plains; on the other hand it sometimes happened that in order to reach suitable locations, a short day's march compensated for the possibly long day preceding or following. (JRA, 134–35)

The brigades travelled an average of fifteen miles a day, and each brigade was made up of a number of individual brigades of seven to nine horses in the care of two men. James's journal continues:

On dismounting, the first duty was to light a fire and for this purpose the flint and steel were altogether used as matches were non-obtainable in those days; the few that I had seen were looked upon as curiosities and only used on very rare occasions as an exhibition of the white man's power amongst the natives. The weary pack-horses as they arrive on the ground quickly recognize that the resting place is reached and as soon as the packs of furs are removed, take a roll and then devote their energies to feeding or if flies and mosquitoes are much in evidence, crowd round the smoke of the camp fires. Tents are pitched and soon the evening meal is ready, the seniors smoke a pipe, the weary youngsters tumble into bed and ere long the camp is wrapped in sleep. (JRA, 135)

Although the brigades might not begin their journey until mid-morning, the men started their work at four o'clock in the morning:

At the first appearance of dawn the cry of "Lêve, lêve" is heard and with many a yawn and many a sigh we turn out and immediately all is bustle and whilst breakfast is being prepared the horses are rounded up and in an incredibly short space of time the tents are struck, packs loaded and the day's march begins. In spite of the fact that the horses are hobbled, it sometimes happens owing

"Tulameen River, looking up from opposite Granite Creek, B.C., July 23, 1888." Photograph by George Mercer Dawson.

perhaps to scarcity of feed or an extraordinary pestilence of flies and mosquitoes, that they will wander far afield and before they can be rounded up, perhaps half a day is lost. The impatience of the gentleman in charge under such circumstances can better be imagined than described; as he would glance every few minutes at his watch and impotently pace the camp ground probably thinking unutterable things. (JRA, 135)

From Red Earth Fork, the men herded their horses over a ridge (Coalmont Summit) that blocked their way, following the Tulameen River west to Campement des Femmes. They did not know how much the snow would delay them, but fortunately it was hard and they crossed with relative ease. At Fort Hope:

We were met by bateaux sent from Fort Langley to await our arrival. The horses were from this point sent back to the Similkameen to recuperate, a most necessary measure, inasmuch as the unfortunate animals were only able to obtain the barest of sustenance during the arduous journey across the Cascade Range. After a night's rest at Hope we made a start in the boats for Langley ... the boats were lashed together and allowed to drift with the stream, a bowsman and steersman in each boat taking turn about to keep the boats in the channel. Early the next morning nearing Fort Langley we were aroused, the men decorated with gay ribbons on their caps, singing Canadian boat songs and pulling lustily, soon brought the boats in sight of Fort Langley. The gentleman in charge, the late J.M. Yale, was at the landing to welcome us and we soon were installed in quarters in the Fort; our first experience of a house since leaving Colvile. (JRA, 137)

Douglas had advised the London Committee that "the Brigade was expected on the 15th Inst [July] at Fort Langley and I propose going there in a few days to meet them."[5] Anderson noted that "the schooner, *Cadboro*, Captain Scarborough, arrived at Langley during my visit there from the Interior, bringing supplies for the trade."[6] James described the arrival of this small ship as it "sailed majestically up the river and anchored in front of the Fort." As Douglas disembarked, he "was ceremoniously received,

"View of Mount Baker from the Fraser River." Watercolour by Alexander Caulfied Anderson, June 1848.

as became his position, being then the Chief Factor in charge of the Hudson's Bay Company's affairs in the North West with headquarters at Fort Victoria" (JRA, 139). Douglas was greeted with the celebratory *feu de joie*, or "fire of joy," the fort's employees lining up with their flintlock guns and firing into the air, one shot at a time but close together so that the boom of the guns rolled through the river valley. Everyone near the fort, whether First Nations or voyageur, would be drawn to the celebrations that resulted from that traditionally noisy welcome.

James described Fort Langley and some of the people who were employed at the place:

> At this period, Fort Langley was but a shadow of its former importance. It had been denuded of its stockades, which had probably been used for firewood. Mr. James Murray Yale, the gentlemen in charge, was a man of retiring disposition, but of unquestioned ability. The rest of the people employed were workingmen, one of whom was named Allard, who was usually known by the name of Shortlain [probably Chastellain]. (JRA, 137–38)

A few days later the New Caledonia men arrived and were greeted in the traditional fashion. Excitement was high as the hard-working men prepared to enjoy themselves, challenging each other with competitions of strength and speed. As a child, Jason Allard experienced "the gay times at Fort Langley" when "the annual fur brigades would sweep down the river with the furs from New Caledonia":

Then there would be high celebration; bagpipes and fiddles would be brought out, and reels and square dances—and the inevitable dram—would be the order of the day. The voyageurs would dance and fight all night and have a mighty good time of it. At the Big House, as the officers' quarters were known, there would be feasting and merriment galore. Dangers and privations were forgotten when there was occasion for a celebration.[7]

For the gentlemen, however, there was work to be done. "Then ensued a period of activity at Fort Langley, such as only occurred at the periods I have described," James remembered. He goes on:

The year's outfits for the various interior stations had to be prepared and packed in convenient bales for horse loads; the officers' yearly requisitions had to be selected and the men belonging to the different interior stations selected for themselves, their friends and for their wives or sweethearts, such articles of use and finery as they could afford and, restricted in all cases to the exigencies of the Company's regulations, altogether a heterogeneous collection of odds and ends which required no little exercise of judgement and skill to apportion properly to each separate interest. (JRA, 139)

In October, Douglas reported to Governor Simpson on his journey to Fort Langley to meet the brigades:

I met the Brigade last summer at Fort Langley, and thank God, we got them off quietly. The men were troubled with visions of California [the gold rush] and one attempt was made by a small party to excite trouble, but it was put down by a little severity. Four men deserted from the Brigades afterwards, but they were all recaptured.

Manson, [Paul] Fraser, and Anderson are as zealous as could be wished, and are doing everything in their power to keep things straight in the present crisis. Manson feels that he is neglected, having been now five years in charge of New Caledonia District without promotion—which is contrary to all precedent ... No man can be more zealous and interested than Manson, and I am not clear that many will be found capable of doing more justice to his District than he does. He has moreover claims from his past services which I trust you will take into consideration for really the poor fellow is getting discouraged.

Fraser as usual promises great things, more I fear than can be reasonably expected from him. He has an unfortunate tongue, which is a never failing source of trouble to himself and all around him. Anderson was very bitter with him at Langley about some reports to his prejudice and was disposed to go to great length with him but I advised him to drop the matter and patched up a reconciliation on Fraser's promise of amendment for the future—which I fear was forgotten as soon as the parties separated.[8]

In 1849, Douglas had been placed in charge of Fort Victoria and now resided there. On his return home he wrote his report to the London Committee:

I have been to Fort Langley, where the Brigades from the Interior arrived safely with the furs between the 15th and 19th July. They crossed the Fraser's River ridge without difficulty, the snow being compact enough to support the loaded horses, and Mr. Manson is of opinion that the passage may be made ten days earlier in the season with perfect safety. They met with no molestation whatever from the natives, and in general report favourably of the road. It has been much improved and many dangerous points avoided this season, and we have made arrangements to employ a gentleman and ten men in effecting further improvements in the course of next spring. The Colvile people reached Fort Langley in 17 days, moderate travelling, and the other Brigades took 10 days from Thompson's River. The woods have been partially cleared by fire, and grass seed sown at Fort Hope and other points on this road, which will in a short time furnish a sufficiency of food for the horses ... The safe arrival of all the return Brigades at Fort Hope has been since reported.[9]

By 1850, word of the gold finds in California had reached Forts Colvile and Kamloops, and Anderson reported on the gold fever that had infected the HBC employees: "As usual a good deal of excitement prevails among the servants there [Fort Langley] and at Victoria from the exaggerated rumours of Gold and high wages."[10] The excitement among the HBC employees was understandable: these men worked hard under difficult conditions, receiving little in the way of pay, and the idea of becoming wealthy from a little digging or gold panning was enticing. As Douglas reported, this lust for easily obtained wealth caused problems for the HBC gentlemen at Forts Langley and Hope:

> The Gold fever had made its way to the interior but with one or two exceptions, there were no violent symptoms of dissatisfaction with the service—until the departure of the Brigades, when four men deserted from Mr. Manson and one from Mr. Anderson, they were recaptured at Fort Langley, and sent by Mr. Yale to this place [Fort Victoria], shortly after my return.[11]

They would not remain long at Fort Victoria. Peter Skene Ogden, at Fort Vancouver, also reported the desertion of the five men, "but they were secured & sent to Fort Simpson."[12] This northwest coast post was so isolated that it was unlikely any man would escape. Ogden also noted that "the interior brigade reached Fort Langley in due season. The Colvile brigade was 12 days from Fort Colvile to Langley, & New Caledonia 10 from Thompson's River, & it is expected that further improvements will be made & the distance shortened."[13]

For Anderson and his men from Fort Colvile, it was just about that simple, as they now travelled through the Kettle and Similkameen River valleys to Campement des Femmes. Almost a decade later, in 1859, Lieutenant Henry Spencer Palmer accompanied the Fort Colvile brigades over the Tulameen Plateau, riding alongside Angus McDonald. Palmer's journal describes the brigade's eastward passage through the river valleys, beginning at Campement des Femmes (Camp 5).

"We followed the valley of the 'Tulameen' in a general south-easterly direction," Palmer reported, "along a level grassy river bottom rather scantily timbered and devoid of brush."[14] The Tulameen meandered from side to side of its valley bottom, which at its widest was a half mile across. "The trail is generally good, but projecting rocky points and occasional slides from the mountains on our left now and then rendered travelling unpleasant" (Palmer, 84).

> At midday we reached a point where the river takes a considerable bend to the south south-eastward, and to avoid the detour the trail passes to the eastward over a portion of the mountain range some 1,000 feet above the valley. From the summit of this hill [Coalmont Summit] the country assumes a perfectly different character.
>
> Bunch grass of excellent quality, probably the best known grazing food for cattle and horses, occurs everywhere in great quantities, forest land disappears from the slopes and gives way to a park-like country prettily ornamented with trees of somewhat inferior growth; the river instead of roaring through caverns and mountain bluffs is now bordered by low and easily accessible banks, and the eye of the traveller so long accustomed to the dull monotony of the forest dwells with pleasure on considerable tracts of prairie land in the valleys before him. (Palmer, 84)

From the heights of Coalmont Summit, the riders viewed the scantily timbered valley that stretched out below them. "From the south a long torturous line of willow and other trees marked the course of the 'Similkameen,' which rises in the mountains near the forty-ninth parallel, and forks with the 'Tulameen' in this plain" (Palmer, 84). Descending the hill, they rode eastward, striking the Similkameen River a mile below what Palmer called the Vermillion Forks. (Palmer's Vermillion Forks was another name for A.C. Anderson's Red Earth Fork.) At this point they were at the junction of the Tulameen River with the Similkameen, where modern-day Princeton stands. Palmer continues: "We camped this evening on the left bank of the Similkameen one mile below the forks, and shortly after our arrival were visited by some of the natives of the district" (Palmer, 84).

On his map, Palmer wrote that the creek flowed down a "Broad Open Valley, leading to Nicholas [Nicola] Lake."[15] The Fort Colvile brigades camped for two days on the banks of Rampart Creek, whose valley led north to the Zouchameen Road (described in Chapter 4). His journal continues:

> September 24 and 25. The weather continued fine and clear, and we resumed our journey at an early hour. Passing over one of the mountain spurs, 300 feet high, at the narrow entrance to the valley [Darcy Mountain], the trail

descends into a fine prairie, scantily timbered, and containing excellent bunch grass ...

Like most of the mountain streams, the Similkameen is extremely torturous, and the prairies, which alternate pretty regularly from side to side, vary in width from one-eighth to three-quarters of a mile, gradually increasing till towards Camp 8, they attain a breadth in places of a mile. (Palmer, 85)

According to Palmer's journal, the Rampart Creek camp was Camp 6. Camp 7 was on the north banks of the Similkameen River under the high hills of Stemwinder Mountain, on present-day Chuchuwayha #2 Indian Reserve just west of Hedley. Camp 8, which the brigades reached on September 25, was four miles west of the place where the river takes a sudden dive to the southeast. They may have camped on the river where Keremeos stands today. Palmer's journal continues:

September 26th—A fine, mild morning. Travelling along from Camp 8, towards the Keeree-maous bend of the "Similkameen," the valley gradually widens to upwards of a mile; the prairies become more extensive, and the soil

"Valley of the Similkameen River near Hedley, B.C., from Fifteen Mile Creek." Photograph by Charles Camsell, 1908.

richer; timber is chiefly confined to the uplands and banks of the river, and the mountains, though undiminished in height, are covered with grass, and assume a pretty park-like appearance.

We soon reached the bend, distant four miles from Camp 8, where the river changes its direction from east to south. Looking southward from the head of the bend is seen a fine open valley, 12 miles long, varying from 1 ½ to 2 miles in width at its upper and middle portions, and tapering to a narrow gorge at its lower extremity. (Palmer, 85)

Camp 9 was at Crow Encampment, on the southernmost of two small lakes or widenings of the river that lie under the brow of Richter Mountain to the east. Four miles south of them was the second bend in the river, called the Big Bend. This was in American territory, so they must have camped very close to the boundary line. Palmer's journal continues:

September 27th … About four miles from our camp (No. 9) occurs a second bend, commonly known as the "Big Bend" of the Similkameen … The trail, on leaving Camp 9, passes over a divide [Richter Pass] in the range of hills bordering on the river, the ascent and descent being long and gradual, the land terraced and grassy, and the road good …

The road through Richter Pass, west of Osoyoos, passes close to Crow Encampment, a regular camping place used by the Hudson's Bay Company brigades.

> Camp 10 is situated in latitude 49° 01' 52" N, at a point
> on Lake Osoyoos where two long sandy bars [eskers]
> projecting from either side to nearly the middle of the
> lake, and connected by a ford, admit of a passage across.
> (Palmer, 86)

Today the town of Osoyoos stands near or on the site of Camp 10, and
the Crowsnest Highway might well cross the lake by these twinned eskers.
Palmer's journal continues:

> September 28—To-day was cold but fine. We started
> late, having but a short day's journey before us, and
> crossing the lake at the ford, traveled three miles in a
> south-easterly direction along its margin. The trail here
> takes to the eastward, following a long and gentle sweep
> up a divide in the Okanagan Range.

> We took this route and camped five miles up the divide
> on a small stream [Nine Mile Creek] which runs into the
> Osoyoos Lake a short distance south of where we left it.

> September 29–October 2—as nearly the whole of the
> remainder of the route is in American territory, a general
> outline of the features of the country will be as much as
> is necessary.

> The trail, on leaving Camp 11 (which is in latitude 48°
> 58' 59" N) runs a little north of the divide we had already
> commenced ascending. The slope is gradual, the trail good,
> the land terraced and covered with excellent round bunch
> grass, timber plentiful (viz. larch, pine, and aspen), and
> the soil of excellent quality. The summit 2,850 feet above
> the level of the sea commands a fine view of the Cascade
> Mountains west of the Similkameen, extending north
> and south, and affording the usual ocular illusion of ranges
> perpendicular to the line of vision. (Palmer, 86)

The country south of Anarchist Mountain is rough, wrinkled, and
mountainous. When Jason Allard travelled over the brigade trail in 1866
he called these hills the "Boundary Creek Mountains."[16] Palmer's journal
continues:

Passing the summit of the divide, the traveler soon strikes the head waters of the "Siyakan" [Baker Creek in USA/Rock Creek in Canada], a rapid mountain brook which forks with the "N-whoy-al-pit-kwu" [Kettle River] 25 miles from the "Osoyoos." The trail follows down this stream to its mouth and is generally good and at a gentle slope, except at the immediate descents to the "Siyakan" and the "N-whoy-al-pit-kwu." The distance from the Siyakan Forks to Fort Colvile by the valley of the latter river is about 85 miles. After striking the "N-whoy-al-pit-kwu" the trail runs south of east, and soon crosses the frontier. Pretty alternating prairies, extending to a considerable size at the embouchure of valleys, light soil, good grass, mountains here and there falling bluff and perpendicular into the river, then retreating from it in

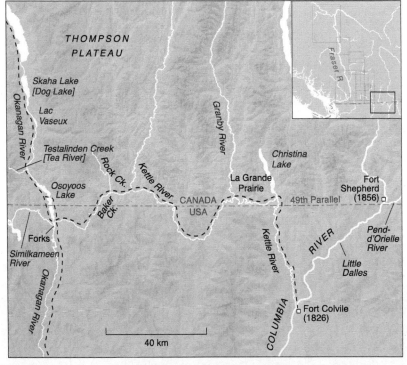

Map 7: Similkameen Forks to Forts Colvile and Shepherd via Kettle River. The brigade trail from Okanagan River to Forts Colvile and Shepherd began at the south end of Osoyoos Lake, in American territory, but brought the HBC men back to British Territory via Rock Creek.

low, broken, grassy masses, and a country generally park-like and pretty, complete the characteristic features of that portion of the N-whoy-al-pit-kwu valley comprised in the next two day's travel. The river is about the same size as the Similkameen, from 20 to 50 yards broad, swift, shallow, and clear, and its banks are generally low and easily accessible. The trail, bad only in two or three places where it passes over unavoidable spurs, crosses the river from time to time, wild fowl are abundant, and excellent camping places exist all along the route. (Palmer, 86)

East of Rock Creek (at Midway), the Kettle River dives south across the boundary line and, cutting through the Monashee Mountains, approaches modern-day Curlew, WA. East of Curlew Creek, the river curls north again to cross the boundary west of Grand Forks, B.C.

Palmer's journal continues:

October 3rd–5th. On the evening of the 2nd October we again approached British territory by a long bend of the river to the northward, and camped on its right bank, in lat. 48° 59' 10" N. From here the river passes north beyond the frontier, and augmented by a considerable branch from the northward [Grandby River], soon resumes its easterly direction.

At the confluence of the three valleys occurs a large open plain, three miles by two, designated in the plan "La Grande Prairie." That plain, which according to my observations lies within the British line, had, previous to our arrival, been devastated by fire, and the young green grass, just springing up, contrasted refreshingly with the dry yellow hue of the surrounding herbage.

Little snow falls here in winter, and its sheltered position renders it an excellent "guard" for cattle and horses during that season.

Past "La Grande Prairie" the character of the valley changes entirely.

The open timbered country gives way to a tolerably dense forest of young fir and other trees; the valley sensibly contracts and is walled in by mountains of solid quartz [Christina Range of the Monashee Mountains]; pasturage hitherto so good and plentiful is difficult to find, and the river again roars along over a rocky bed, and through precipitous mountain defiles.

In this portion fords frequently occur, unavoidable owing to the steep mountain bluffs, and the river takes several remarkable horse-shoe bends. The same general character of country, relieved here and there with patches of prairie and level bottom, extends to the mouth of the river (33 miles) where it empties with a roar into the Columbia one mile above Fort Colvile.

We crossed the Columbia, opposite the Fort, in bark canoes propelled by long six foot paddles. The river at this point is about 400 yards wide in the fall of the year, very clear, and very swift. The Fort stands in a large open prairie, about 1,200 acres in extent, portions only of which are cultivated by Indians, the remainder being liable to inundation when the Columbia is at its height. One mile below the Fort are the "Kettle Falls" of the Columbia,

"Fort Colville [Colvile] from near the Columbia River, April 1846," by Henry James Warre.

called by the natives "Schwan-a-te-koo" or "Sounding water." I visited these falls during my stay at the Fort, and the clear blue water of this noble river dashing with a dull roar over a ledge of rocks 15 feet high, and sending a huge white cloud of foam into the air, is a sight well worth the short walk from the Fort. (Palmer, 87)

In 1850, Anderson reported to the Governor and Council on his journey to Fort Langley and return. He wrote:

I left this [Fort Colvile] with the Brigade on the 2nd July and on the 19th reached Langley, where I delivered, in good condition, the returns, amounting to 90 packs of furs. After an absence of 8 weeks, the Brigade reached Colvile on the 26th ulto [August]. The servants continue to behave well; the arrangements of the season are in the usual state of forwardness; the grain crops, which are good, are secured; and the trade, all things considered, is sufficiently prosperous.[17]

Things did not go so smoothly for the New Caledonia brigades, and both they and the Kamloops men were forced to make two trips over the mountain to Fort Hope. The Kamloops men reached home on August 17, travelling ahead of the New Caledonia brigades. "Owing to the want of Horses," Paul Fraser wrote, he was "under the Necessity of leaving 20 pieces at Fort Hope. So soon as the Horses recruit I shall send for these."[18]

The New Caledonia brigades arrived at Kamloops on August 24 and left for Fort Alexandria the following day. From Fort Hope, Manson had sent a small party over the Tulameen Plateau to Fort Alexandria, bearing letters stating that all was well, "although they are sadly deficient in Horses." The messengers reached Fort Alexandria on August 5, and Chief Trader McLean noted that "D. Manson Esquire requests me to send all the Horses I can muster, and if possible to meet him myself en route."[19] McLean borrowed five horses from his First Nations neighbours, and on the last day of August rode south with Manson's wife and children, who had spent the summer at Fort Alexandria. They met the brigade at "The Pont" (Bridge Creek) on September 2, and McLean returned to Fort Alexandria. Two days after his return home, the brigades reached the fort, and on September 19 Manson and his family, Ferdinand McKenzie, and Charles John Griffin began their journey up the Fraser to Stuart's Lake.

News travelled fast: the clerk-in-charge at Fort St. James had already heard of the brigades coming upriver and dispatched a boat to Fort Alexandria to meet them. The journal read:

> September, Thursday 13 ... Form a crew of six men in a boat and immediately dispatched them down to [Fort] Alexandria to meet the upcoming Brigade in charge of Messrs. Griffin and McKenzie, old Lapierre accompanies them down by order of C.T. Manson as his services are required on their way up for sending provisions &c &c ...

> Saturday, October 5th ... Arrived the Brigade from Langley with part of the Outfit in charge of Mr. Donald Manson C.T. accompanied by Messrs. Griffin and McKenzie.[20]

So the main party of the New Caledonia brigades arrived home safely, having left Fort St. James at the end of April and returning home in the first week of October: it had taken a week more than five months to make the journey out to Fort Langley and back in. Three years earlier, in 1847, they had left Fort St. James in April for Fort Vancouver and returned five months later, almost to the day.

For the New Caledonia men, the trail over the Tulameen Plateau was not yet a shorter journey, and it was certainly harder on the horses. And even when the main brigade had reached home, there was still work to be done: the men from Fort Alexandria were responsible for bringing in the second load of goods from Kamloops and Fort Hope.

On September 21, Paul Fraser dispatched Michel Ogden and four men from Kamloops to Fort Hope "for the remainder of the outfit which was left there, say 29 pieces."[21] A day later, Leolo and Louis Marineau (Louis Destasten [Martineau]) arrived with a party of First Nations men from Fort Alexandria, on their way to Fort Hope for the remainder of the New Caledonia trade goods. This would be their second trip over the mountain this year. "They have hired horses for the purpose from Indians," Fraser noted, "and from their appearance I am of opinion many of them will not return. However of this time will tell."[22]

And so, the First Nations men living near Fort Alexandria had stepped forward, once again, to save the HBC community on which they depended for goods and trade. This fort had stood in their territory for a full twenty-five years, in various locations, and the local First Nations were firmly connected to it. Old conflicts might have distressed the HBC men in the early years, but by 1850, the local Dakelh and Secwepemc were interested in the post's well-being and wanted it to remain successful in their territory. The Dakelh were not horsemen, but the Secwepemc were, and they had horses to loan to the HBC men—as long as they were fairly paid for the use of them. The Dakelh supplied the HBC men with thousands of salmon every fall, except in years when the salmon run failed; the Secwepemc planted and ate the potatoes that the HBC gentlemen gave them, and learned how to grow their own.

They had a shared communal interest; unlike the Secwepemc who lived around the Kamloops post, those First Nations who lived near Fort Alexandria seemed not to prey on the HBC animals when hunger struck. Many First Nations men appeared in the Fort Alexandria journals because they were trusted by the HBC men to carry messages to Kamloops. Others, such as Toutlaid (who babysat A.C. Anderson's children), were regularly employed inside the fort or as assistants in the brigades. Fort Alexandria was an integral part of their lives, and members of these two First Nations had good relationships with the HBC traders.

The Fort Alexandria men set off on their journey to Fort Hope on September 27 with thirty-four sickly horses. On October 15 Jean-Baptiste Vautrin arrived at Kamloops from Fort Alexandria, with thirty additional horses "for the purpose of Conveying the property St. Paul [Leolo] & party may bring from Fort Hope."[23] Michel Ogden returned to Kamloops from Fort Hope on October 21, bearing the news that "the greatest number of St Paul's [Jean-Baptiste Leolo's] Horses are dead in the Mountains."[24] Hoping to pick up the abandoned and lost packs and convey them down the mountain to Kamloops, Vautrin travelled towards Fort Hope with the Fort Alexandria horses.

The shortages and deaths of horses continued to be the most important issue in the territory. In 1850, Anderson reported to the Governor and Council that:

> the scarcity of horses [in 1849] again compelled me, as last year [1848], to leave a number of pieces at Fort Hope; to procure which I have had recourse once more to the inconvenient and expensive alternative of a second trip. I had some conversation last spring [1850] with Governor [Eden] Colvile (whose attention to the subject had [been] previously engaged) on the facility of importing a supply of horses from Edmonton, via the Kootenais Country ... One hundred and fifty stout pack-horses,

in the proportion of two thirds for New Caledonia and one third for Colvile, would, if procurable, relieve the business from great prospective embarrassment. I see no prospect of trading any number in this quarter at anything like a reasonable rate of purchase.[25]

Because Americans living in the territory paid more for Walla Walla and Cayuse horses the HBC men had traditionally purchased for a blanket, those Indigenous peoples were now charging higher prices for their animals. As Anderson reported a few years later:

At, or about, the time when the question of importing horses from the Saskatchewan was mooted [in 1850], as much as sixty dollars in cash were, at times, paid for a horses of common quality. When paid in goods, three, four, or even five, blankets, with other articles, were offered. The Company could have procured a few horses at these rates, or possibly cheaper, but then each Blanket was the representation of from ten to fifteen dollars in Cash, and such was the deficiency of our means of transport that our annual importation to the interior was barely sufficient to meet the ordinary demands of the trade.[26]

The Fort Colvile men could make a second trip to Fort Hope to pick up their goods, but the men from Fort St. James could not. Most of the goods that came in with the New Caledonia brigades that year likely travelled upriver to Fort St. James, and the Fort Alexandria men were forced to bring in most of their own trade goods, or have none. In February 1851, Manson reported on his long journey home to Fort St. James:

I am sorry to inform you that our business in the Interior, at present, is in a very unsatisfactory state & this is entirely owing to our deficiency in the means of transport. Last summer I had to leave the Depot with only 63 loaded horses, and, as a matter of course, I was compelled to leave one half of the Outfit behind. The total number of horses now attached to New Caledonia will not exceed 90 & many of them are unfit for the difficulties of the new route, indeed only strong powerful animals will answer for our present transport, and it is a needless expense to the concern sending us weakly animals as they cannot render any service in such a country.

The circumstances of having been obliged to leave so great a portion of the outfit at Fort Hope would have been attended with a very serious loss to the trade, had I not succeeded in getting the [rest] of the property brought in to Alexandria [later] in the autumn by means of Indians, a Party of whom, with the [requisite] number of horses, were hired for the purpose, and this Party were conducted by Lolo & Marrineau. A considerable expense was incurred in effecting this object. The hire of Indians & horses for the trip was no trifle, and this is not all, 29 Indian horses perished on the route, which number I must return to them ensuing summer. This loss of horses is again entirely owing to the material difficulties of that abominable road, not one horse in twenty is able to carry his load all the way from Fort Hope to Alexandria.[27]

Douglas complained that "Manson certainly made a fearful blunder in sending Lolo [Leolo] to Fort Hope for the 2nd trip of goods, 29 horses died on the way, all belonging to Indians who are now clamouring for payment."[28] As late as July 1851 he was writing to Paul Fraser on the continued problem of paying for the animals: "Twenty three still remain due, say, five to the Indians of Kamloops, which you will make good to them with young horses rising three years, the others which were borrowed of the Indians of the Pont [Bridge Creek], the Barge, and Alexandria, will be settled for by Mr. McLean, who will either make payment in goods, or draw on you for two-year-old horses, which orders you will please to honor with strict attention."[29]

In August 1850, James Douglas mentioned, for the first time, the horse-breeding farm the HBC had established at Kamloops. Some horses remained at Fort Alexandria for the winter, but all the mares were sent to Kamloops, where they were serviced by stallions. Naturally, the pregnant mares were no longer used in the brigades, which contributed to the shortage of horses. Douglas reported to the London Committee on his plans for the newly established farm:

Our attention having been attracted by the alarming loss of horses experienced during the last two years by the Brigades traveling to and from the Interior; to the importance of

securing means of transport for the future, a band of 87
brood Mares, to be hereafter increased to 100, are to be
retained at Thompsons River exclusively for the purpose
of rearing horses.[30]

Predators were one of the problems the Kamloops men faced, and Douglas
warned, "The wolves should be destroyed by means of poisoned baits as
fast as they appear, or they will commit dreadful havock among the cattle
and horses."[31] According to the Kamloops post journals, wolves destroyed
a number of horses, but there is no indication that Paul Fraser reported this
to Douglas.

And the brigade horses continued to die. From Lachine, Simpson
accused Manson of carrying in more goods than they had in the past. Manson argued, "I have reduced the number of pieces every year and for the
last three the District Outfit has been from 30 to 40 pieces short of what it
was in [Peter Skene] Ogden's time, & at present it may amount, at most,
to 250 or 260 pieces and this includes Servants Orders, Provisions, &c
&c." He continues:

> To transport this amount of property into New Caledo-
> nia [district] we ought to have in [hand] not less than 200
> good geldings. This number may appear great in your
> eyes, but permit me to assure you it is not one too many,
> as from the rugged and difficult road we have to follow,
> it is absolutely necessary that we should have a relay of
> animals, in order to relieve (as I said before) those who
> may be maimed in passing the mountains, and to lighten
> the labour of the whole Brigade, & thus enable them to
> reach Alexandria in that condition which would ensure
> their safety through the winter—for the past three years
> our horses have been so much harassed & worn out on
> reaching Alexandria that many of them have perished
> there in winter. I have repeatedly stated this to the Board
> of Management, and urged, in the strongest terms, the
> necessity of providing a sufficient number of horses for
> the transport, but, with the exception of a few very indif-
> ferent animals (say, 30) received in 1849 and 1850, good
> able ones last spring, we have not had any assistance from
> them. I understand there is now great difficulty in procur-
> ing horses at Walla Walla and Governor Colvile, being

well acquainted with this fact, will I trust take the necessary steps to provide a sufficient number from the Saskatchewan, otherwise the New Caledonia transport will be entirely atrophied.[32]

Manson was absolutely correct in his statement: the horses were harassed and worn out. This was, perhaps, the biggest standoff between the chief traders in the territory and the chief factors on the coast. The chief factors lived and worked in posts that were distant from the actual brigade trails over which the chief traders brought the brigades, and they saw nothing of the difficulties that the men who did the actual work experienced. Yet they constantly harassed the chief traders to do better, to save and protect the brigade horses—something the chief traders in the inland posts were unable to do because they did not have enough horses to carry the loads they had to bring out. In the early years the HBC men had used both gelded horses and mares as their brigade horses: now the mares were set aside to protect the foals they carried, and only the stallions or gelded horses were used on the brigade trails. In the early years, the brigades had fifty or sixty horses that travelled light: now all were heavily laden, and they travelled distances that were far longer, over trails that were far more arduous than the early brigade horses had experienced. As for getting fresh new brigade horses, there were none available.

The only solution to the problem for the HBC men in New Caledonia was to borrow horses from the First Nations communities that surrounded their various New Caledonia posts. But First Nations men would not loan their horses if they were not guaranteed replacements for animals killed on the trail. In New Caledonia and at Kamloops, the HBC horses continued to die from exhaustion or injury in numbers large enough that the animals could not be replaced by the colts raised at the Kamloops farm. Even if the numbers of colts born were large enough to replace the horses killed on the trail, many of those colts died of predation or were damaged and killed before they were well-trained enough to become steady, useful brigade horses. The overworked and inexperienced horses continued to die on the trail in ever larger numbers.

Not only that, the horses that wintered at Kamloops were herded north to Fort Alexandria in the spring when they were still lean from the snow-covered grass of wintertime. At Fort Alexandria they were loaded and sent south to Kamloops, where they rested for a few days while the men finished their work. When all was ready, the animals were loaded once again and crossed the mountains to Fort Hope, where there was little grass. They recrossed the mountains, without loads, and spent a few weeks resting and eating at the horseguard. When the incoming brigades were due to arrive at Fort Hope, the horses were again herded across the Tulameen Plateau to Fort Hope, where they were loaded up with the incoming trade goods and crossed the mountains to Kamloops.

Every summer the horses made a minimum of four journeys between Campement des Femmes and Fort Hope: sometimes loaded, sometimes light. Many also made four journeys between Kamloops and Fort Alexandria, sometimes light, sometimes loaded. The constant travelling, the lack of grass on parts of the mountain and in the rocky valleys to the west, the rough trail that wore out their unshod hooves, and the unhealed wounds caused by the ties of the pack saddles left them vulnerable at the end of the season. Magpies picked at their wounds, which caused more damage and sometimes killed them. Wolves preyed on them in their winter feeding grounds, and so did the First Nations peoples in years when the salmon runs failed. Horses scraped for grass through snow, but in some years the snow that covered the grasslands was so deep they suffered from lack of food. There is no indication that hay was grown for their winter feed. Oats were grown at the posts, but it is not known if they were fed to the horses. It was no surprise the horses died of exhaustion and starvation in staggeringly large numbers every year.

In spring 1851, Ogden reported that "the loss of Horses last season has been again great." He hoped that, with the new road, "the general loss of Horses will now be considerably reduced."[33] It did not happen. The damage to the horses continued to be one of the most difficult and persistent problems the HBC men faced. It was a problem that had no solution.

1851 BRIGADES: THE ROAD CREW

As early as 1843 a new brigade trail had replaced the old mountain trail to the North Thompson River that the early HBC men had used. Both the old trail and the new passed through the grasslands on the north side of Williams Lake and Lac la Hache. Both trails rounded the east end of the latter lake and followed the west bank of Salmon River (Watson Creek) past a series of lakes to Watson Lake itself.[1] A short ride over a range of hills that separated two watersheds brought the HBC men to Little Bridge Creek. To go out by the old mountain trail they might have followed the north shore of Little Bridge Creek and crossed the Beaver Dam River (Bridge Creek) to the trail that ran along the north shore of Drowned Horse Lake.

In 1843, however, the outgoing brigades from New Caledonia crossed Little Bridge Creek and followed its south bank past today's Exeter Lake to the south shore of Drowned Horse Lake. From there they might have followed Atwood Creek southward through its grasslands in a big swoop around the end of low wooded hills. That long, curving trail brought them to the north shore of Butte or Green Lake,[2] about halfway along its length. As they rode west along the lakeshore they passed a landmark called La Butte, which stood a few miles east of the embouchure of Eightythree Creek.[3]

Green Lake's alternative name, Butte Lake, may have come from the beautiful mountain, shaped like a termite mound, that graces the lake's south shore and is known today as Horseshoe Hill. In French, the word *butte* means "mound" or "knoll." To geologists, however, a butte is an isolated hill with steeply sloped sides and a small, flat top, formed when a layer of hard rock is laid down over less resistant rock, which then erodes. Many of British Columbia's so-called buttes are actually volcanic plugs. Lone Butte and Huckleberry Butte are to the north of Green Lake, and Olsen's Butte, although not mentioned among the volcanic plugs in the region, is a few miles east. Another volcanic plug, called Tin Cup Butte,

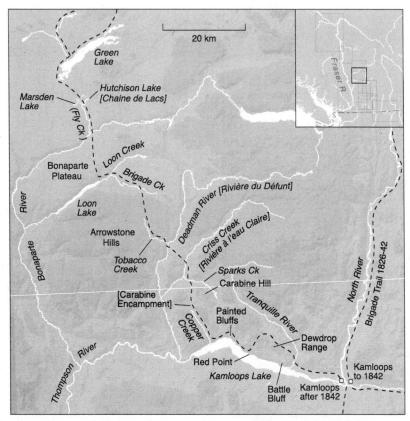

Map 4: 1843 Trail. This trail from Green Lake southward to Kamloops was used by the HBC brigades for the first time in 1843, and proved successful. The section of trail north of Green Lake is in Chapter 1.

is south of Green Lake, while Mount Begbie is some distance west, near today's Highway 97. No buttes exist where La Butte is drawn on A.C. Anderson's map of British Columbia (CM/F9, BCA), so La Butte must have been the remains of an old NWC outpost that is known to have been in this area, or of a Secwepemc village and fishing site. Green Lake's waters are higher than they used to be. Perhaps La Butte has been buried by the unique green-tinted lake whose beauty Anderson admired:

> Lac Vert, or Green Lake, so called from the sea-like tint of its waters. This lake, in length some thirty miles, is a beautiful sheet of water. Several streams run into it; but it has no free outlet. There is a slight subterranean drainage, only, into the Bonaparte, a tributary of the Thompson. The water, therefore, kept within limits chiefly by evaporation, is brackish.[4]

As they continued west from La Butte, the brigades crossed the mouth of Eightythree Creek and rounded the west end of Green Lake, riding about seven miles to a group of lakes that they called the Chaine de Lacs (now Marsden/Hutchison Lakes). Ponderosa pines grew here, according to Anderson:

> The P. Ponderosa extends on the northward to the vicinity of the Bonaparte; the last isolated members being observable at a point ... near the Chaine de Lacs, a few miles from Green Lake.[5]

South of the lakes the brigades topped the rugged, wooded plateau that was part of the Green Timber. This is roughened, rocky land with numerous moraine ridges left behind by the Cordilleran ice sheet that covered much of ancient British Columbia two million years ago. The plateau's glacial features include both *kames* (mounds) and *eskers* (snakelike ridges). Some of the eskers are fifty feet in height and one hundred feet in length. Those along the southward-flowing Fly Creek are particularly well developed, and the brigades followed them for miles.[6]

From the southern end of the Fly Creek eskers their trail led them, by many switchbacks, down a steep hill that Anderson described as being "clearly wooded." They had reached the upper waters of the Bonaparte River, which they crossed by a ford about ninety feet wide. Ahead of them was the Bonaparte Plateau, and they mounted it and rode an estimated nine miles to the east end of Loon Lake. John Stuart's provisioning

Riders and heavily laden packhorses crossing a small river in the wilderness. Photographer unknown, ca. 1913.

brigades (mentioned in the prologue) might have travelled over this same stretch of road from Green Lake to Loon Lake. And in 1833 a cattle drive from Kamloops to Fort Alexandria did take this route. Botanist David Douglas accompanied the drovers and drew maps of the trail. His journals were lost in the Fraser River, but his maps survived,[7] and they show there were trails in this district that later HBC men knew about but no longer used as brigade trails.

From Loon Lake the brigades rode eastward up Loon Creek to Brigade Creek. Following the latter stream past its many lakes (which included Hudson Bay Lake), they made their way to the Beaver Swamp, or Chartrand Lake, following its outlet downstream to Tobacco Creek, which they crossed. A few miles south they rode down steep switchbacks, which in six miles took them from the heights of the high hill to Rivière du Défunt (Deadman River), through a country that was, as Anderson noted, "wooded with trees of no great diameter, chiefly Douglas Pine and Pinus Banksiana, a tree closely resembling the Scotch Firs."[8]

Once they had forded the thirty-six-foot-wide Rivière du Défunt, a new set of switchbacks led them up and over a hill to the banks of Rivière à l'eau Claire (Criss Creek). They forded the creek east of its junction with Sparks Creek, and Anderson noted the ford was about twelve yards wide. Sparks Creek flowed out of Red Lake, but the HBC men rode upstream only as far as Hudson's Bay Spring.

From the spring they made their way across to Carabine Creek (sometimes identified as Copper Creek), riding south along its east bank. On their left-hand side was Carabine Hill, and beyond that Red Lake. According to Anderson, Campement à la Carabine was situated on the second or third small lake along Carabine Creek. To reach the shores of Kamloops from that encampment, the HBC brigades rode across a steep hill to the lakeshore, where they could admire the muted rainbow colours of the coarse-grained batholithic rocks at the Painted Bluffs.[9]

At Red Point, the HBC brigades mounted the sagebrush hills of the Dewdrop Range, avoiding the steep ridges of Rosseau Hills to the west. They rounded Battle Bluff and forded Tranquille River, and Anderson noted that west of that river the trail passed through "open country, clear wood in parts."[10] They rode across the grasslands some distance from the shoreline of Kamloops Lake, and in relatively short order reached the Kamloops post. This newly rebuilt post had been moved from its old location across the North Thompson River in the same year that the 1843 trail was opened.

When he drew his 1867 map (CM/F9, BCA), Anderson pencilled in the approximate route of the 1843 trail that rounded the series of hills north of Green Lake. In red ink he indicated a newer trail that cut off that big loop of road. From the west end of Green Lake, this trail followed Eightythree Creek north on its east bank, then followed Taylor Creek north to Taylor Lake. From that point the trail appears to head straight north to Horse Lake, possibly following Ninetythree Mile Creek. In the middle of that new route, and on the shore of today's Taylor Lake, Anderson noted the name "Mr. Ogden's Camp." In 1851, Peter Ogden Jr., son of Chief Factor Peter Skene Ogden, was charged with the duty of straightening out many of the big curves on the brigade trail between Fort Alexandria and Fort Hope. Anderson had left New Caledonia by this time, but at Fort Langley he would have learned that the meandering trail from Horse Lake to Green Lake had been straightened and shortened by Peter Ogden's axemen.

Almost all the men who worked in the territory went out with the brigades in the summer, and there were never any men to spare for the job of straightening the trail. To solve this problem, Douglas had ten men shipped into New Caledonia via the Rocky Mountain Portage (Yellowhead Pass). They reached Fort St. James in fall 1850 and spent the winter there and at nearby posts. In the spring they were available to work as axemen along the brigade trail, and when the work was done they were distributed throughout the territory.

And thus the larger HBC community on the east side of the Rocky Mountains supported the needs of the HBC communities in the west, supplying manpower to build and clear the new roads needed in New Caledonia and over the Tulameen Plateau. Manpower was one item the HBC in the enormous Saskatchewan district could easily provide, as the mixed-blood communities at Red River and on the North Saskatchewan River were overflowing with young, energetic Métis men who were looking for adventure and work. Most if not all of the men sent over the Rockies were Métis descendants of earlier HBC connections; the HBC gentlemen in New Caledonia would have little conflict with these young Indigenous men who were used to the kind of work that was done at the various HBC posts they had grown up in, both at Red River and in the Saskatchewan district. They were strong, hardy, and unafraid of the hard physical labour of chopping down trees for hours and days at a time. And like all young Métis men, these fiddle-footed young men were always ready for the adventure of exploring a territory that was new to them.

In early May of 1851, Peter Ogden Jr. left Fort St. James with the brigades. He arrived at Fort Alexandria five days later, as noted by Donald McLean in the post journal:

> Thursday 8th [May]. About 1 o'clock PM Mr. Peter Ogden arrived with a Brigade of four Boats ... Chief Trader Donald Manson is incapable [from sickness] to go out with the Brigade and I (D. McLean) am deputed to take charge of it from this to Langley. Mr. Ogden is to proceed on in advance in order to work at the Road ...
>
> Friday 9th. Arranging axes &c &c for the road party.
>
> Sunday 11th. Mr. Ogden with a party of 10 picked axemen took his departure for the purpose of arranging the Route ...
>
> May, Saturday 31st. Started for Fort Hope via Thompson's River taking out the Returns of this District.[11]

At Kamloops, Paul Fraser had instructions to assist the road builders, "supplying them with guides and abundance of goods for their journey."[12] At the end of May he learned that the axemen were approaching his post. The Kamloops post journal reads:

> Saturday 24th [May]. Michel Ogden arrived, he was sent by his Brother [Peter] who is working at the river for provisions. He left him with 10 Men at the River de pont [Bridge Creek].
>
> Sunday 25th. Early this morning St. Paul [Jean-Baptiste Leolo] left this for Alexandria for the purpose of assisting the New Caledonia brigade hither. In the Evening, Mr. P[eter] Ogden arrived with his party.
>
> Friday 30th. Mr. Ogden and party off on their way to Fort Hope. Provisioned them with 600 [salmon] and Horses to Convey them to Campement des Femmes.[13]

Douglas had told Yale that "Mr. Fraser expects to be at Langley by the 25th inst. [June]."[14] However, things at Kamloops did not go as planned. On Monday, June 9, Fraser recorded that the Kamloops men "finished Stamping [branding] the Horses. Arrived Mr. McLean with the New Caledonia brigade. This was their 9th day from Alexandria."[15] On Tuesday Fraser had two oxen shot for provisions, and in the days that followed the men crossed the baggage and horses. On Monday, when they had planned to begin their journey, Fraser recorded that "Owing to the rain we could not Start."[16]

Because of the rain delay, the combined brigades reached Fort Langley five days later than Fraser had planned. Douglas reported:

> The New Caledonia Brigade in charge of Mr. McLean arrived here on the 30th June with the Furs in good order. Since then Mr. Ogden has come in with the road party having completed the service on which he was detached in a very satisfactory manner. The perilous passages in Manson's Mountain have been either avoided by altering the direction or so much improved the pack horses may travel in safety. The road through the back country between Fort Hope and the Similkameen, beyond the high table land known as the Garden of Eden, had been cleared of roots and fallen timber, and made wide throughout wherever the breadth was before too contracted for the passage of loaded horses.
>
> The hills have been in many places obviated and others improved by means of the hoe and spade and about 200 yards of boggy ground, before nearly impassible, have been substantially bridged over with round timber and on the whole the road has been vastly improved and may be considered in as thoroughly passible a state as it ever will be until by the advent of trade converted into a thoroughfare for wagons. I am much pleased with Mr. Ogden's activity and attention to duty which will not be forgotten.[17]

Douglas obsessed about making this trail into a wagon road. No matter how often Yale or Manson told him how difficult the trail was, and how nearly impossible it would be to turn it into a road, Douglas would never understand the harsh geography of the country. The same happened with the Chilliwack River: in 1847 it was explored and eliminated as a possible trail because the HBC men could not find their way past the box canyon that bound in Chilliwack Lake. Nevertheless, a decade later Douglas gave Yale instructions to explore the river once again, and once again it was eliminated.

Douglas was like this in every decision he made, and every man who worked under him suffered the consequences of his stubborn belief in himself. A tall and imposing man, Douglas took pleasure in intentionally crowding James Murray Yale, a small man who was easily intimidated. Douglas also sealed his reports to Governor Simpson so that the Fort Vancouver gentlemen could not read them.

Before Peter Skene Ogden left Fort Vancouver, he told his replacement, John Ballenden, about his disagreements with Douglas. When Douglas attempted to control Ballenden, the new man fought back. He wrote to Douglas: "You said in your last letter Mr. Ogden was rather 'intractable' lately—might this not have arisen from circumstances similar to those to which I now allude—a want of mutual confidence respecting the Company's affairs."[18] In spite of Douglas's aspirations, Ogden was the senior man in the territory: he had been a chief factor since 1835, Douglas since 1839.

Thus, even among the upper echelon of HBC gentlemen there were disagreements. Against all odds, Ogden held his Fort Vancouver district together, fending off attacks from American immigrants who encroached upon HBC lands and stole their cattle and horses. Douglas, however, behaved as though he were the superior gentleman in the district, considering his HBC community more important than Ogden's. Perhaps he was right; nevertheless, he ignored HBC protocol and demeaned Ogden's work,

Fort Vancouver and its village as it was in 1853. Artwork by Gustavus Sohn.

deeming it less important than his own. In so doing, Douglas contributed to the breakdown in HBC connections between his own district and the HBC headquarters at Fort Vancouver.

In spite of his flaws, including being difficult to deal with, Douglas was a good organizer. In mid-July 1851, he met the brigades at Fort Langley. In his letter to Manson, he expressed satisfaction that the brigades had arrived so early in the summer:

> The early arrival of the Brigades at this post is most sat-isfactory, and Mr. McLean has been very active and expeditious since his arrival in making preparations for his departure on the 15th instant [July] which will enable him to reach Stuart's Lake early in September. He leaves this place with 82 horse loads of 164 pieces, a more bulky outfit than was sent into the district in its most prosper-ous days.

> From the experience of the last two years we are con-vinced that the Fort Hope road is practicable for pack horses at a much earlier season than was at first supposed: it has been therefore decided that the Brigade shall in future leave Kamloops on or before the 10th of June and you will please to regulate the movements of the out-coming New Caledonia brigade accordingly.[19]

But Douglas also had a complaint. Communication in this territory was done by letter, and it is possible that Manson thought that all the men sent out with the road crew would return to his district. Whatever communi-cation breakdown existed, it resulted in a shortage of men for the incom-ing New Caledonia brigade, and earned Manson another sharp rebuke from Douglas:

> The incoming party consists besides the Officers, of 17 labouring servants, a force insufficient to take charge of the property, and the number of pack horses going into the District, and it is out of my power to increase the number, as all our disposable men have been already dis-tributed: and moreover, the complement of the District is now complete, as it appears that the scarcity of men at this point arises from the unusual number of men who have been injudiciously kept inland, there being no less

than 28 men in the summer establishment, a number far exceeding any former precedent.

In future I beg that the complement for the Return Brigade may always be made up to 21 men exclusive of the servants whose contracts expire and who come out here for the sole purpose of remaining in the settlement, an arrangement which will relieve us from the inconveniences experienced this year from the scarcity of men.[20]

Fortunately, Douglas was able to report to the London Committee that the excitement caused by the news of the California gold rush had subsided, and the men were not so eager to desert as they had been in previous years. "The new road is ... gradually losing its terrors," he wrote, continuing:

The passage of the Fraser's River Mountains was effected this year at a much earlier season than was supposed practicable. Snow was found in abundance on the summits of the mountains, but it offered no impediment to the horses, and was rather an advantage, as it afforded good footing and was compact enough to support them. The snow was all gone from the valleys, and vegetation far advanced, so that the horses had food at every halting place. Next year we propose that the outcoming Brigades shall leave Kamloops for Fort Langley on the 10th June which will be a great advantage to all, by insuring an early return to their respective Districts.

There is still a scarcity of transport horses, but hereafter there will not be so great a loss from the effects of hunger, fatigue, and careless driving; while the measures taken to recruit our stock can hardly fail to be successful. We have now collected a herd of 180 brood mares at Kamloops reserved solely for the purpose of rearing horses. Many of these being only rising two years will not produce before next year, but when Mr. Fraser left Kamloops there were 115 colts of spring 1851, and many more were expected. At that rate of increase annually we will, if prospered, soon rear all the horses required for the interior transport and be independent of foreign supplies.[21]

On his return to Fort Victoria, Douglas reported on an additional improvement to the trail. As the men rode (or walked) over the mountain, they sowed grass seeds that would provide feed for the horses in future years. In July, Douglas had shipped a quantity of grass seeds up the Fraser River to Fort Langley:

Invoice of Grass Seeds Forwarded per Canoe to Fort Langley and consigned to James M. Yale Esq.

1 Bush. Perennial Rye Grass

½ Bush. Cockefoot Grass

1 bushel Italian Rye [Grass]

8 lbs. Red top Clover

6 lbs. White top Clover

2 lbs. Foxtail Grass

2 lbs. Rib Grass

2 lbs. Cow Grass

4 lbs. Trefoil Grass

2 Bush. Italian Rye Grass[22]

Cockefoot grass was common in seed mixtures in England; it is a perennial that grows in spring, and grows in clumps when left to nature. Perennial rye grass is a cool-season grass that lasts for about five years but yields less than the short-lived Italian rye grass; some varieties are highly digestible, and it is a favourite of cattle and horses. The meadow foxtail is a nutritious and palatable grass that flowers early in the spring. White clover is a persistent slow-growing clover that thrives when grazed; nutritious red clover lasts two years once planted. Ribgrass (ribwort plantain) is a popular perennial forage herb, and trefoil grass is a close relative of clover, a low-growing annual used to suppress weeds. The HBC men also planted timothy at Fort Hope. Timothy is a flexible, persistent grass that grows abundantly on most soils and gives forage that is acceptable to most stock. Douglas reported in July that "there are now about eight acres of timothy Grass at Fort Hope, and that or other kinds of grass at every encampment on the mountains, in sufficient quantities for one to two night's consumption."[23]

The outbound 1851 brigades reached Kamloops in safety, as Paul Fraser reported in his post journal:

> Sunday 3rd [August]. Returned from Langley with all the Outfit in good Order in Company with the New Caledonia Brigade and found Mr. [John] Simpson and people well but sorry to say all the Stockades down and the wheat Crops &c &c are destroyed by the Cattle and Grasshoppers.
>
> Thursday 7th. Messrs. McLean and [Peter] Ogden with the New Caledonia brigade off to Alexandria.[24]

If we ignore 1849, with its many delays caused by Manson's choices, we can see improvements over time in the arrivals of the New Caledonia brigades at Kamloops. In 1848 they arrived on August 22 by the difficult Anderson's River trail. In 1850 they reached Kamloops on August 17. In 1851 they arrived two weeks earlier than they had done in both 1848 and 1850. However, in spite of all the improvements, the new horse trails to Fort Langley were still slower than the old Columbia River route to Fort Vancouver. When the brigades went out and came in by the Old Brigade Trail to Fort Vancouver, they had always reached Fort Alexandria in August. As well, the straightening of the trail between Kamloops and Fort Alexandria contributed to a quicker journey north. In 1851 the brigades arrived at Alexandria in mid-August rather than early September:

> August 1851. Saturday 16th. I [Donald McLean] reached this with the Outfit of the District all safe this evening but not in sufficient time to cross all the Baggage to the Fort.
>
> Sunday 17. Crossed the goods and gave out the Summer mens private orders, also got the Boats hauled out of the Shed in order to commence gumming in good time tomorrow. I shall not await the arrival of Mr. C.T. Don Manson [from Fort St. James], but shall accompany Mr. [Peter] Ogden to Stuart's Lake with part of the Outfit, as there is no means of feeding the men there being no Salmon, I shall be under the necessity of feeding the people upon Flours ...
>
> Monday 18th. Men employed gumming &c.

Tuesday 19th. All ready for a start tomorrow.

Wednesday 20th. On putting the Boats into the Water, one
was found to make so much Water that she was taken out
to regum, and finally made a start with two at 11:30 am.[25]

Manson met the brigade boats on their way upriver, and they reached
their headquarters at Fort St. James on September 3. On September 12,
McLean returned to Fort Alexandria with the New Caledonia men, who
were picking up the goods they had left behind three weeks earlier. A day
later he received news from Kamloops that there was an extreme shortage of
salmon there, as there was at Fort Alexandria, Fort Langley, and throughout the entire district.

The Fraser River salmon have a predictable four-year cycle, with one year
being very good, the next extremely poor. The fishery recovers in stages
over the next two summers until the Fraser River has, once again, a good
year. As always, a bad year for salmon meant starvation for the First Nations
people, and for the HBC traders. At Fort Victoria, Douglas reported that
the result would be a poor return in furs:

I lately received letters from Chief Trader Frazer, dated
Thompson's River, which mentions the safe arrival of all
the Inland Brigades at their several Districts. Salmon are
reported to be exceedingly scarce in Frazers River, which,
there is too much reason to suppose, will cause a decrease
in the returns of Thompson's River and New Caledonia,
and has already led to a serious falling off in the Fisheries at
Fort Langley, which have this season produced a little over
900 Barrels, under half the yield of last year.[26]

It was fortunate for the New Caledonia men that they were able to
obtain salmon from Babine Lake, which was connected to the Pacific
Ocean by its own short river. This salmon run rarely failed, and in years
when the Fraser River salmon disappeared, fish could always be traded
from the Babine First Nation. In his report to the governor, Manson gives
a little more information on the numbers of salmon consumed by the
HBC men. "Had we not procured a small supply [of salmon] from the
Babines," Manson reported to Governor Simpson, "we should have
been reduced to the greatest distress, fortunately Mr. [Charles John]
Griffin who is in charge of that place, secured about 30,000 which has
enabled me to afford a small supply to each of three Posts, and this with

the produce of our gardens, which providently provided good crops last Summer, had enabled us to weather out the winter, & I trust, to leave a sufficiency, with the usual summer resources, for the people who remain inland."[27]

In his annual report to Governor and Council, Manson included additional information on the effect the shortage of salmon would have on the First Nations:

> The poor unfortunate Natives have been great Sufferers throughout the winter from this dearth of Provisions, and have almost all gone to the Babine country, where, alone, they had any chance of subsisting throughout the winter. This state of affairs has I regret to say, ruined our Marten Trade, as Indians, t'is well known, when in a state of starvation will not hunt martens, as that animal yields little in the shape of food. In Beaver and other fur the returns are considerably greater than last year and, notwithstanding the failure of Martens, I trust the result of this Outfit will be found more satisfactory than that of the last.[28]

The American pine marten is a forest-loving weasel with a long slender body, short legs, and a bushy tail. As Manson wrote, because of its small size and diet of animals, fruit, and carrion, marten cannot have provided a tasty meal for the First Nations, so when food was short, the marten hunts suffered because First Nations people had no energy or incentive to trap a non-food animal. It was also easy to overtrap these elusive animals, and when that happened, marten became scarce. According to A.C. Anderson, "Like the Lynx it disappears partially at intervals, and then reappears in great numbers."[29]

As for the Fort Colvile brigades, Anderson and his men left their home post on July 1 and reached Fort Langley on July 15. He reported on his successful journey in September:

> The Brigade reached Colvile on the 14th August, after an absence of forty-five days. The Returns, amounting to 97 packs, with Cash to $800, were delivered safe and in good condition on Board the "Cadboro" in the Gulf of Georgia. I am happy to state that the whole journey was effected without loss of horses or accident of any kind.[30]

In earlier years the *Cadboro* had been towed upriver to Fort Langley by the steamer *Beaver*. This year the Fort Langley bateaux delivered the furs to the ship as it anchored off the mouth of the Fraser River near present-day Steveston—another efficiency for the HBC business.

Anderson noted that he had delivered cash to Fort Langley as well as furs. The money came from American gold miners who were following small gold rushes north from California. The excitement of the California gold rush had died, but in Oregon Territory men still searched for the valuable mineral. Even HBC and First Nations men tested their local streams for gold, and sometimes they found it. In April, Anderson reported that "a lump about the size of a ball is now said to be in the possession of an Indian who lives a day's march from this."[31] Gold was also found on the Flint River near Fort Connah (Flathead Post), and Angus McDonald had sent down for a specimen. Anderson wrote:

> This, sir, may be dry details to you. I must confess there
> is something almost ludicrous in this constant playing in
> the word GOLD, as is now the case in the Columbia ... I
> suppose all this gold now flung about since the discovery
> in California will help with the dividends, but really I am
> sometimes tempted to wish that the good old times were
> back again. If profits were less, they were more secure;
> and we had the benefit of tranquility into the bargain
> which is out of the question nowadays.[32]

The work of the fur trade continued after the gentlemen returned to their home posts. Anderson dealt with a special problem: the delivery of horses from Edmonton House. The Saskatchewan horses had not yet arrived at Fort Colvile when Chief Factor Peter Skene Ogden's temporary replacement arrived with the incoming Columbia Express. Chief Factor John Ballenden found Anderson and his entire family sickened by the influenza that raged through the district. As Ballenden reported to the secretary of the London Committee:

> We reached Fort Colvile on the 5th November and there
> found Mr. Chief Trader Anderson seriously indisposed,
> and almost all his family suffering from the prevailing
> epidemic—the influenza. I had no officer with me appointed
> to relieve him but considering the circumstances of his
> Case I felt obliged to place Mr. William Sinclair, one of

> the Clerks who had accompanied me from the East Side,
> in charge of that Post "pro tempore" and to take Mr.
> Anderson and family with me to Vancouver.[33]

On November 20, Ogden met the incoming express on the beach in front of Fort Vancouver. The influenza-stricken Anderson had mostly recovered by the time they reached headquarters, but his wife was seriously ill. Anderson had arranged that if Ogden disapproved of his leaving Fort Colvile, he would return to his post. But Ogden was pleased. Many of the Fort Vancouver employees had abandoned their fur trade jobs for the excitement of the California goldfields, and the Columbia River headquarters stood almost empty. Americans were settling on the farmlands that surrounded the fort, and were tearing down the fences and stealing the HBC cattle. With the help of the American Army, whose military post had been erected on the hill above the old HBC headquarters, Ogden had defended Fort Vancouver against American aggressions for four or more years and was exhausted. He left Ballenden's training in Anderson's hands and boarded the steamship for New York.

✤ 12 ✤

1852 BRIGADES: THE BULLY

The winter passed quietly, and at Fort Victoria, James Douglas turned his mind to the brigades. In March he sent a warning letter to Anderson, asking him to "bring out a sufficient number of men to take out your Brigade, as there is no probability of any spare men being at Fort Langley."[1]

Anderson, however, had wintered at Fort Vancouver, where he had many long discussions with John Ballenden. One of those discussions centred on the Fort Colvile brigades. With Ballenden's agreement, Anderson travelled upriver to Fort Colvile in the spring, carrying trade goods from the Fort Vancouver warehouses. Eden Colvile's report to the London Committee explains how Anderson took in the Fort Colvile supplies:

> Formerly the supplies of goods for Fort Colvile were taken in small boats, but there was more loss of lives and property by destruction of boats in the rapids of the Columbia than in all the rest of the Company's territories, and of late years the outfits have been conveyed by the route of Fraser's River, although, to obviate difficulties with the United States Government on the subject of duties, the outfit was last year forwarded from Fort Vancouver, and by pack horses from the Dalles to Fort Colvile.[2]

Fort Colvile's trade goods would have been carried from The Dalles over the Shawpatin Trail. This historic Indigenous path crossed the treeless scablands of the interior of Washington State, from the southernmost trailhead at the Snake River to a place on the wooded Spokane River where the Spokane Tribe of Indians traditionally ferried men and goods across the river. The horses were swum, and the HBC men continued their journey to Fort Colvile. Anderson advised the Governor and Council that from Fort Colvile, "I am directed to convey the returns by horse and bateaux transport to Fort Vancouver, where the District will in future be outfitted, instead of through Fort Langley as for several years past."[3]

Anderson reached Fort Colvile on April 15 and reported on the superb job his clerk, Angus McDonald, had done. McDonald was in charge of both Forts Colvile and Connah (Flathead) but had spent his winter at the more difficult Flathead post, where the company faced brisk competition from Americans and free-traders. When all was arranged, Anderson returned to Fort Vancouver, where he retired from the company, leaving McDonald in charge of the Fort Colvile district.

Over the next few years, McDonald packed his furs across the scablands to Fort Vancouver. For the New Caledonia brigades, however, nothing changed. In March 1852, Douglas reported to Eden Colvile on his arrangements for them:

> It is arranged that the outcoming Brigades are to leave Thompson's River on their way to Fort Langley on the 10th of June next, being a month earlier in the season than was supposed practical on the first opening of the Fort Hope road. It was found by the experience of last summer [1851] that the snow on the mountain summits at that season is compact enough to support the weight of horses passing over it, and that it is rather an advantage, as forming a smoother road and affording better footing for the horses. At that season the grass is also well grown up in the valleys, and in sufficient quantity to supply the pack horses with food at every halting place.[4]

Once again, men who had entered the territory via the Rocky Mountain Portage in the fall would winter at Fort St. James. In the spring, Douglas further wrote, they were to be sent out ahead of the brigades to clear and straighten the road:

> A party of ten men, under the direction of Mr. Peter Ogden, were employed upon the new road for nearly two months last spring [1851], and made many substantial improvements ...
>
> It is arranged that a party of equal strength will be employed upon the road this spring [1852], and we shall continue the process of improvement from year to year until the

new road loses its terrors. There is still much to do in the way of clearing land and sowing grass seed before all that we propose be accomplished, and this is not without an object even should we only take into account the annual loss of transport horses in that part of the route, without considering the future commercial importance of having a good road to the interior ...

I have before remarked that we are not yet fully supplied with pack horses for the inland transport; but hereafter there will not be so great a loss from the effects of hunger, fatigue, and careless driving in the mountains, while the measures taken to recruit our stock from the brood mares at Thompson's River can hardly fail of meeting all our wants.[5]

In all seasons of the year, First Nations men and HBC employees walked over the trail to Fort Hope, carrying letters from Kamloops. In April 1852, Douglas reported to the London Committee on recent news from New Caledonia:

I have lately received intelligence from Fort Langley to the 10th April, Thompson's River to the 1st of April, and New Caledonia to the 28th of February.

The general failure of the Salmon in the latter District has occasioned great distress among the Native tribes, but happily there had been no loss of life, as by constant exertion they had contrived to exist on Rock weed [Black Tree Lichen],[6] and casual supplies of food obtained by hunting. The worst of the winter was then over, and they were beginning to derive much assistance from trout and other early fish, which they were taking in considerable quantities. The returns had not suffered to the extent usual in times of dearth, for Chief Trader Manson reports that they are fully more valuable than the trade of last year. At Thompson's River, C.T. Fraser had procured an early supply of salmon from the Tribes of Fraser's River, equal to the support of his own people and to succor the lower Posts of New Caledonia as well, and the Indians of his own District, thereby enabling them to devote their time to hunting furs. The returns are rather under the standard of last year, but the decrease in value is not great. The horses and neat cattle had come well off the winter which was remarkably mild all over the Interior.[7]

Neat cattle, mentioned above, were mature cows that had calved.

Douglas also reported to Yale that "Mr. Manson will leave Stuart's Lake on his journey to the Depot rather earlier than usual, and will be scarce of provisions ere he reaches Thompson's River."[8] At Fort St. James, Manson prepared for the departure of the outgoing brigades. In the post journal, he noted: "The Indians report that the water in the river between this and Fort George is indeed very low and expect will have some difficulty with the brigade before they reach Alexandria."[9]

For many years Donald Manson was the chief trader in charge at Fort St. James, New Caledonia. By 1865 he was retired from the company and living in Oregon. Photographer unknown, ca. 1865.

The New Caledonia brigades left Fort St. James on the morning of April 23, arriving at Fort Alexandria six days later. "About noon C.T. Manson arrived from Stuarts Lake with a Brigade of 4 Boats," McLean wrote. "He is accompanied by Mr. Ferdinand McKenzie. I am happy to say that all is well in the interior."[10]

Over the next few days the men hauled up the boats and sorted the horse *agrets* —a voyageur word for "equipment." On Tuesday McLean noted that "Laferte, St. Paul [Leolo], and Toutlaid arrived from Thompson's River. They have brought the New Caledonia horses, many of which have been stolen by the Indians and some have died. Mr. Fraser has also forwarded by this opportunity 5 kegs of wheat & 7 of potatoes."[11]

That spring, in a letter to Eden Colvile, Fraser bragged about the attention "paid to the Brood Mares attached to this place since my assuming the charge of them; as not one of them has been either disposed or worked since knowing the difficulty of procuring Horses now from the Columbia."[12] However, he later discovered that some horses and colts were missing. In July 1851, Douglas had stated there were 180 broodmares on the

Kamloops farm. According to Eden Colvile's report to the London Committee, it appears that thirteen mares were lost over the winter:

> I have much satisfaction in stating that the band of Brood Mares attached to this post having done remarkably well, and the Stock consists at present of: 167 Brood Mares; 47 Colt, 3 years old; 21 Colts, 2 years old; 91 Colts, 1 year old; 22 Colts of this spring up to the time of the departure of the Packet [York Factory Express], at which date of course there were many of the mares yet to foal. I go into these details because it is to this establishment that we have to look for the future, for the horses required for the Interior transport, as the price asked by the Indians at Walla Walla and the Snake Country, on whom we formerly depended, is so exorbitant, that none can be profitably procured from that quarter.[13]

With the news of the loss of horses ringing in the New Caledonia gentlemen's ears, the brigades left Fort Alexandria on April 8, with Donald McLean second-in-charge under Manson. It appears that McLean travelled with the brigades in order to act as "the bully."

In the early days on the east side of the Rocky Mountains, *bully* was an actual position in the fur trade for both the HBC and the NWC. A bully was a strong man who was willing to intimidate: he protected his company and enforced the rules, punishing offenders whether they were employees of a competing company or First Nations people who traded at the competitor's posts. In 1802, the NWC bully James King claimed furs that the much younger Joseph-Maurice LaMothe, of the short-lived XY Company, had collected—and lost his life as a result. Two later Nor'Westers, Samuel Black and Peter Skene Ogden, could also be said to be enforcers and were so effective at their job that when the HBC took control of the NWC in 1821, Governor Simpson refused them positions in the new company. Ogden eventually succeeded in convincing the governor to employ them, but both spent years in the

"Donald McLean, chief trader of the Hudson's Bay Company's post at Kamloops, British Columbia, ca. 1850s." Photographer unknown.

183

worst positions that Simpson could think of: Black explored the wilds of the Finlay River, and Ogden spent years in the desolation of the Snake River district.

Forty years later, the role of the bully still existed in the west, and it appears that Donald McLean most often acted as the HBC's enforcer in New Caledonia. Historian Bruce McIntyre Watson wrote of McLean: "Throughout his long career with the HBC, he left a trail of heavy-handedness, a condition that his superiors appeared to overlook."[14] In February 1849, McLean searched for the murderer of Alexis Belanger, who had died at Fort Alexandria. He "went up [to Quesnel River] with the intention of killing the murderer of poor Belanger & as there was no chance of his falling in with him he killed the instigator (the chief). The other young man (a son-in-law of the chief) was shot in mistake."[15]

In 1852, McLean acted as enforcer once again, riding out with the HBC brigades as they made their way over the brigade trail to Kamloops. As we see above, McLean had always held the position of bully for all the company communities in the region. The bully enforced HBC rules on First Nations people who were connected by trade to those communities, but whose behaviour conflicted with the HBC's expectations of honesty and trustworthiness. It was McLean's job to locate the offending First Nations man, and to punish him by thrashing him in front of his own Indigenous community. Then, in a forceful conversation with the First Nations present, he made them agree that the man deserved his punishment. In this way, every First Nations man learned what would happen to him if he was caught stealing or damaging a horse that belonged to the company.

Manson described McLean's duties to the Governor and Council:

> I am sorry to inform you that throughout the winter of 1851 and spring of /52 great depredations were committed on our horses by the Kamloops Indians, indeed to such an extent and so daring were these vagabonds in this wholesale slaughter of our horses and cattle at that place, that I saw if not immediately [stopped], they would soon become so formidable as to affect our business in the interior very seriously. I therefore determined before [leaving] this place [Fort St. James] last spring, all those who had been causing the destruction of our horses or cattle, if they could be found, should be severely punished, and to enable me to carry through this necessary tho' disagreeable duty, and

at the same time to provide for the safety of the brigade, in case of accident to myself, I took Mr. McLean along with me to the Depot. On our way out several of the Culprits were caught, and on every occasion punished as he deserved, that is by flogging, and this punishment on every occasion was witnessed by their friends and countrymen, who all acknowledged the justice of their chastisement. This severe but salutary lesson will, I trust, have its desired effect.[16]

The rumour has always existed among modern-day historians that McLean loathed the First Nations population that the company traded with. Yet it appeared from the Fort Alexandria journals that McLean ran his post with a gentle but strong hand and did not exhibit any obvious inability to get along with the First Nations men who traded at the fort. But it was his job to punish First Nations men if they stole from the company. Today people say he did not respect First Nations (and that is probably true).[17] But if he did not, he kept his feelings under wraps until such time as his specialized service was called upon once again.

There is little information on the brigades' passage over the Tulameen Plateau to Fort Hope in the summer of 1852. On July 12, Douglas reported to the London Committee that he had met the brigades at Fort Langley. His letter continues:

> Chief Traders Fraser & Manson arrived at Fort Langley with the New Caledonia & Thompson's River Parties, and the Returns of those Districts, on the 22nd June, having left Thompson's River on the 10th preceding.
>
> Though a month earlier than the usual season for commencing the journey to the Depot, no difficulty was experienced in crossing the Fraser River mountains, as the snow which still covered the higher passes to a great depth was compact enough to support the horses and did not cause the slightest inconvenience, while at the different halting places the grass was sufficiently grown to supply the animals abundantly with food. The practicability of passing these mountains with horses at so early a season, a subject which gave rise to much anxiety, may be now regarded as an established fact and has removed all

fears about the business of the interior as the Brigade may always reach their respective destinations in full time to secure the harvest and supply the distant outposts before the approach of winter.

I am sorry to report a great decline in the Returns of Martens in New Caledonia in consequence, chiefly, of the failure of the salmon fisheries last season in Fraser's River, which was the cause of much suffering, both to the whites and natives. There is on the other hand an increase of the Beaver returns and on the whole the money value of the furs collected will not fall much short of the returns of last year.[18]

As Manson had predicted, instead of hunting marten in the winter of 1851–52, the First Nations hunters had turned their attention to trapping beaver, which in addition to giving them an income, provided them with a meaty meal. Douglas's letter continues:

The returns of Thompson's River rather exceed those of the preceding year, and the business of that District is in other respects in a prosperous state. The horses and neat cattle on the farm at Thompson's River, besides being healthy and in good order, exhibited a satisfactory increase. About 60 three-year-old colts bred and reared on this farm will be disposable in 1853 and about 80 colts of the same age will be fit to break in for 1854. After that the farm may supply from 90 to 100 young horses annually, which will exceed the number required for the service, in which case they will be sold off to Indians or other parties who may wish to become purchasers.

Messrs. Manson & Fraser with their respective Brigades left Fort Langley on their return to the interior on the 8th of this month [July], and will I trust have a safe and expeditious journey to their several stations.[19]

In a letter to John Ballenden at Fort Vancouver, Douglas reported that his stay at Fort Langley had been quiet, but not uneventful. "I paid my annual visit to Langley where I met the gentlemen of the Interior. Everything passed off quietly and they started on their return to the interior on the 8th July. Four men since deserted from the Brigade and are now here in confinement."[20] They would be shipped to the northwest coast post of Fort Simpson, from which there was no escape.

In his report to the Governor and Council, written in February 1853, Donald Manson expressed satisfaction with the present state of the brigade trail:

> I am happy to inform you that it is now ascertained beyond all doubt that the route, for the past three years to Langley, can be traveled through at a much earlier date than was supposed when it was first opened by me. I then was of the opinion that the depth of snow on the two intercepting mountain ranges could completely prevent the passing of horses. The past two years' experience has, however, convinced me of my error, and that from the compactness and hardness of the snow on those Alpine heights, our horses have less difficulty in passing them than in threading their way through the deep ravines where no snow has ever yet been met with by us on our way to the Depot. I last year [1852] left Kamloops with the brigade on the 10th June and without forcing the horses, arrived at Fort Hope on the 21st. We found considerable quantity of snow on Campement de Chevreuil (Mount Colvile) [Mount Davis] but had little or no difficulty in passing either it or the other intersecting ridge.[21]

It is not known when the brigades reached Kamloops on their incoming journey, nor on what day the New Caledonia brigade started for Fort Alexandria. On August 2, Ferdinand McKenzie wrote in the Fort Alexandria journal, "I had the agreeable intelligence of the Brigade by the arrival of a messenger from Thompson's River. Mr. Manson writes me that they are sadly in want of horses."[22] McLean rode into Alexandria on August 16, when he wrote, "The brigade arrived from Langley all well."[23] On August 20, Manson continued his journey upriver to Fort St. James, taking with him Ferdinand McKenzie and some Fort Alexandria men, and leaving McLean at the post with only one man. McKenzie had not done a good job over the summer, and McLean complained:

> Clear sunny weather, arranging various matters. No Salmon to be had. Our potatoes a complete failure as also the Oats, the Wheat very indifferent and no hay made. Starvation

with all its horrors will no doubt be our Lot. D. Manson Esquire has not left the Equipment for this post, merely the whole pieces say Tobacco, Powder, Ball & Shot, so that I have no great variety to induce the Indians to bring in provisions, admitting they have any to share.[24]

By the end of the month, however, salmon began to show up in the river, and McLean felt more optimistic about provisions for the winter. "A few Caisse [Chinook] and Salmon [Sockeye] traded this morning. God send that Salmon may yet arrive in sufficient quantities to enable me to obtain a supply of provisions for the post without depending upon others."[25]

Food was also an issue at Fort St. James, where the men who had remained behind heard news of the boats coming upriver on August 31. On September 1 "two young men arrived and informed us that Mr. Manson with one boat was a little below the rapid on his way up from Fort Langley, and had left one boat a short distance from this, and the two other boats were left behind from below Fort George in charge of Mr. McKenzie."[26] The second boat arrived the next day, and four days later the two boats under Ferdinand McKenzie made their appearance.

In July 1852, Douglas had instructed Manson that he was once again responsible for the job of clearing the Fort Hope Road the following spring:

I beg to inform you that the recruits from York Factory are again ordered in by the way of New Caledonia, and may be expected at Tete Jaune's Cache about the 10th October next, and you please to send boats and provisions to meet them at that point and bring them to Fort George.

These men will spend the winter in New Caledonia, and their services may be made available in rebuilding and repairing the Forts of the District, several of which are, I hear, in a dilapidated state. In the spring of 1853 they will be drafted off to supply the deficiencies of the establishments of New Caledonia, and the remainder should be brought to Fort Langley for general service ...

We shall depend upon reaching Kamloops with the Caledonia people about the 20th of May next year [1853], and that you will employ the whole force of the two Districts in repairing and improving the Fort Hope road, until such time as the mountains become accessible to horses, which will not be before the 10th of June, so that you will have about 20 days disposable for the improvement of the road, and with a large force under your own able and energetic management a great deal may be done in that time.[27]

However, the idea of additional men arriving for the winter sent Manson into a panic when the salmon run failed. Manson reported to the Governor and Council that on September 1, when he arrived at Fort St. James, he found:

the stores empty, not one days rations at the place, no appearance of salmon in the River, and from the lateness of the season, but faint hopes of any eventually casting up. I therefore dispatched Mr. Griffin to the Babines in order to procure a few for immediate use, and at the same time to ascertain what quantity I might depend upon from thence. On the 16th September he returned without having procured any, and informed me that altho' the natives of that place had a good many amongst them, still they refused to dispense of them unless we paid double the usual price. Fortunately, during Mr. Griffin's absence, a few Salmon made their appearance here, but the Natives had some time before despaired of any coming up and consequently had stowed away all their fishing apparatus, and ere they got this in order the greater part of the fish had passed, and I regret to say, they only secured a very scanty supply for their own use. The Season, by this time, was so far advanced that (from my own experience for the past ten years, together with what I could learn from the former records of this station) I had not the slightest hopes of securing even a scanty supply for the winter, and dire starvation with all its accompanying evils stared me in the face, and in this state of things I was, most reluctantly, constrained to dispatch an express to Jasper's House, in order to prevent the expected incoming Party from passing by the Tete Jaune's Cache, as the addition of so many more mouths, had they come into this district, would have greatly helped to increase the difficulties I then anticipated.[28]

From Fort Victoria, Douglas expressed disappointment in Manson's hasty decision, calling it "an arrangement which I much regret, as there will be great difficulty next season in replacing the returning Servants from the Interior should those men desert during the Winter."[29] The men would come all the way downriver to Fort Vancouver, where desertion was common because of the many opportunities to make good money among the American settlers. However, when the Columbia Express arrived in early November, Ballenden forwarded the new men to Fort Victoria before they could desert.

In February 1853, Douglas reported to the London Committee that "I lately received intelligence from New Caledonia ... Provisions were abundant and not the slightest fear of scarcity existed, notwithstanding the alarm & anxiety caused by Mr. Manson's previous reports. Martens were reported to be on the increase and there was every prospect of fair returns."[30]

Another letter from Manson, written in 1853 to the governor, explained an additional problem that plagued the brigades: a shortage of leather. As early as the 1840s their usual supplier of leather goods, the Peace River post of Dunvegan, had begun having difficulty collecting skins of large animals because of the shortage of moose and bison in their territory. Fort Colvile could no longer obtain buffalo skins from the east side of the mountains as the Blackfoot had successfully barred the Ktunaxa from their buffalo hunts. Deer may have provided skins, but they were small and hard to find in the heavy forests of New Caledonia, and the First Nations people had their own need for the deerskins they collected. Cowhides were collected at Kamloops, but not in sufficient quantities to supply the brigades. Manson thought his only hope was to get a supply of leather from the Saskatchewan district. "I learn from the minutes of Council of last summer that a portion of our leather supplies is to be sent in this fall by the Tete Jaune's Cache route," Manson wrote. "May I therefore beg that from 20 to 25 dressed Buffalo skins, for arranging our horse appointments, may likewise be sent in by the same route. We formerly received such supplies from Colvile district, but for the past 4 or 5 years it has furnished us with nothing in the shape of leather, and I have been constrained, much against my will, to cut up moose skins for this purpose."[31]

Simpson expressed his impatience with Manson's request and tartly suggested he find other sources of leather. His somewhat sarcastic suggestions for the replacement of this necessary product may have shocked Manson. As leather was becoming so scarce in New Caledonia, the governor noted, Manson must devise new ways to replace this expensive material. Simpson wrote:

One way in which you may supply within the district a large proportion of common leather would be to skin the horses that are killed annually in such number in transport &c; the leather is very good & by making use of it, it will be turning even the dead horses to account. You should also prohibit the destruction of Moose Skins for making horse harness, shot & saddle bags &c, for which a less expensive article would answer perfectly well. For hobbles; horse hair or twisted withies [tough, flexible branches of willow] may be substituted for leather.[32]

Manson also discussed this problem with Douglas, who was more sympathetic. In 1853, Douglas told Paul Fraser that he should cross the mountains without a hide covering on his packs, and Fraser reported on his arrival at Kamloops that "my Bales without Hide or parflesh [parfleche] reached this without a Covering being torn. Mr. Douglas was right about the hides."[33] Later, Douglas forwarded sheepskins to Fort Langley for the use of the brigades, and in April 1857 he informed Manson that he was "now collecting all the leather that I can possibly procure for the use of New Caledonia, and shall make it a point to send you a number of tanned seal skins which I have no doubt will be found admirably adapted for general use among the men and Indians. I shall also send you a supply of sheep and parchment deer skins for horse appointments."[34]

A few months after he penned that letter, however, Douglas learned that the supply of leather from Dunvegan was so small as to make it "scarcely worth the expense of sending for it. I am therefore starting a tannery on Vancouver's Island for the preparation of Deer skins, and expect to furnish New Caledonia abundantly with leather next year."[35]

This was, in fact, a few years in the future. In October 1852, Fort Langley's James Murray Yale had more positive things to say, as he reported to Governor Simpson on the brigade trail:

We hear no more complaints about the new route to the interior. Fraser, to whom the credit is due of bringing out the Brigades some twenty or thirty days earlier than was considered practicable, praises it highly, and that luxuriant Man, McLean, seems to think it a matter too slight to advert upon, and in reality there appears to be but one considerable obstruction to a Waggon road on leaving the banks of Fraser's River, called Manson's Mountain, and that affords the pleasing prospect of a distant view of Campement de Chevreuil in the Land of Promise. Manson himself begins to appreciate its great advantages.[36]

By November, reports that the brigades were travelling much more easily over the new trail had reached the London Committee, and everyone believed that its many problems were resolved. The solution to the shortage of horses would come when the two-year-old colts at Kamloops were put into service as pack horses. The travelling times on the trails between the various posts were shorter. New men came into the district regularly every autumn over the Rocky Mountain Portage in sufficient numbers to keep the posts in good order and to work on the trail. The trail itself was becoming easier to travel, and under Douglas's leadership it would continue to improve.

→ 13 ←

1853 BRIGADES: CLUB LAW

By March 1853 the slow-moving gold rush reached Oregon Territory, and Paul Fraser reported from Kamloops that some of his men had departed for the new gold grounds at Grande Ronde, east of Walla Walla. But for the most part the HBC had other worries: shortage of provisions, loss of horses, and shortage of leather and agrets (equipment). The territory had also suffered extreme cold that winter, but in spite of that, Douglas reported that the Kamloops horses and cattle "had come off the severe winter with little loss, and in tolerable condition, which was then rapidly improving."[1] At the same time, Manson defended himself and his territory against Governor Simpson's charges that the fur returns of the district were falling off. Manson's letter contains interesting, and surprising, information about the district:

> In regard to the 1st part of your letter where you say that the Returns of New Caledonia have been declining for several years back, I beg leave, with much deference, to say that this falling off is not in the bulk of Returns annually collected, which for the past ten years will average, or very nearly so, as high as what was procured by my predecessor. The great falling off is caused by the non-demand for Beaver [in London], and the low price they have commanded for the last ten years ... I am however, happy to state Martens and Lynx appear to be plentiful again to this quarter, and that there is a very considerable increase in this fur in the returns of this year [1853] when compared with those of Outfit /52. Indeed, this increase, I am happy to state, is general in every description of fur, with the exception of Bears, in which there is a slight falling off.[2]

On April 17, Manson and the Fort St. James men were "rushing themselves as [they] intend starting for Langley tomorrow."[3] Beginning a brigade journey excited the Métis, who were always ready for a change of scenery. On April 18 the clerk recorded:

> Weather cloudy but a little frost during the night. C.T.
> Manson accompanied with Messrs. [Ferdinand] McKenzie
> & [William] Todd with the boats loaded 78 Packs and 7
> Kegs Castoreum and 47 Bales of Salmon, manned 5 men
> per boat, principally Indians which are to return from the
> Grand rapid.[4]

There were two bad rapids on the Fraser River south of Fort George: the "white water" rapids in Fort George Canyon, fifteen miles south of the post, and the Grand Rapids in Cottonwood Canyon below the West Road River. Once beyond these rapids, the few HBC men who remained with the boats experienced little trouble coming downriver to Fort Alexandria. McLean reported on their arrival on May 1:

> This afternoon the Interior Brigade of 4 Boats (under charge
> of D. Manson, C.T.) made its appearance. I am happy to
> state that the Returns are superior to those of last year
> and that all is well and quiet at the different posts.[5]

Although it was unusual for the gentleman in charge of Fort Alexandria to go out with the brigades, McLean did make the trip, as he had done the previous year. There is little information on the brigade's journey south, but they left Kamloops on June 5 and reached Campement des Femmes before June 12. Ferdinand McKenzie had been placed in charge of the road crew this year; it rained heavily the whole time his crew worked on the trail. On June 15 McKenzie reported from Fort Hope that the steady rain had created a massive problem on the trail:

> I am happy to inform you that the interior Brigades,
> New Caledonia & Thompson's River, are on their way
> hither. I left them at the Guard [Campement des Femmes]
> on the 12th inst. [June] from which place I was dispatched
> ahead by Mr. Manson with four men to make repairs on
> the road. Everything so far has gone favourable with us,
> but Manson's Mountain is one state of [mess] from top to
> bottom & in the peak [plenty] of snow, so I expect they

will experience some difficulty in crossing this piece of road. Ever since I left them it has been raining incessantly & from this I judge they have not yet started from their Encampment, & if the weather proves at all favourable to them, I give them four or five days grace at the furtherest [*sic*] to be here.[6]

No one had complained about Manson's Mountain before 1853, but in the years that followed the ridge was always reported to be the most difficult part of the trail. Susan Allison, who as a fifteen-year-old lived outside Fort Hope, described the trail down the mountain as she knew it in 1860:

In the early days we had no roads, only rough trails mostly those used by the Hudson's Bay Company and Indians—with no attempt at grades. In crossing the Hope Mountains the Hudson's Bay Company brigade always took twice as many horses as were needed and went well armed. The horses were taken to enable them to negotiate "the Slide" on Manson's Mountain where they invariably lost half their horses. There was no road, the

"Interior of Fort Victoria." Painted by Matthew Fortescue Moresby in 1851.

trail ended at the top of the Slide and the horses were driven over the bank and once started had to go on sliding to the bottom. A few of the horses who had been used before had learned to brace themselves and went without being forced to go, and usually came through without accident. Going back it was easier on them.[7]

The trail over Manson's Mountain would continue to be a headache for the HBC men, and many hours were spent trying to find a fix. In 1859, Royal Engineer Henry Spencer Palmer rode over the ridge and recorded that his horse party had "commenced the laborious ascent of the mountain by a zig-zag trail, very steep and rocky, but, fortunately, for ourselves and the horses, free from mud. After struggling up this difficult mountain path for an hour and a half we reached the summit of the pass."[8] (More from his journal, and others, is included in the epilogue.)

Many gradual changes had occurred over the years after 1849, both in the interior and at Fort Victoria. In 1851, Douglas had been made governor of the Colony of Vancouver's Island, which had been established two years earlier. The first colonists had come in 1849, and by 1853 there were as many as three hundred settlers outside Fort Victoria. Douglas was also still a chief factor in the HBC, and the colonists grumbled whenever he looked after company business. As a result, Douglas shortened his annual visits to Fort Langley. On his return to Fort Victoria in 1853, he reported on the apparent success of the trail:

> The outward passage was effected without serious accident, and though they left Thompson's River on the 5th of June, the horses passed the mountains safely on the hardened snow, and found food enough during their stay at the usual halting places, and we therefore propose to make a move from Thompson's River next spring on the 1st day of June, which will be a further advantage to the business, and as early in the season as is desirable.
>
> The fur returns from the Interior exceed in value those received in Outfit 1851, and I have much satisfaction in reporting that the spring trade in Martens was unusually good, and that martens as well as lynx are evidently on the increase, and will probably give a large yield on the current outfit.

The farm at Thompson's River [Kamloops] has not been productive in grain, as neither the soil in the vicinity of the fort nor the climate are favourable for farming, and the number of labouring servants, 16 in all attached to the District, cannot with due attention to the trade and running stock devote much attention to tillage operations.[9]

In the past, Fort Alexandria had been the most productive farm in the territory, and for many years provided the other posts with grain and vegetables. But almost all of the post's Canadien employees had retired, and First Nations men, who were not so reliable, looked after the horses. As a result, Kamloops became the provisions post for the territory. The men there had less trouble obtaining salmon from the First Nations, and although the soil was not good for farming, they were successful at raising the horses and cattle. Douglas reported that at Thompson's River there were now 500 broodmares and 326 cattle, young and old, and "the stock farm at Thompson's River performed a very important part in reference to the interior, both as respects the supply of food, and of the means of transport."[10]

Of his return journey from Fort Langley, Douglas reported to Yale: "We arrived here last night with the Boats and got the Furs all dry and safe on board the *Cadboro*, and we are now ready for sea and waiting a favourable breeze to proceed on our voyage."[11] *Here* was the mouth of the Fraser River, where the ship had remained at anchor off Point Pelly (modern-day Steveston, B.C.).

In July, Douglas reported from Fort Victoria:

The brigade arrived at Fort Langley on the 18th June, and left on the return to the interior on the 3rd and 5th July. The men were as usual somewhat difficult to manage, but they were all induced to return to the interior, with the exception of 3 who deserted from the Boats, but were afterwards captured and put to a severe penance. The interior furs were shipped by the Schooner *Cadboro* and safely landed at this place to remain here for the next return ship.[12]

At a later date, Douglas penned an angry letter to Donald Manson regarding the three deserters from the New Caledonia brigade:

The desertion of three of your men on the morning you went to leave Fort Langley with the Brigade, is really a most annoying circumstance, calling for very stringent measures of prevention: but there appears to be a great reluctance on the part of all my colleagues to resort to the only measure which will ever put a stop to such proceedings. I am of course [illegible] and should be the last person in the country to advocate violent measures, but every one must be convinced that a deep-rooted evil requires a severe operation before it can be vindicated, and Gentlemen, the remedy is in your own hands, and can be used when necessity requires it. I am quite convinced that none of your men had any just cause of complaint, and that their conduct in deserting your Brigade is altogether inexcusable. I have not seen the parties, who will remain at Fort Langley until your arrival next year.[13]

Douglas's letter, which strongly suggested that Manson should use violence to punish his men for desertion, was written in November 1853. At about the same time as Douglas penned his letter, Manson received Governor Simpson's letter on the same subject, which arrived with the incoming Columbia Express. Simpson told Manson that the "service in New Caledonia is very unpopular among the people in consequence of the reports spread of the rough treatment experienced at the hands of the Company's officers":

There is at present a retiring Winterer from your district, one François Lacourse, who states that he was very severely beaten by Mr. P. Ogden, who knocked him down, kicked him and injured him so seriously that the man has since then been subject to epileptic fits. He states that on another occasion when angry with him, you aimed a blow at him with an axe, but fortunately missed him & only cut open his coat, which he exhibited here, & he further adds that you afterwards presented him with a suit of clothes as reparation for this injury. These are the exparte statements of Lacourse & may be in part false, but taken in connexion with other cases of late years, they afford ample evidence of the existence of a system of "club law" which must not be allowed to prevail. We duly appreciate the necessity for maintaining discipline & enforcing obedience, but that end is not to be attained by the display of violent passion and the inflection of severe & arbitrary punishment in hot blood: when a servant is refractory or disobeys orders, he should be allowed a full hearing, his case examined fairly & deliberately, & if he be guilty either taken out to the depot, put on short rations, or under arrest—in fact almost any punishment rather than knocking about or flogging. I have to beg that you will make the foregoing remarks known to Mr. P. Ogden, Mr. McLean and other officers in the district, and I trust we may hear of no more of these disagreeable affairs.[14]

Club law was by no means unknown in this district. As early as winter 1827, clerk George McDougall was sent east across the Rocky Mountain Portage (Yellowhead Pass) on foot up the frozen Fraser River from Fort St. James. He and his four men arrived at Tête Jaune's Cache, where he discovered a Canadien man had discarded the provisions he carried to lighten his load. The section of the journal that has been published does not tell how McDougall punished the man, but it is clear that he was left behind, dead or alive, at Tête Jaune's Cache.[15] In February 1849, as noted in Chapter 12, Donald McLean killed two Dakelh men for the shooting of Alexis Belanger, although neither was guilty of his death. In 1855, Paul Fraser is supposed to have killed a man by beating him to death. The man was Michel Fallardeau, a Métis from Red River who had arrived in the district in 1827 with Edward Ermatinger's incoming Columbia Express. The story of his death was recorded in A.G. Morice's *The History of the Northern Interior of British Columbia*, but the Fort St. James journals that cover this time period are lost or destroyed. This is the story that Morice told:

> At that time clubbing and flogging were the devices resorted to in order to enforce obedience or punish a wrong. Now, it happened that for some offence, the nature of which is not remembered, he gave (at Kamloops) to one of his men, a French Canadian named Falardeau, such a beating that the poor fellow died of it. As Baptiste, an Iroquois, was planing and bending the planks intended for the luckless man's coffin, Fraser happened to pass by.
>
> "What are you doing with these boards?" he asked of the Iroquois. "Rough, unplaned boards are good enough for that rascal."

> The Iroquois, surprised at such a remark under the cir-
> cumstances, stared a moment at his master; then, with
> the brutal frankness proper to his race: "Hehm! When
> you die you may not have even rough boards to be bur-
> ied in," observed the laborer.[16]

In 1853 it can only have confused Manson to have received two such conflicting instructions from the two men who were his immediate supe-riors. Although Simpson disapproved of flogging, Douglas did not. Flogging was very much part of the discipline of the Royal Navy at this time, and James Anderson, who attended school at Fort Victoria in the early 1850s, remembered an occasion when Douglas ordered that one of his men be flogged. (His story reveals that some of the children who attended Reverend Staines's school at Fort Victoria suffered the same punishment.) James wrote:

> One of the men attached to the Fort was flogged, for what
> reason I do not know. It took place on the Company's
> jetty. The man was stripped, bound to a post and the cat
> o'nine tails applied to his back. Being a novel sight and
> not for a moment thinking it cruel, accustomed as we were
> to the cruel castigation inflicted by Mr. Staines on some of
> the boys, we viewed the performance with equanimity.[17]

In the isolated HBC communities of New Caledonia, where difficult employees were sent as punishment for misbehaviour at other posts, com-plaints of violence were common. Both Peter Ogden Jr. and Paul Fraser were noted for their violent acts. Ogden beat his men for disobedience, but Fraser had a streak of meanness that caused him to hit his men for any reason whatsoever. Donald Manson also punished his men, but in his case it appears that his inability to control his temper was the reason for his vio-lent outbursts.

Whenever men are mistreated they will resist in some way, and one of the ways that the New Caledonia men resisted was by taking every oppor-tunity of abandoning the HBC community they no longer felt connected to. As the gentleman-in-charge, Donald Manson was left with the prob-lem of sorting out how best to balance the required punishment of his misbehaving men with the fair treatment Governor Simpson demanded. Did he expect his gentlemen, and himself, to follow Simpson's instructions and punish his men by methods other than beatings, methods that would prove ineffective when he considered the overall level of dissatisfaction among his employees? Could Manson discourage his gentlemen from beating their men when he could not control his own foul temper? Almost certainly the beatings would continue; so too would the attempted desertions and numerous complaints.

Manson's actions were those of an angry man who could not control his feelings, but he had good reason for his simmering rage. As mentioned in Chapter 10, in 1850 he had not been promoted to chief factor, against all precedent. Three years later, he had still not received his long-awaited promotion. Every year, Manson was shamed in front of his own men when his promotion did not arrive. He did the work of a chief factor and had a chief factor's responsibilities, but he did not receive a chief factor's pay. Although he worked extremely hard at his job, he was angry and disappointed, and he took it out on his men. As a natural consequence, Manson's bad treatment of his own employees caused chaos and conflict among the men, and they abandoned their jobs—some from Fort Langley, and some directly from Fort St. James.

The work of bringing in the trade goods had to continue, however, and the constant distraction of scolding letters from Douglas had to be ignored. The incoming brigades left Fort Hope and arrived safely at Kamloops on July 20. In his letters, Fraser gave more information about the condition of Manson's Mountain:

> I have much pleasure of informing you that the Thompson's River brigade reached this on the 20th ulto [July] with Horses and property in good order. Mr. Manson reached this on the 28th and on the 30th left for Alexandria. From the three day Rain we had at Fort Hope, made Manson's Mountain very bad. Nevertheless we passed all the bad part of it in one day. So from Langley to this the voyage was performed in 14 days, with not a Horse injured in the Smallest degree.[18]

Douglas was pleased to hear of the brigade's safe arrival at Thompson's River. "I was very happy to learn by your letter of the 9th August of the safe arrival of the Brigades at Thompson's River without accident, and that the New Caledonia brigade proceeded towards Alexandria on the 30th July, and had reached Green Lake in safety."[19]

At Fort Alexandria, John Leonard reported in early August that no salmon were found at the rapid (Soda Creek) and there was no word of the incoming brigade. However, a week later the brigade arrived at the fort, and "all the property crossed over before night to the west or Fort side of the River."[20] On August 15 "the Interior brigade of 5 boats started for Stuarts Lake under the command of C.T. Donald Manson, Esquire, accompanied by Messrs. McKenzie & Todd, clerks."[21]

At Fort St. James the clerk reported that on August 27, "I was agreeably surprised of the early arrival of the Brigade this morning with 5 boats from Langley and this being the 13th day from Alexandria, the boats manned principally by Indians."[22]

In April 1853, Chief Factor John Ballenden left Fort Vancouver with the outgoing York Factory Express to Hudson Bay soon after Peter Skene Ogden returned from his furlough. Because of the danger of losing men to the goldfields, Ballenden had arranged that the Fort Colvile men would once again pack their furs out to The Dalles. At the end of April, Ogden told Governor Simpson, "I am daily expecting the arrival of Mr. McDonald from Colvile; his outfit is already prepared for him, and will be duly forwarded to The Dalles by the Indians, it not being considered good policy in the present times to bring the Servants here." Both Ballenden and Ogden knew that if the men came downriver to Fort Vancouver, they would be tempted to abandon the fur trade for the highly paid work now available in the district.

McDonald later reported to the Governor and Council from Fort Colvile:

> I have gone with our Returns to Vancouver, upwards of 120 Packs of furs with some Castoreum & Casks, and I made a safe arrival here [at Fort Colvile] with all the Outfit that I could bring, but could not bring the whole at one hit, as Chief Factor Ogden sold fifty of our horses to the American Government at $100 per head. The Balance of the Outfit was left at the Dalles but we are daily expecting it by a party sent for it a month ago.

> We have excellent crops. Our Returns have been good. Peace and death all around us. The small pox is playing a very mortal game with the poor natives of the Country. They were not numerous before and that disease has decreased a great many more of them. Upon this account and the increasing supplies independent of ours that find their way to the Rocky Mountains, I plainly see that the returns of '53 will not be so heavy. I may be mistaken, but I speak as prejudgement dictates.

I have already spoke to Mr. Ballenden about a blacksmith. If you think this establishment can be kept with its usual success without a man of that description let me state that it is a mistake. The way that our returns were conveyed from the Dalles was disagreeable and uncertain. A similar way has been tried to convey a part of the Outfit but it was no go. But I trust that these failures will quicken the perceptions of those who failed in order that we may make a more advantageous trip to the Depot in future.[24]

The blacksmith held an important position at Fort Colvile, as he made the axes and other farming utensils they used at that post and elsewhere. But the major problem this year was the sale of fifty of Angus McDonald's brigade horses to the American Army. Peter Skene Ogden almost certainly agreed to the deal because the American Army, now located in their own fort on the slope above Fort Vancouver, was the HBC's only protection against the ravages of the American settlers. The resulting shortage of horses made it impossible to bring McDonald's packs back to Fort Colvile in one trip.

His statement also indicates that there was trouble in the interior, or at The Dalles, that McDonald thought might threaten the Fort Colvile brigades. He considered it wise to try a different plan, and it does appear that a new road was available to his brigades. In November 1853, John Work, the third member of the Board of Management, suggested to Ogden and his second-in-command, Dugald Mactavish, that "as a road is now open from Nisqually to the Yakima Country, allow us to suggest that it might be even better for the Colvile returns to be brought to Nisqually and the outfits taken from that place than from Vancouver."[25]

Fort Nisqually was on Puget Sound, and the new road led west through Naches Pass from Yakima (now spelled Yakama) tribal territory. Although the route was well known to Indigenous communities on both sides of the Cascades, the HBC men did not often use the pass, which they called "Sinahomish." The lone exception appears to be Alexander Caulfield Anderson, who in 1842 had crossed the pass to deliver cattle from Forts Nez Percés and Okanagan to the new farms at Fort Nisqually. Peter Skene Ogden likely told Angus McDonald about this trail in 1854, and in 1855 the Fort Colvile men used it for the first and only time.

But this is still a year in the future.

❯ 14 ❮

1854 BRIGADES: HORSE RAID

Every February the gentlemen in charge of the northern posts wrote their reports. In his letter to Douglas, Manson once again brought up the subject of the shortage of horses in his district. Not surprisingly, Douglas responded in a fit of fury. "You also refer to the subject of the transport horses," he replied, "a certainly endless theme, and one which I did not expect to hear renewed after the great trouble and expense we have had in providing the large supply of horses, no less than 63 sent into New Caledonia last year [1853]. It is needless to tell us that the horses were old and useless animals, people will listen to such reports with incredulity, and no counter statements will ever remove the suspicions that the New Caledonia transport horses are miserably mismanaged."[1]

Douglas insisted that with proper care and management, Manson's horses could each carry two ninety-pound bales. However, the length of the trail between Fort Alexandria and Fort Hope was much longer than that travelled from Fort Colvile, where McDonald considered his horses too small for the heavy loads suggested by Douglas. As an HBC clerk noted:

> Each bale weighing eighty pounds, two of which made a load for a horse and weighed 160 pounds, a load quite heavy enough for a common pony weighing from 700 to 1,000 pounds to pack over such roads and trails as are found in this mountainous country.[2]

When Manson left Fort St. James on the first day of May 1854, the clerk who kept the post journal recorded that Manson and "Mr. Ferdinand McKenzie took their departure for Fort Langley in 4 Boat loads containing 106 packs of furs & 10 kegs Castoreum, returns from the upper forts not including the posts of Alexandria and Fort George."[3] The returns from Alexandria and Fort George added up to "146 pieces Returns (137 packs & 9 kegs castoreum)."[4]

At two packs per horse, the New Caledonia men needed seventy-three horses to pack out their goods. While we don't know how many horses were sent into New Caledonia in 1854, Douglas said that sixty-three had been forwarded in 1853. Clearly, in some years there were not enough horses available for the loads they had to carry out. It is unlikely that the chief trader at Kamloops, Paul Fraser, who was not a generous man at the best of times, would make his own journey to Fort Langley more difficult by sending additional horses to New Caledonia. Yet the traders had to bring all the furs to the coast, whether to Fort Langley or Fort Vancouver, in the summertime. The distance from Fort Alexandria allowed for only one trip to the coast every summer. And furs that did not reach London in time for the sales caused the company a loss—something that everyone took seriously.

Thus the gentlemen of the HBC communities in New Caledonia had a problem they could not solve without increasing the number of pack horses at their disposal. At this time, the HBC was using only stallions, geldings, and inexperienced two-year-old colts as pack horses: the mares were kept at the Kamloops farm for breeding purposes. Manson could not reduce the loads the individual horses carried as that would add to the number of horses required. In fact, it is highly likely that Manson increased the loads that some of the strongest horses carried out, which conflicted with orders sent to him by Governor Simpson and James Douglas. What other choice did he have? The HBC was a business first and foremost, and there was no profit in leaving furs behind at Fort Alexandria: they had to reach the London markets as quickly as was possible. The overloading of horses might have worked if the New Caledonia men were only travelling as far as Kamloops, as they had done in the past. But since the HBC men had begun to use the trail over the Tulameen Plateau, their horses travelled all the way from Fort Alexandria to Fort Hope and return, with only short rests at Kamloops.

Everyone, including the First Nations neighbours, looked forward to the arrival of the boats at Fort Alexandria. In 1859 an Englishman described the arrival of the New Caledonia boats in early April. The excitement generated among the fort's employees was intense and contagious:

> The fort at this place [Fort Alexandria] was a very important one. Here came every spring the huge Batteaux of the Company from Fort George and further north, bringing down the year's furs for shipment to Fort Hope. When I

arrived there about April 1st, the Fraser was still frozen
over solid and I crossed over to the Fort several times on
the ice trail. About April 4 I heard a tremendous explo-
sion early in the morning. I ran to the river bank close at
hand, and saw a most wonderful sight. The ice was breaking. The river was opening. First the well-worn trail over
the smooth white ice began to slowly move, the whole
river mobbing, at first in a solid sheet, but constant
explosions took place, in an hour the ice began to break
up in huge cakes, and by evening it came only in large
broken masses. The river was very wide at the Fort but
not turbulent. Late in the afternoon I heard great noise
and shouting. Running down to the river bank I saw a fine
sight, one seldom seen—several large heavy Batteaux
pulling long oars were coming in and amongst the ice
cakes, all filled with Canadian voyageurs and half Breeds,
in their wild mountain dress.[5]

In 1854 the boats arrived a month later than these boats had. McLean
reported on May 4: "The river still rising rapidly. Afternoon thunder and
Hail and Heavy showers of rain. The Indians are gathering round in
expectation of the Brigade," although McLean was "much afraid that the
Brigade will have much difficulty in passing the Rapids owing to the very
high water in the River."[6] Manson's boats arrived safely at Fort Alexandria
on May 6, and there is no record of any difficulties they may have experienced upriver.

The men had work to do: storing the boats in the shade of the now-
empty hayshed, packing the furs, and arranging the packs for the horses.
On Sunday, May 14, McLean noted in the post journal: "Did not start
with the Brigade on account of it being the Sabbath but God willing will
make a start tomorrow leaving Mr. Ferdinand McKenzie in charge of the
Establishment during my absence with the Brigades."[7]

The brigades experienced some unexpected difficulties on their way
out to Fort Hope that summer. On July 4 Ferdinand McKenzie reported
that "late in the afternoon William Atnah arrived from Kamloops. He left
the brigade at Campement des Femmes. They were remaining there as
snow was plentiful in the mountains."[8]

William Atnah was the Secwepemc chief at the Barge, forty miles south
of Fort Alexandria. At Campement des Femmes, the HBC men kept their

horses under guard of one or two men who kept smoky fires burning to drive off the flies. As the brigades waited for the trail to clear, some Nlaka'pamux men raided the horseguard and drove off the HBC horses. The enraged HBC gentlemen followed their trail, and when they located the chiefs, they threatened them with loss of trade if the animals were not promptly returned. The Nlaka'pamux surrendered their rustled prizes, and the horses were safely delivered to Fort Hope with their loads. When Douglas heard about the attack, he was both angered and relieved. "It is well that they [the Nlaka'pamux] returned the horses as it saves us from the trouble of going for them."[9]

Young Susan Allison, who lived outside Fort Hope in the 1860s, described the horses that arrived at the post as "splendid animals, hardy and enduring, with lots of good horse sense."[10] She also wrote of the excitement that occurred as the brigade horses galloped into the post.

> From the doorway of our shack we could see the Hudson's Bay Company's Post and watch the pack trains come in from Colville, Keremeos and other places. Sometimes there would be a grand stampede and the pack trains would disrupt. Horses and men could be seen through a misty cloud of dust, madly dashing all over the Hope flat, lassos flying, dogs barking, hens flying for safety anywhere. Suddenly the tempest would subside as fast as it had arisen, the pack boys would emerge from the clouds of dust leading the ring leaders in the stampede.[11]

This year, Douglas sent another man to Fort Langley in his stead. He reported that "the Brigades arrived at Langley about the usual time with very large returns in Martens. Those valuable animals are numerous, almost beyond precedent, and we expect very large returns this year."[12]

The brigade's time at Fort Langley was not without incident: after the boats left for Fort Hope four men deserted and returned to Fort Langley. Douglas planned to send them to the new coal mine at Nanaimo, but, contrary to orders, Yale kept the deserters busy at his post. Douglas grumbled: "I am sorry you did not forward the New Caledonia deserters to Nanaimo, as with such encouragement as those have received this year, the men from the Interior will be hereafter deserting in crowds."[13] He had a point, as life at comfortable Fort Langley was much easier than that at Fort St. James.

In August, Douglas responded to a letter from Manson, who had reported that the problem of keeping the horses well fed at Fort Hope appeared to be solved: "a plain [had] been discovered near Fort Hope of sufficient extent to keep the horses during the passage of the brigade to & from Fort Langley."[14] It was no longer necessary or desirable to send them across the mountains to Campement des Femmes until the brigade was ready to return to the interior. As Douglas noted, "This will be a great advantage."

Paul Fraser returned to his Thompson's River post well before the beginning of September, when he made his first journal entry. At Fort Alexandria, McLean recorded in the post journal on August 22 that he "arrived here from Lac la Hache, Mr. Manson in Company."[15] The gentlemen had ridden ahead of their brigades, which reached the post on the next day. The men brought the trade goods across the river to the fort, and on the following day the "Brigade men employed gumming &c &c. St. Paul [Jean-Baptiste Leolo] employed castrating some of the Brigade horses."[16]

Castrating the male horses was necessary, as the procedure prevented testosterone-fuelled chaos on the brigade journey. On this occasion, the castrated horses were probably two-year-old colts fresh from the Kamloops farm. It may always have happened that some horses died, but in 1854 more than a few of these valuable animals bled to death as a result of Leolo's operation.[17]

By the end of August the Fort St. James men were ready to begin their journey upriver. McLean reported: "The brigade is all ready for an early start tomorrow, the Boats being loaded and crews appointed to each of them."[18] The Fort St. James men took their departure on August 30, travelling north in five boats with a crew of thirty-five men. McLean's Fort Alexandria journal records that "two more of the Horses castrated by St. Paul [Leolo] died since his departure."[19]

In early September the clerk at Fort St. James recorded that Donald Manson's son, William, "left this morning for the purpose of meeting the Brigade."[20] There was a fall of snow overnight, but on September 13, "early this [morning] we were agreeably surprised by the arrival of the Brigade from Langley with Mr. C.T. Manson accompanied by Mr. McKenzie with 5 Boats. All hands employed carting the property and immediately gave out the servants' orders &c."[21]

In the meantime, Jean-Baptiste Leolo arrived at the Kamloops post from Fort Alexandria, bringing the news that the New Caledonia men had arrived safely. Fraser sent him over the mountains to Fort Victoria with a bundle of letters for Douglas. In September, Douglas responded to Manson's report with information about a possible new trail to Fort Langley. Douglas's letter read:

Another object probably of greater importance, as respects our inland transport, has just been announced by Lolo [Leolo], who states that a new route from the Similkameen Valley, leading through a continuous valley direct to Fraser's River, where there are extensive alluvial plains capable of supporting all the Brigade horses for any [illegible] length of time, has been discovered by Indians of his acquaintance, who report most favourably of the route and country through which it passes.

I have employed Lolo to examine that route, and to report upon it to Mr. Fraser on his return to Thompson's River. Should that route prove accessible, I am of opinion it will be found to combine all the advantages in regard to the pasture and its proximity to Fort Langley which we have in vain sought for in the Fort Hope route.[22]

Douglas wrote to Yale at Fort Langley, informing him of Leolo's new trail and asking him to explore the route from his end. His letter read:

He [Leolo] has informed me of the probability of a new route from the Similkameen to Fraser's River, opposite its confluence with Harrison's River, being soon discovered, a great part of it had already been traversed by Indians of his acquaintance. Should that route prove accessible, it will combine so many advantages, as respects our inland transport over the terminus of the present route by Fort Hope, that I conceive it of the utmost importance to have it thoroughly explored. With that view I have desired Lolo to take that route on his way to Thompson's River, for the purpose of examining it carefully, and as an encouragement for doing so, I intend to make him a small present before he leaves this place. He will require some assistance from you in the shape of provisions and guides, and I hope you will supply him with every necessary aid for carrying out that very desirable exploration.[23]

Yale was being asked to explore the same river that had been explored, and discarded, as a possible horse road to the interior as early as 1847. But it was important to find a new trail, if there was one. The trail over Manson's Mountain had washed out in the heavy rains of summer 1853, and it presented difficulties the men were no longer prepared to deal with. Although no one mentioned any loss of horses at Manson's Mountain in 1854, this was likely the place where the heaviest losses occurred. Leolo did not explore the new trail on his return home, however, as Fraser reported to Douglas:

> It appears by his statement that he could not prevail on any of the Similkameen Indians to accompany him on his way to Victoria, and on his return Yale could not procure him a guide. Be that as it may, I shall have the road Examined before the Brigade leave[s] this in the spring [1855], and have to request that you instruct Mr. Yale to send a Man with an Indian who knows the country to where the Indians of the Similkameen, and those of Harrison River, usually meet ...

> I have had some Conversation with an Indian who knows the Country well and reports favourably of it. Should this information prove correct the road might be opened by both Brigades this summer. It cannot be worse than Manson's Mountain.[24]

"It cannot be worse than Manson's Mountain"—an ominous phrase. And it may well have proved to be worse: although a great deal of trouble was spent exploring and building pieces of the new trail, it was never used, and the Brigades continued to come out over the Fort Hope trail.

In the meantime, the Fort Colvile brigades made their way out to Fort Vancouver once again. Peter Skene Ogden reported:

> Mr. Angus McDonald arrived here some time ago with the furs &c from Colvile, he left on his return with the Outfits for that district on the 11th inst. [July], and it is pleasing to mention that he had reached The Dalles in safety, from whence he will take up the goods with horses.[25]

Around this same time, James Sinclair was due to arrive at Fort Nez Percés from the Red River district to take charge of that post. As Governor Simpson wrote to the Board of Management: "By the Minutes of Council you will observe Mr. James Sinclair (who has entered the Company's service as a clerk for a term of years) is appointed to Walla Walla & we have little doubt will by his superior management retrieve the affairs

"Fort Nez Percés, Hudson's Bay Company post on the Columbia River, Washington Territory," painted by John Mix Stanley in 1847.

of that post and of the Snake Country, which may be considered as an appendage thereto. Mr. Sinclair is now on his way to Oregon with a party of emigrants from this settlement [Red River]."[26]

Clerk James Sinclair may have been, but Governor Simpson (now Sir George Simpson) clearly thought a lot of Sinclair, the mixed-blood son of an Orcadian HBC officer. Unlike his father, James did not work for the HBC for long, but became a merchant and private trader at Red River. He and his partner freighted goods for the HBC and were engaged in a number of businesses, some of which conflicted with HBC interests in the Red River Colony. In 1841 he delivered a party of immigrants to the Columbia, where they settled in the Willamette Valley and elsewhere. In 1848, Sinclair panned for gold in California and returned to the Red River Colony wealthy. He decided to settle in the Columbia district, and although he had been a thorn in Governor Simpson's side, he reconciled with him and re-entered the HBC service. Simpson informed the Board of Management that Sinclair had made special arrangements with the company. Sinclair and a second party of immigrants had left Red River in May and were expected to arrive in the Columbia district in October. Simpson's letter continues:

> I think it might be advisable that one of the members of
> the Board of Management proceeded to Walla Walla to
> concert arrangements with Mr. Sinclair in reference to

his charge & to the delivery of 200 head of cattle according to agreement. I have informed Mr. Sinclair that while
in charge of Walla Walla he will have a Commissioned
Officer's allowance, that you will be good enough to
provide him.[27]

Sinclair reached the headwaters of the Columbia River in late Octo-
ber, and in early January he was at Fort Vancouver, where he impressed
Chief Factor Dugald Mactavish with his energy.[28] In a letter to a friend,
Sinclair told of his plans for the future:

> I return in a few days to assume my charge of Walla Walla.
> Sir G [Governor Simpson] writes me that I am to assume
> charge also of the Snake Country, Fort Hall & Fort Boise—
> these have all gone wrong, completely disorganized ...
> This will keep me in hot water—in the meantime no
> ammunition is sold to Indians—what is the result of this
> time only can tell.
>
> Mr. Mactavish is everything I could wish—we get on very
> well and Sir G also is disposed to be liberal. Every effort
> shall be made to meet his approbation—however more
> of this at another time.[29]

James Sinclair was Métis—and by no means the only mixed-blood man
in this district. The Métis had been here since the early 1800s, but in the
1840s they came in from Red River and the Saskatchewan district in larger
numbers than ever before. It is probable that most of the men who came out
from the interior posts with the brigades, whether voyageurs or gentlemen,
were Métis. Both Ferdinand McKenzie and William Todd, who worked
under Manson at Fort St. James, were Métis; when McKenzie was later placed
in charge of Fort Alexandria, he was known to the packers of the time as
"Red River McKenzie." William Todd was son of Dr. William Todd of Red
River. Robert Todd, who worked under Donald McLean at the Kamloops
post, was probably his brother. George Stewart Simpson and his half-brother
John McKenzie Simpson, who also worked in this district, were mixed blood,
as their mothers were Métis. Michel Fallardeau, who was killed in 1855 at
Kamloops, was Métis from Red River. Montrose McGillivray, who accompanied Anderson on one of his cross-country expeditions but died of measles
and tuberculosis at Fraser's Lake in 1850, was the son of Simon McGillivray
and his First Nations wife. William McBean, who was in charge of Fort

Nez Percés at the time of the Waiilatpu Massacre, was the mixed-blood son of John McBean and his Métisse wife. Peter Ogden, now in charge of Fort Alexandria, was mixed blood, as was his brother, Michel, who had worked under Anderson at Fort Alexandria. Another Métis man was Edouard Montigny, probable son of Narcisse Montigny, who had manned the post at the top of Okanagan Lake at the time John Stuart passed through it. Napolean Dease, who in 1853 was in charge of Fort Hope, was the mixed-blood son of John Warren Dease and a First Nations woman.

The Métis were everywhere in New Caledonia and other parts of the Columbia district. By the 1840s, there were more mixed-blood people in the territory than there were Canadiens or Scotsmen. The Métis were the workhorses, the men who could be depended on to trade for essential salmon or for furs; they moved among First Nations communities with relative freedom, and they communicated with the First Nations people and sometimes fraternized with them. In their regular travel throughout the territory they heard the stories of the First Nations people they traded with, and with that specific knowledge they were able to communicate with them easily, and to sometimes prevent conflict with the HBC community. It is probable that some of the requests for trapping specific furs, or for information on exploring and opening up of new trails, came to the First Nations via the Métis. For many First Nations men, the Métis were their connection to the HBC community. And the reverse was also true: the Métis were the fur traders' connection to the First Nations communities.

The Métis were not always reliable, but they were clever and adaptive. They had a combination of skills that came from both their parents. They were the interpreters for the HBC traders as they spoke the French language of their fathers and the First Nations language of their mothers. The Métis were connected to and an active part of the HBC community, but they could also fit into the First Nations families they married into. Best of all, in the HBC's eyes at least, they never returned to Quebec. They had never lived there, and wherever they now lived they made their home. For this reason and others, Alexander Caulfield Anderson called them a useful breed of men.[30]

James Sinclair hoped to make his name in a territory filled with men just like him. There is no doubt that he was a charming and talented young man, but things were changing rapidly in the Columbia district. At Fort Nez Percés he was caught in the midst of them. He would live and thrive in exciting and dangerous times, but all too quickly it would come to an end.

⇾ 15 ⇽

1855 BRIGADES: DEATH ON THE TRAIL

The Fort St. James men left their home post on April 22, 1855, and in five days reached Fort Alexandria. A week later the Fort Alexandria clerk recorded:

> Monday 7th [May]. Morning cloudy & chilly; gave out the Horses to each Brigade and divided the Baggages, but could not make a start as it rained very heavily. Several claps of thunder.

> Tuesday 8th. Brigade took their departure for Langley. Messrs. Manson & McLean in command. The returns consist of 124 packs furs & 7 kegs castoreum, rather better than last years' transactions.[1]

Normally the journey to Kamloops took nine days. In 1855, however, the brigades may have been delayed by heavy rains and flooded rivers, and Paul Fraser noted:

> Saturday 19th [May]. Weather fine. Arrived Pierre Paul's son from Green Lake where he left the New Caledonia brigade who[se] arrival we may Expect on Tuesday. By him I am sorry to learn that New Caledonia has lost 60 horses during the winter & Spring. However, of this loss I have my doubts.

> Monday 21st. Men employed at sundry jobs. In the Evening, an Indian arrived informing us of the New Caledonia brigade being Encamped at the Tranquille River and will be here Early tomorrow, weather permitting.

Tuesday 22nd. The New Caledonia Brigade arrived, the Returns of that district are the best that has been for Some years back ...

Thursday 24th. The New Caledonia Horses, say 2 of the four Castrated last Evening died. That added to the great loss of last winter, Numbers 30—which we have to replace from our Bands.

Saturday 26th. Made up our 36 packs. Potatoes making their appearance. Arrived Spintlum from the Similkameen who reports of there being much snow in the Mountains.[2]

Although spring had come earlier than normal, the depth of the snow in the mountains and the deaths of so many Fort Alexandria horses indicate it might have been a hard winter while it lasted. Fraser noted in his journal that there was overcast and snow in early November 1854. The New Year came in with weather that was "cold in the extreem [sic] with a strong wind from the north,"[3] and by the middle of January it snowed again. Nevertheless, the Kamloops post did not appear to have been adversely affected by the cold. On June 1, Fraser "supplied the New Caledonia brigade with 30 Marrons."[4] (Marrons is a French word that today refers to chestnut horses, but in those days referred to horses generally.) The Kamloops men, and those from New Caledonia, prepared for the work of taking their loads over the mountains to Fort Langley:

Saturday 2nd. Very warm. A Number of Indians arrived to See the Brigade.

Monday 4th. Men Employed at Sundry Jobs. Water rising much, arrived an Indian from the Similkameen who reports much snow in the Mountains between this and Fort Hope.

Tuesday 5th. The New Caledonia Horses were Crossed over to the South Branch. Got 2 Oxen shot [for provisions] ...

Saturday 9th. Warm Weather. Crossed over our Baggage, and tomorrow will make a Start ...

Sunday 10th. Very warm. Owing to some of our Horses having crossed to this Side we Cannot Start today but God willing tomorrow we will.[5]

Horses everywhere like to return home or go back. In this case, these horses were left to their own devices on the south bank of the river and returned on their own to the grasslands around the fort where they normally grazed.

In July, Douglas reported to the London Committee that he had recently returned from Fort Langley, where he had met the gentlemen from the interior:

> Their arrival was later than usual in consequence of heavy rains and flooded Rivers, which caused much delay on the journey. The furs were however landed at Fort Langley in perfect order and entirely free from damage. The Trade for the past year has been on the whole unusually good, but I observe with regret that the spring hunts in both those districts have slightly declined; arising, in New Caledonia, from the early disappearance of the snow in spring, and from the non-arrival at Thompson's River of a large part of the North River Hunters with their furs, previously to the departure of the brigade from that place. The journey to the depot was effected without loss or accident of a serious nature, and the people were in excellent health and spirits.[6]

The North River hunters mentioned by Douglas referred to the First Nations men who traded their furs at the North River post, an outpost of Kamloops located some distance up the North Thompson River. This post had been established by Paul Fraser over the winter of 1850–1851. Douglas's letter continues:

> We succeeded in re-hiring the men whose contracts with the Company had expired with less trouble than usual, and we made up the New Caledonia complement of servants to the usual number by the addition of half-white lads brought up in the country, who will soon become efficient men. The establishment of Thompson's River district was made up partly by the same means, and partly by drafts from other districts.[7]

As mentioned, many of the new men who had come into the territory with the incoming Columbia Express were Métis from Red River. They had accompanied the New Caledonia brigades to Fort Langley and were distributed throughout the district, replacing Canadiens, who continued to retire. Douglas arranged that "the Brigades were to leave on the 12th of inst. [July] on their return to the Interior."[8] On August 1 Douglas reported to the London Committee that he had "received intelligence of the safe arrival of the New Caledonia and Thompson's River Brigades at Fort Hope, on their return to the interior."[9]

Less than two weeks later, news of a shocking accident was spreading quickly through the territory, reaching Fort Alexandria when Charles Touin rode in ahead of the brigade. The Fort Alexandria journals record that Touin arrived from Kamloops on August 12, carrying the news of "the death of Chief Trader Paul Fraser who was killed accidentally by a tree felled by one of his men."[10]

Fraser was killed in late July, but the scenario for his death was set up some time before. The story of Michel Fallardeau's beating death is told in Chapter 13, but the conclusion of that story is here:

> Two months later Paul Fraser was on Manson's mountain, seated in a large tent by the side of Manson, who accompanied his brigade, and the men were variously employed in preparing the camp, when a crash was heard, and a big tree, which a Canadian was falling, came down on the tent instantly killing Paul Fraser, who was reading his correspondence. So it was that he who had grudged a decent coffin to the victim of his own brutality had to be returned to Mother Earth without any kind of coffin.[11]

The camps are sometimes misidentified; this accident occurred at Campement du Chevreuil, near the summit of the mountain.[12] In 1859 a Royal Engineer accompanied Angus McDonald over the trail and recorded the story of Fraser's death as he heard it from McDonald. "It is here that Mr. Fraser met his death by a tree falling on him when asleep," the Royal Engineer noted, "and within a few yards of the spot where we had pitched our tent, a neat pile of rough hewn logs mark[s] his lonely grave."[13]

At Fort Victoria, Douglas heard of Fraser's death and wrote to Governor Simpson: "The death of poor Fraser is most unfortunate, a grave on a lonely mountain is the reward of 40 years wandering in the Indian Country. I have just learnt that the tree which caused his death was felled by one of the men and took a wrong direction. Strange that they should fell trees so near a tent and in the very midst of the camp."[14]

Paul Fraser was under the age of sixty when he was killed. Except for the occasional furlough, he had worked on the west side of the Rocky

Mountains for twenty-three years. He did his job and was made chief trader, but stories of his violence and his drinking had followed him for years.

The story of Fraser's death in the mountains has since become a murder mystery: the story of an intentional murder of a despised man by a voyageur who rode with the brigade. But is that story true? It is likely not true, but as usual, the story persists. In the 1880s, the missionary A.G. Morice read of Fraser's death in the Fort St. James post journals, and retold the story in his book, *The History of the Northern Interior of British Columbia*. It appears that at the time, even the HBC men had their suspicions, but nothing was proven. The post journals no longer exist but the story remains. In all these HBC communities, as in all Métis communities, Métis history is told in its stories.

As a result of Fraser's death, there are no records of the brigade's journey through Kamloops. In August, Ferdinand McKenzie rode into Fort Alexandria ahead of the incoming brigades:

> Thursday 23rd [August]. Arrived here from Lac la Hache. Mr. Manson sent me ahead in order to send up Jean Boucher with a couple of Indians to Stuart's Lake, to get salmon to feed the people on the way up, as his men will not admit of feeding them on flour yet there being no salmon coming up the River.
>
> Saturday 25th. Mr. McLean arrived here from Lac la terre Blanche [McLeese Lake]. The Brigade will be here tomorrow ...[15]

Donald McLean noted:

> Wednesday 29th. About 9 o'clock am, the brigade started for the interior under charge of Chief Trader Donald Manson, Esquire, Mr. F. McKenzie & self (D. McLean) remained.[16]

Because of the shortage of men, freeman Charles Touin was temporarily placed in charge of Fort Alexandria, while McLean took charge of Kamloops. The New Caledonia men arrived at Fort St. James carrying the news of Fraser's death. The post journal read:

> Saturday 1st September. Sunshine and showers. Men employed principally in cleaning fort stores &c &c. Late this evening [Jean Marie] Boucher [arrived] with two Indians; he is sent by Mr. Manson for Salmon [for the]

incoming brigade as none can be had below. He also informed us of the death of Mr. Fraser of Thompson's River, who was accidentally killed on his way in with the Horse Brigade by a felled tree having fallen on him in one of the Encampments.

Sunday 2nd. All hands making Salmon Bales for incoming brigade, and I am started with two canoe loads this afternoon, say 12 Bales Salmon ...

Sunday 11th September. About noon Mr. Manson arrived with one Boat and towards evening Mr. McKenzie cast up with the others.[17]

In September, McLean wrote to Fort Langley from Kamloops to advise Yale that he was "about to send off a party to Fort Hope in order to bring from thence the property which owing to the want of Horses the late P. Fraser Esquire was under the necessity of leaving behind in July last." McLean's letter continues:

I have to request that you will be kind enough to furnish the party with provisions for their return, as it is not in my power to do so, there being a great scarcity of Salmon in this quarter and its vicinity, so much so indeed that I am fearful that the Aborigines will from the pressure of Starvation be induced to commit depredations upon the Horned Animals & Horses belonging to the Company. The Wheat Crop at this place I regret to say had proved very indifferent, and as Chief Trader D. Manson made a demand of Ninety Bushels for New Caledonia, with which I have complied, I now find myself with barely sufficient to save for seed the ensuing Spring.

With the number of individuals whom I have to feed at this Establishment, I will no doubt be put to my shifts, but trust to get along without absolute starvation.[18]

With McLean sent to Kamloops, Peter Ogden took charge of Fort Alexandria. On his arrival he listed the horses that were left dead or injured on the trail. On the outgoing journey, one had died at Fort Alexandria and four at Kamloops. One succumbed at Campement des Femmes, and another was left behind on the trail. A horse called Blanche Toutlaid was killed at

Manson's Mountain, and two died at Peers Creek (one drowned). In addition to the thirty horses that had died over the winter at Fort Alexandria, ten were dead or lost to the New Caledonia men in the summer brigades.

In December, Douglas received letters from Manson, at Fort St. James, and McLean, at Kamloops, and reported to Simpson:

> I have also lately received intelligence from New Caledonia up to the 30th September and from Thompson's River to the 3rd November. Chief Trader Manson reports that he arrived at Stuart's Lake with the New Caledonia brigade on the 11th of September, having met with no serious accident on the route—that the fur trade was with the exception of Martens somewhat better than at the same date last year. He also reports the total failure of Salmon all over the District to an extent greater than ever before known, a misfortune that will be felt both by the whites and natives. I am however in hopes that Chief Trader Manson may have succeeded in procuring a larger quantity of Salmon than he appears to anticipate as the fish have been frequently known to arrive in con-

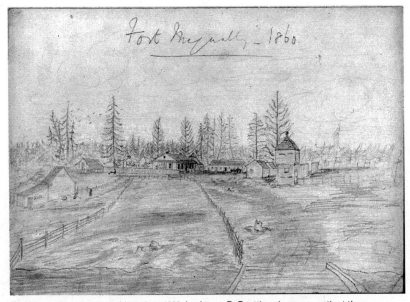

Fort Nisqually at its second location, 1860, by James R. Beattie, who was a patient there.

siderable quantities at a period later than the date of his letter. I trust the event may prove so for otherwise there will be much suffering and privation in the district.

Chief Trader McLean reports from Thompson's River that a distemper supposed to be the glanders had appeared among the horses of that District, and carried off about 20 head of working horses and colts.[19]

The Indians of the District had secured a considerable quantity of salmon for their winter use, and he does not appear to apprehend that there will be any scarcity of food among the natives generally. Mr. McLean makes no report on the state of the Fur Trade, as the natives had not more than commenced their winter hunts.[20]

The New Caledonia brigades faced many troubles that year, but Fort Colvile had its own set of problems. For the first time they came out to the Puget Sound post of Fort Nisqually via a mountain trail through Naches Pass. In June, Dugald Mactavish had advised the London Committee from Fort Vancouver that "the returns of Colvile & Walla Walla will this season be taken out to Nisqually with horses and it is my intention to go over there in a few days for the purpose of meeting Mr. McDonald, who I am in hopes will reach Puget's Sound with his brigade by the 1st May [July]."[21]

On July 2 the Fort Nisqually clerk noted that "Mr. A[ngus] McDonald arrived this day with the Colvile and Walla Walla Brigades consisting altogether of about 200 pack horses."[22] In his reminiscences of his time at Fort Nisqually, Edward Huggins wrote:

On the 2nd of July at about midday, I was startled to see a tall, rather slim man ride in the Fort, dismount and walk towards the large house where he was met and kindly received by Doctor [William Fraser] Tolmie. This was Angus MacDonald [McDonald] of Fort Colvile, and now in charge of the Brigade of upwards of 200 horses, most of them packed with furs, the result of the years trade of Fort Colvile, Walla Walla, Boise, Hall, Okanogan, Nez Perce and the Snake Country.

I had heard a great deal about MacDonald and was anxious to meet him, which desire was soon gratified, for

Doctor Tolmie brought him to the packing room where
I was working and gave me an introduction to him. He
was rather a good-looking man, about six feet in height,
straight and slim, but was said to be very wiry and strong.
He had a dark complexion with long jet-black hair reaching
to his shoulders and a thick, long and very black beard
and mustache. He wore a dressed deer skin over shirt and
pants, a regatta or rowing shirt and had a black silk hand-
kerchief tied loosely around his neck. He had a black
piercing eye and a deep sonorous voice, with a low and
rather monotonous manner of speaking.[23]

In his letter to Governor Simpson, Mactavish also reported on McDonald's arrival at Fort Nisqually. "I have the satisfaction of informing you that
Mr. Angus McDonald arrived at Nisqually on the 2nd inst [July]," Macta-

Angus McDonald of the
Hudson's Bay Company, who
was in charge of Fort Colvile and
district, ca. 1860. Artist unknown.

vish wrote. "He found the road from the
Yakima very wet & stony. Twelve horses of
the Walla Walla brigade got knocked up and
were left en route but they will probably be
found on the return of the party."[24]

In an earlier letter Mactavish had reported
that "McDonald came out in high style by the
new road. He is a very experienced man."[25]
However, the later letter reveals that the
road through Naches Pass was not a good
trail for horses. Horses often wrecked in deep
mud, and stones injured their unshod hooves
and lamed them. This alone might account
for the animals left behind on the trail.

The brigades spent some time at Fort
Nisqually, where the packs of furs were
opened and packed into larger bales that
would be sent on to Fort Victoria. Part of
any brigade journey to headquarters was the storytelling and singing that
occurred while the men were at their destination post. The voyageurs
were, of course, ready to party, but so too were the men who worked at
whatever fort they arrived at. Every man who worked in an HBC post in
the territory kept himself in shape by playing games imported from his
homeland. At some posts, the Canadiens played a traditional French game

called *boules*, substituting rocks for the steel balls that were aimed to land as close as possible to a small wooden ball. At Fort Vancouver, Thomas Lowe tells of the clerks at the post curling with rocks on the frozen Columbia River one cold winter day. Competitions of strength and speed also took place throughout the year, and at Fort Nisqually the meeting place appeared to be just outside one of the fort's gates. These challenges must have occurred regularly at Fort Langley and other posts in the interior, although they were rarely mentioned by the gentlemen who kept the journals. However, Huggins worked at Fort Nisqually for many years and later owned the property on which the old fort stood. He was a storyteller who chronicled the history of the post as he had known it.

Among his collection of stories were tales of the traditional celebrations that took place at Fort Nisqually in 1855, when the Fort Colvile men rode in with their furs. These celebrations took place whenever a visiting brigade arrived at its destination, whether they were travelling across the continent to Hudson Bay in the annual York Factory Express or bringing their furs across the Pacific Slopes to Forts Vancouver or Langley. Once they reached their destination the gentlemen worked, but the voyageurs partied, and their exuberance annoyed the gentlemen but strengthened the connections between the men who worked in the different HBC communities. Conflicts occurred, of course, and more conflict occurred in some years than in others, as we know. But for the most part these men were happy to be together at a new-to-them fur trade fort that was so much larger and more exciting than their own post that stood all alone in the wilderness, sometimes a thousand miles away. In his story, Huggins wrote:

> The men accompanying MacDonald were a cosmopolitan crowd. There were Scotchmen, French Canadians, Halfbreeds and Iroquois Indians. The foreman was a Scotch Highlander and when at home was in charge of the little trading post amongst the Blackfoot Indians. The Canadians were strong, wiry fellows, and amongst them were men who had been in the employ of the company for fifty years. The Iroquois or Halfbreed Iroquois were the best looking men in the band. The handsomest and strongest man amongst them was a halfbreed Iroquois and French Canadian. He was very strong and agile, and being the champion athlete amongst his own people, he challenged our hands to run a foot race and other games requiring strength and

endurance. Although amongst our staff were some strong and powerful fellows, this Iroquois beat them all, and at running a foot race he beat them badly.[26]

The Fort Nisqually employees knew that among their own men was one who could beat the Iroquois champion. "They begged him to accept the braggart's challenge,"[27] and the clerk (likely Huggins himself) eventually gave in and agreed to compete in a one-hundred-yard race. Huggins described the competition:

> The starting point was down the road, west of the gate. A line was drawn and 100 yards measured off, terminating almost opposite the small gate where another line was made. The first man to cross this line was the winner. Between 6 and 7 p.m. a large crowd had assembled at the gate, for the coming race had caused quite an excitement and many Indians from the Nisqually and Puyallup rivers had come to witness the struggle, for the clerk was well known to the Indians and was rather a favourite. At the time appointed the contestants appeared. The Iroquois, Edouard Pichette was his name, wore a gaudy, loud coloured shirt fitting tight around his big, barrel-formed chest. A handsome red silk belt around his waist and a pair of thin cotton drawers which showed his handsome, muscular legs to good advantage. He was a splendid figure of a man ...
>
> The young Englishman stripped well also, and I noticed that MacDonald was astonished when he saw his well-developed chest and powerful arms, for the young man was a leader in the prevailing games, throwing the hammer, putting the stone and pitching the heavy iron quoits ...
>
> Well, all was ready and at an agreed-upon signal from MacDonald a fair start was made. The young Englishman jumping [sic] ahead at the start and, to our astonishment, he increased his lead until the end of the first 50 yards when Pichette, the Iroquois, shortened the distance between them to about three yards. From then on to the winning sprint the handsome young Iroquois shortened the distance, but to the intense disgust of MacDonald and

his company, the Englishman won the race by a distance of about four or five feet.

Oh, the howling and hurrahing by the English part of the crowd, "Sacreeing" and other demoralizing French expressions from the Canadians, and the silent jubilant looks of the Nisqually Indians. It was all very pleasant to the English victor. Edouard Pichette earnestly begged the Englishman to run him the distance of one mile, or half a mile and down to two hundred yards but the Englishman was wise and refused to run any more and was content to rest on his laurels. The young man's reputation as a great runner, who had defeated the Rocky Mountain champion, spread over the Indian country between Colvile and the base of the Rockies.[28]

The Fort Nisqually clerk, possibly Huggins, was afterwards known as the "bully of Fort Nisqually." If the brigade had come out to the fort again, he would have been challenged once more, and would have had to prove his superior strength and speed. But this was the only year that the Fort Colvile men came out to Nisqually.

While the men played, the horses put on weight, and their wounds healed. Finally the packing was finished, and on July 25, "Mr. McDonald with the Colvile Brigade started this day with 151 pieces goods."[29] Before they left, Dr. Tolmie organized a party. Huggins recorded:

A dance was given by Dr. Tolmie to the MacDonald band of packers before leaving for their homes. One of the large stores was emptied of goods and it became a fine dancing hall. A room about 60 feet in length and 30 feet in width, its floor was rather rough but that didn't trouble the dancers. One or two of the Canadians were fair fiddlers and, of course, a liberal supply of whiskey was provided and nearly all the young Indian girls and Halfbreeds in the neighbourhood were there ...

We had in our employ at that time about ten Kanakas (Sandwich Islanders) and to vary the entertainment I would persuade these men to dance some of their native dances. They would cheerfully comply, and standing in a row would begin a wild and monotonous chant, keeping time by

> moving their bodies with great exactitude and twisting
> about, in which I could see no dancing but merely pos-
> turing and sometimes it seemed to me to be an unseemly
> performance in the presence of ladies.[30]

On their way home, the HBC men learned of troubles ahead. A hot-headed Yakama man named Qualchen had murdered some American gold prospectors who made use of the Yakima River shortcut on their way to the goldfields at the Pend-d'Oreille River.

At the same time as McDonald made his way from Fort Nisqually to Fort Colvile, two retired HBC men—Alexander Caulfield Anderson and Archibald McKinlay—made a trading journey up the Columbia River to the goldfields. They set up some kind of trading post near the mines (leaving Anderson's brother, William, in charge) and did a little gold panning on the side. As they made their way home, they camped on the Spokane River, close to a large camp of disappointed gold prospectors who planned to return to The Dalles by the Yakima River shortcut. Anderson recorded what he heard as the two HBC men finished their supper:

> One of the Spokane chiefs approached and said with an
> air of mystery he had something to say to us. He then
> said, "I do not want to hear of bloodshed. Tell these men
> not to cross the Columbia and take the Yackama route"
> (as was indeed their intention) "but let them follow the
> left bank of the Columbia to Dalles, the Yackama route
> is foul, if they follow it not one will reach Olympia."
> On further questioning he told us distinctly that an
> ambuscade had been laid and that he already knew from
> authentic report that more than one life had been lost of
> passing travelers on their way upwards through the
> Yackama Valley. Knowing the chief and satisfied that he
> would not speak without just cause, we at once commu-
> nicated with Mr. Patton Anderson, who as delegate to
> the Territorial Legislature might be assumed to have
> influence with the rest, and told him what had been told
> us, at the same time recommending him to follow the
> advice of the Chief. The following morning he assem-
> bled the whole party and communicated the intelligence,
> asking for their opinions.

Owing to the tempting shortness of the distance many were averse to abandoning their plans of proceeding direct to Olympia [via Naches Pass], others thought more prudently. We jumped on our horses and left them disputing, but eventually the better sense prevailed and we afterward heard that they followed the Dalles route. Fortunately for themselves, for meanwhile Major Haller had been defeated in the Yakama Valley, the country was in arms, and the Yakama War had commenced.[31]

This was the beginning of the Yakama Indian Wars, which plunged the whole of Washington Territory into a turbulent war zone. From Fort Victoria, Douglas reported to the Secretary of State of Great Britain that "Major [Granville] Haller's detachment of United States Troops had been compelled to retire before the Indians, and were hotly pursued by the enemy to one of their military stations on the Columbia."[32] Haller, a noted Indian fighter, was stationed at the U.S. Army's post at The Dalles. He was not the only Army man who lost a fight with the Yakama. The United States Army had little success in subduing the First Nations warriors, and two years later the Upper Columbia was as turbulent as it had ever been.

Fortunately, McDonald made his way home to Fort Colvile in safety, as Mactavish reported to the governor. "I am advised by Mr. Angus Macdonald that he reached Colvile with his brigade in order on the 12th August," Mactavish reported. His letter continues:

> The reports from the gold regions are not encouraging. It seems that gold is found all the way up the Pend'Oreille, but in such small quantities that miners have to work very hard to get from 1 ½ to 3 dollars each per day. A great many of the people who went up from this quarter are already coming back, not feeling satisfied with the idea of so small a return for their labour.[33]

In the meantime, at Fort Victoria, Douglas orchestrated another project that would replace the road over the Tulameen Plateau: the opening of the Chilwayook (Chilliwack) River road to the Skagit. Douglas reported to the London Committee that:

> there being however no continuous land route from Thompson's River, we have commenced the exploration of the country by the valley of the Chilwayook River,

by which the Indians report there is a practicable passage through the mountains into the level plains of Thompson's River.

The Chilwayook unites with the Fraser's River 30 miles above Fort Langley, and the intersecting district is level, as well as the country between Fort Langley and Point Roberts, on the Gulf of Georgia, so that if the Chilwayook route prove [sic] to be as good as reported, we shall have the advantage of a practicable road from Point Roberts to Thompson's River, the whole distance between those places being scarcely over 170 miles, and by the route, sheep, horses, or cattle may, at any time, be driven to or from the sea coast, but the great present advantage to us will be that the brigades may come the whole way to Fort Langley by land, thereby relieving the trade of the expense of maintaining the post of Fort Hope, and the fleet of Boats now used on Fraser's River for the outgoing and incoming brigades.

Mr. Gavin Hamilton and two men with Indian guides will form the exploring party.[34]

On the first day of August, Douglas reported to the London Committee on Hamilton's exploration of the Chilwayook River:

Mr. Gavin Hamilton who was employed with a party of two men and Indians, in exploring the route to the interior by the Chilwayook valley, has completed that service, and reports very favorably of that line of road; the country being generally level, rising to the dividing ridge, which is there scarcely perceptible, by a gradual slope, pasture for the horses everywhere abundant, and there are extensive grassy meadows at the point where the road strikes Fraser's River, to pasture the horses during the stay of the Brigades at Fort Langley.

It therefore possesses great advantages over the Fort Hope road, and entirely avoids the Mountain barrier which forms the principal difficulty of that route, with which it unites on the banks of the Similkameen River. We propose to employ a few men and Indians in opening this road in the course of the present summer, but we will not go to any expense until it has been further examined.[35]

By September 1855 Douglas reported that a party of HBC employees and First Nations men was building the road from Fort Langley. A later trail, the Whatcom Road, followed this same route through Chilliwack Lake, but a modern-day historian tells us that it was the most difficult trail that could be designed:

> The Whatcom people then employed a U.S. Army engineer, Captain W.W. DeLacy, to locate a trail through the mountain area to the Skagit and Sumallo, and in July 1858 he announced he had found a pass from headwaters of Sumallo River to intersect the fur-brigade trail to Fort Thompson (Kamloops). *The Northern Light*, a newspaper published at Whatcom then, gave the various stations and mileage along this trail—showing a distance of 273 miles from Whatcom to Fort Thompson ... It was pointed out that Summit Lake—one of DeLacy's stations—was probably Chilliwack Lake. To obtain a practical route from head of Nooksack River to the Skagit mountain passes would compel a course by one of the tributaries of the Chilliwack River, along it to the lake; then south by way of Dolly Varden Creek to the summit and so on to the Skagit. Whatcom celebrated the location of this trail, and subscribed money to open it, but little was done; only a score or two travelled over it with difficulty and it was soon abandoned.[36]

This was the intended route for Douglas's new road. He encouraged McLean to "open the road to the Scatchat [Skagit] River so that with the assistance of a party in the spring the road may be made passable for next summer."[37] But in June 1856 he received bad news. "Those men make a fearful report of the Chilwayook Road," he wrote to Yale. "I fear Mr. Hamilton has not made a discrete report, from want of knowing better."[38] The road builders had finally reached the box canyon that surrounded Chilliwack Lake, and all work on the trail was halted. Douglas explained this to the London Committee:

> We have for the present abandoned the proposed new route to the interior by the Chilwayook valley in consequence of the unexpected obstacles which the explorers of the route had overlooked, near the Chilwayook Lake, which is enclosed by precipitous rocky hills, apparently inaccessible to horses either in a direct line across their summit or by following the margin of the Lake. We are therefore now about to direct all our strength to improve the existing road by Fort Hope.[39]

The mountain ranges that stood between the coast and the fur-rich interior of New Caledonia and the Thompson's River district were proving to be a major barrier to horse transportation. Once again Douglas was frustrated by his inability to find a trail that would bring the brigades safely to the coast. The HBC men had no choice but to continue to make their way out to Fort Langley by the mountain trail that led them over the Tulameen Plateau and Manson's Mountain to Fort Hope and the safety of the lower Fraser River.

⟡ 16 ⟡

1856 BRIGADES: FORT SHEPHERD

In Washington Territory, the lust for gold showed no signs of abating. A short-lived gold rush in 1853 drew miners to the Grande Ronde, in the Blue Mountains behind Fort Nez Percés. The gold strike of 1855 was different. From Fort Colvile, McDonald advised the gentlemen at Fort Vancouver that "one of his men, while employed hauling firewood, had almost undesignedly amused himself by washing out a pannikin of gravel on a beach near Colvile. Some particles of gold appeared—enough, however, to excite curiosity and invite further research—explorers went out; and at the mouth of the Pend'Oreille River, close by the boundary line, diggings which were moderately productive were discovered."[1]

Douglas's report to Henry Labouchere, then Secretary of State for Great Britain, gives additional information:

> That gentleman [Angus McDonald] reports in a letter
> dated on the 1st of March last [1856], that Gold has been
> found in considerable quantities within the British Ter-
> ritory on the upper Columbia, and that he is moreover
> of opinion that valuable deposits of Gold will be found
> in many other parts of that country, he also states that the
> daily earnings of persons then employed in digging gold
> were ranging from £2 to £8 for each man.[2]

The Pend-d'Oreille River flowed into the Columbia forty miles north of Fort Colvile and just north of the forty-ninth parallel. The rush of miners soon interfered with the HBC's trade, as James Sinclair, then in charge of Fort Nez Percés, complained from Fort Vancouver:

> The confounded gold discovery at Colvile is creating quite
> an excitement all over the country, as I expected all our
> men at Colvile and Walla Walla have cut and run. I had

> only one man left, which has induced me to come down
> here to endeavor to hire two or three, but this is a hard
> matter in such times as these.[3]

Sinclair had taken over the charge of Fort Nez Percés in January 1855. By June, most of his men had abandoned his post for the gold mines. This was not surprising. Sinclair had seen some of the gold that came from those mines. "The largest bag of gold dust that I saw from Colvile was about the size of a half pint tumbler, beautiful thin flakes—containing from $1200 to $1500, and this was the work of one man for about a month or rather less."[4] From Fort Vancouver, Dugald Mactavish also reported on the gold discoveries at Fort Colvile: "There is considerable excitement in Oregon about the Colvile mines, and I have no doubt there will be three thousand people digging before the end of summer."[5]

The gold rush was real, but so too was the Yakama War. As mentioned in the previous chapter, the Indigenous communities who lived on the Columbia Plateau were infuriated by the numbers of American miners who were invading their territories in search of gold, and they declared war. In October, Sinclair reported that the U.S. government Indian agent had destroyed all the HBC's ammunition belonging to Fort Nez Percés and ordered him to abandon the post. He came downriver to Fort Vancouver, then returned in November to find Fort Nez Percés ransacked. The oldest continually running post in the territory, built by the NWC in 1818 and an HBC post for thirty-eight years, was finally abandoned.

Mactavish assigned Sinclair the duty of building a new post in British territory, north of Fort Colvile and close to the gold mines on the Pend-d'Oreille River. Sinclair was on his way up the Columbia River in March 1856 when he and others were killed in an attack by the Yakama Indians at the Cascades.

The Yakama War effectively stopped the rush of gold miners north to British territory; even the HBC men rarely travelled up and down the river. The miners already on the Pend-d'Oreille continued their work, and small but steady streams of gold dust reached Fort Victoria via Forts Hope and Langley. In April 1856, Douglas reported that "some very fine specimens of Scale Gold have been lately discovered in one of the Tributary Streams of Fraser's River, at no considerable distance from the sea coast."[6] Douglas also mentions a box of gold that was delivered to Fort Langley in mid-March, which appears to have come from Thompson's River: "The accounts and Box of gold dust was safely delivered, the former at this place, and the latter at Fort Langley."[7]

Around the same time, Douglas learned that Governor Simpson had approved construction of a new trading post on the Columbia River. As Douglas reported to the secretary of the London Committee:

> Those instructions were lately made known to me by a letter from Chief Factor Mactavish dated the 12th of April last [1856], and received here on the 26th of the same month, who moreover stated in the same communication that Sir George Simpson had appointed the late Mr. James Sinclair to build the new Fort, and goes on to observe, "but as he, poor fellow, is removed from among us, somebody else must take the matter in hand, for my own part I can do nothing, and must leave it with you to say what is to be done, as I have neither officers, men, nor in fact anything to work with."[8]

Many changes were being forced on the HBC men. Because of the Yakama War, Douglas instructed the Fort Colvile brigades to bring their furs out to Forts Hope and Langley in 1856. The last time the Fort Colvile brigades had used this route was in 1851, when Anderson was in charge of the post. Five years later, McDonald had to travel over a road he had never seen, and which few of his men had travelled.

McDonald also received detailed instructions from Douglas for construction of the new post north of Fort Colvile, which was to be named Fort Shepherd, after John Shepherd, the newly minted governor of the HBC's London Committee. "In deciding the locality of the new Post, two conditions must be kept steadily in view," Douglas wrote. "First, that the locality be accessible for the transport of supplies from Fort Langley, and secondly, that it be within a convenient distance of the gold producing country. The Post and the entire line of the route from Fort Langley must also lie within the British limits." Douglas's letter continues:

> With respect to the access from Fraser's River, we must carefully avoid carrying any part of the intermediate road through American territory, the road should therefore run in a due west direction over the range of hills situated on the north side of the proposed site, till it strikes the Colvile [Kettle] River about 30 miles distant, and from thence about 40 miles further nearly in the same direction to the Okanagan River, which I propose crossing

near the confluence of Tea River [Testalinden Creek],
a little beyond which point is the present road to Fort
Langley. As that part of the country is chiefly prairie and
open wood land the road can be opened with little labour
and expense.[9]

Douglas clearly had no idea what the country looked like or where the
trail through the Kettle River valley ran. He did not know that any new
trail must cross the Rossland Range, a section of the Monashee Mountains
that lies between the Columbia River, where the new post was to stand,
and the Kettle River near today's Christina Lake, which was presumed to
be in British territory. He was unaware that the trail already crossed the
boundary line as it followed the Kettle River valley around the end of
another section of the Monashee Mountains. It dipped again into American territory as it followed the Kettle River south to the Columbia at Fort
Colvile. Fortunately, there were no American citizens residing in those
places who would report the brigade's presence.

To enable McDonald to build the new post, Douglas hired André
Balthasard and Leon Morel, two ex-HBC employees who were experienced
carpenters. With these carpenters sent off from Fort Victoria, Douglas
turned his attention to the next problem: the brigades. On May 5 he wrote
to McDonald on the probable shortage of horses for the Fort Colvile brigades. "I fear the number of horses at your disposal will be far from sufficient
to transport all the goods required this year at one trip."[10] On July 2,
Douglas met the Fort Colvile brigades at Fort Langley and found many
problems with their overall organization. Douglas's list of complaints gives
a great deal of information on how the Thompson's River and New Caledonia gentlemen ran their brigades. Douglas's letter read:

> The trip men have all been paid at the rate of 8 pounds
> sterling per man, according to your agreement. That price
> is however far beyond the value of the service, especially
> where the other allowances given are taken in consider-
> ation: to each man, a riding horse for the trip and freight
> for one piece, making 3 horses for every 2 men over and
> above their money wages. We pay 13 Made Beaver or 2
> Blankets and a half for the trip to and from Kamloops, the
> men finding their own horses, or performing the jour-
> ney on foot according to their means, and the distance
> to that Post is within 40 miles of the extreme distance to

Fort Colvile. This will give you an idea of what ought to be paid to your trip men in future. Mr. Shuttleworth performed the journey to Fort Hope in 14 days of very slow traveling and the trip under ordinary circumstances to and from Fort Colvile and Fort Hope may always be performed within the month without distressing horses, and the route is accessible at any time between the 1st of June and the first of November, so that four or five trips may if necessary be made every summer.[11]

The Fort Colvile brigade had come out under twenty-two-year-old Henry Shuttleworth, while McDonald remained at his post. Douglas commented on this in his report on the brigades:

Mr. Shuttleworth, apprentice clerk, accompanied the Fort Colvile brigade, assisted by Mr. Patrick McKenzie, a retired Postmaster now a settler at Fort Colvile, as conductors; a serious responsibility to cast upon a young person of Mr. Shuttleworth's age and experience, but it appears that Mr. Angus McDonald could not conveniently leave Fort Colvile as I expected, in consequence of some difficulty with the Americans, who falsely accused him of supplying the hostile Indians with ammunition, and Mr. Mactavish thought it was better that he should remain inland to give the necessary explanations if required.[12]

After the massacre at Waiilatpu in 1847, the HBC had been ordered to stop giving ammunition to the Indigenous people, and it does not appear that the order was ever rescinded. Now, Americans who lived near Fort Colvile had falsely accused McDonald of providing ammunition to his Indigenous neighbours, and both he and Mactavish, of Fort Vancouver, thought it best that he stay to face the charges, if any.

Americans in what was now Washington Territory feared and hated the Indigenous population, and because the HBC traded with them, the Americans also hated the HBC. As early as 1848 the company had brought charges against claim-jumper Amos Short, although the HBC lawyer said that there was "too much prejudice against the HBCo, and those connected [with] it, to permit you to have a fair trial."[13]

At Fort Nisqually, Dr. Tolmie was kept busy warning American squatters off HBC land. In 1850 he had forced two Americans to pay him for HBC cattle they had slaughtered. In the same year the HBC ship *Cadboro* was illegally impounded by American customs agents. Although General John Adair, then collector at Astoria, ordered the release of the vessel and reprimanded the customs agent, two more HBC ships were impounded a year later, and it was months before they were released. Oregon's representative to the United States Congress accused the HBC of giving blankets to the Indigenous peoples as a reward for attacking Americans, and many citizens in the territory believed his stories.

Not all Americans hated the HBC. Many recognized and appreciated the company's presence. But the more prejudiced citizens threatened and bullied the HBC men; they watched their every move and complained to American authorities, who might then lay charges. Although the company men remained neutral in every Indigenous war and obeyed every American law, some Americans accused them of being accomplices to the Indigenous peoples and were especially watchful in times of war. The citizens wanted the HBC gone. Fortunately for the company, for more than ten years the U.S. Army, stationed at the military fort on the hill above the HBC's Fort Vancouver, was the force of law that prevented the company from being overrun.

However, in 1856 there were no immediate threats to the HBC's safety in the region, except in the case of inconvenient charges such as the one against McDonald. In his letters to Douglas, McDonald explained why he had remained behind at Fort Colvile, telling him that Mactavish agreed. Nevertheless, Douglas complained to Mactavish, hoping he would replace McDonald at Fort Colvile. When Mactavish defended McDonald's actions and refused to replace him, Douglas complained to Governor Simpson:

> With respect to the business at Colvile it appears uncertain what it may produce, as Mr. McDonald's curt and unsatisfactory communicating really gives no information that is at all reliable on the subject. The business should, I think, be directed by the Board of Management of the Oregon Department as hitherto, seeing that the communication with this place is difficult and tedious. That fact I endeavoured to impress on Mactavish, who wishes to make over the charge to this Department. Let the management come from Fort Vancouver, as a divided charge can never prosper, and if McDonald receives orders from this place and Fort Vancouver at the same time, he will

attend to neither, and take his own way, which is not at all times intelligent. McDonald is a capital trader and Mactavish thinks he ought not to be removed from Colvile, as his influence with the Indians is, at present, useful. I concur on his views as we have no disposable person fully qualified to succeed him. Chief Trader McLean, to whom I wrote on the subject, is timid and does not think himself qualified for general business, neither does [George] Blenkinsop ... appear ambitious about going there. I mention those things merely for your information, as of course they must go there if required, but at the same time as you well know, a person is always likely to do best in a place which is agreeable to himself, and which he is anxious to fill.[14]

Douglas seemed to find fault with anything done by McDonald or his men from Fort Colvile. Fort Vancouver's Chief Factor Dugald Mactavish was McDonald's direct supervisor, and McDonald had already reported in full to him. In his casually written reports to Douglas, McDonald hinted at incidents he had discussed with Mactavish. But Douglas demanded full reports. He complained that McDonald's wording was vague, and much of what he had written was confusing and irrelevant to the company's business. He scolded McDonald because the road that left Fort Shepherd led the brigades into American territory as it followed the Columbia River south to the mouth of the Kettle River or rounded other mountain ranges that were impossible to cross with horses.

At the same time as he read McDonald's reports at Fort Langley, Douglas gave Henry Shuttleworth instructions that included taking care of the horses on his return journey:

As the transport horses have a great deal of work to do this summer, I have to recommend the utmost care and tenderness in driving them to and from Colvile; by making two spells a day in the morning, and afternoon, and leaving the animals to rest during the hours of heat. By attention to saddling and loading, and careful management, they will do more work in the course of the summer, with less fatigue and loss of flesh than by any other system of traveling.[15]

Douglas was hardly an expert on managing a brigade, as he had last travelled in one in 1829. A large, imposing man, Douglas overwhelmed young Shuttleworth with instructions that were almost impossible to follow, and Shuttleworth had neither the experience nor the courage to ignore those instructions. From Fort Vancouver, Mactavish reported in September that Shuttleworth "had been very unfortunate with the Brigade to Langley, having lost fifty horses on the trip."[16] At the end of September, Douglas penned a letter to Donald McLean, at Kamloops. "There appears to have been a fearful loss among the Colvile Transport horses," Douglas wrote. "The summer arrangements at Fort Colvile appear to have been defective. McDonald is evidently not the man for the place, and I am of opinion that we will ere long have to appoint you to the charge of that district. This however is merely intended as a preparatory hint."[17]

In his own way, Douglas had become an oppressive force, a man who listened to no one and who no one could challenge nor control—his treatment of young Shuttleworth is a prime example of that oppressive behaviour. Even in his early years at Fort Vancouver, Douglas was disliked: in 1849, Francis Ermatinger told Eden Colvile that the reason the clerks at Fort Vancouver were retiring was from "disgust at the way they are treated by the Chief there, meaning I suppose Douglas."[18] At Peter Skene Ogden's death in 1854, Douglas had become the superior chief factor in the territory, and the fact that his power was virtually without limits went to his head. He was the expert in everything. He bullied his men; he controlled them; he demeaned them. He spoke to his employees as if his opinion was the only one that mattered, and he listened to no one who told him that what he wanted done was impossible or that it had already been done and proven useless. He trusted no one to do their job well without his constant input. As he was a forceful man, and his treatment of some employees who he saw as lesser than himself caused conflict among them, some men broke their connection with the HBC community because of him. Unfortunately, Douglas was untouchable, as Governor Simpson thought him the perfect man for his job. And perhaps he was; he just wasn't very likeable.

Although the situation at Fort Colvile was a particular concern in 1856, there were also worries as the New Caledonia and Thompson's River brigades made their way to Fort Langley with their furs. In March, Douglas warned McLean that the New Caledonia men were short of provisions and McLean must be ready to provide some on their arrival at his post. The winter had been hard, and there had been few salmon in the Fraser.

Because there are no journals for Fort Alexandria or Fort St. James after 1855, Douglas's letters are the only source of information about the arrivals and departures of the New Caledonia brigades at Fort Langley. (McLean, who took Fraser's place at the Thompson's River post of Kamloops, did not keep journals that survived his time there.) On his return from Fort Langley in July, Douglas wrote:

> I have now much satisfaction in announcing the safe arrival of the New Caledonia, Thompson's River, and Fort Colvile brigades at Fort Langley, on the 22nd ultimo [June], and the delivery of the Furs from those districts in good condition. Chief Traders Manson and Ogden accompanied the New Caledonia brigades, Chief Trader McLean conducting the Brigade of Thompson's River …
>
> The returns of New Caledonia and Thompson's River exhibit a very heavy decline in Martens, as compared with the large returns of Outfit 1854, but there is an improvement in almost all the other staple Furs. The decrease in Martens is ascribed by the gentlemen in charge of those districts to the scarcity of food last winter among the natives, but I am inclined to think that is not the sole cause, and that the decrease may be in part ascribed to the periodical fluctuations in the number of those animals.[19]

As mentioned earlier, First Nations hunters would not hunt marten when they were short of food because the animals had little food value. The winter of 1855–56 had been long and hard. Salmon were scarce, and the Kamloops farm had lost forty-nine cattle to sickness or "Indian depredations" (when First Nations people were hungry, they hunted HBC cattle). There was also loss among the horses, as Douglas reported:

> The brood mares and neat cattle at Thompson's River had suffered from disease, and the extreme rigour of the past winter, but had recovered their health and condition before the departure of the brigade. The decrease of horses from sickness, old age, fatigue and the hardships of the winter for the several months ending with the 1st of June 1856, amounts to 69 head, say: 30 pack horses, 5 brood mares, 33 colts one-year-old, 1 dozen [two-year-olds]. Total loss 69.

> The inventory of horses on hand on the 1st June 1856 is
> as follows, viz: 268 brood mares, 3 years old and upwards;
> 72 fillies, 2 years old and upwards; 75 mare colts, 1 year
> old and upwards; 26 colts, 2 years old and upwards; 66
> ditto, 1 year old and upwards; 15 stud horses, 38 pack
> [horses], 18 pack horses lent to Fort Colvile; Total 578.

190 colts of spring 1856, Grand Total 768.[20]

On his return to Fort Victoria, Douglas reported that "the outfits were all packed on my departure from Fort Langley, and it was arranged that the brigades should leave that place yesterday, say the 7th of instant [July]."[21] On July 26, Yale wrote to tell "of the departure of the Brigade from Fort Hope on their return to the interior."[22] Douglas continued to receive reports on the New Caledonia brigades' progress. Yale heard "of the safe arrival of the Brigades in the open country beyond Fort Hope, and I trust their subsequent journey has been also without accident."[23] In mid-September a fresh batch of letters reported on the arrivals of the brigades at their various headquarters, as Douglas reported to the London Committee:

> Letters have just arrived from Thompson's River, New
> Caledonia, and Fort Colvile. The Brigades with the out-
> fits had all safely reached their respective destinations
> with some loss of horses in the Colvile Brigade, but
> without any other serious accident. Mr. Chief Trader
> Manson's letter is dated Alexandria, 28th August, and he
> intended leaving that Post for the upper district on the
> following day. Salmon had arrived at Alexandria in small
> quantities, and it was generally feared that there will be a
> great scarcity of fish this year. The summer returns of
> New Caledonia up to that date were better than usual,
> particularly in the article of Beaver.
>
> Chief Trader McLean writing from Thompson's River
> reports that their researches for Gold have not been so
> successful as he at first expected. The Indians and other
> parties are still collecting it in small quantities, but he had
> not purchased any from them in consequence of his
> being without any means of weighing small quantities,
> though one would think he might have devised some
> temporary means of overcoming that difficulty. Samples

of gold have been brought in from various parts of the country, particularly from the Nicoamen Fork, a tributary stream of Fraser's [Thompson] River, and I am in hopes that some more important discovery will yet be made in that District. Salmon are reported to be very scarce at Thompson's River but in other respects business prospects were good.[24]

Another project was underway this year at Fort Hope as a result of the meetings held while the gentlemen were assembled at Fort Langley. The trail over Manson's Mountain was becoming too difficult to travel. Clerk Donald Walker, now in charge at Fort Hope, was to explore for a new route that avoided Manson's Mountain. It appears that Walker's suggested road made its way to the height of land by the Coquihalla and the Sowaqua, avoiding Peers's Creek. That trail would avoid Manson's Mountain and Fool's Pass, but according to Leolo it was little better than the old route. McLean, when he came into Fort Langley to pick up his second load of trade goods, agreed, and the idea was quickly dropped.

On McLean's return to Kamloops, he and his men, with all the First Nations men they could employ, worked to clear the part of the trail that ran between Manson's Mountain and the height of land west of Campement du Chevreuil. "I feel assured that the work is safe in your hands, and that every possible exertion will be made to render the route more easy for

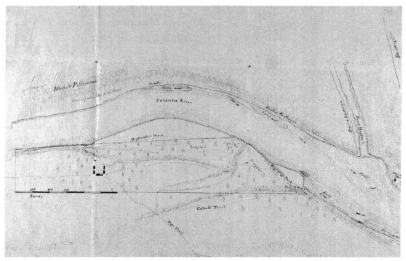

Plan of claim of Fort Shepherd, drawn by William Fraser Tolmie on August 26, 1864.

the annual increasing transport from Langley to the interior," Douglas wrote to McLean.[25] At the same time he told Manson that McLean "is now busily employed on the Fort Hope road with a large body of Indians. His report of Walker's new route is not favorable, and I fear that Manson's Mountain will continue to be an obstacle on the way to the end of the chapter."[26]

Work was also continuing on Fort Shepherd, the new establishment on the Columbia at the mouth of the Pend-d'Oreille River. In July 1857, Douglas wrote:

> The parties who contracted to build Fort Shepherd have, as Mr. Blenkinsop reports in a letter dated 5th June, "completed the buildings in a workmanlike manner, reflecting credit on the contractors, every particular specified in the contract having been fulfilled to the utmost, under no ordinary difficulties."

> The Fort is composed of four substantial one-story houses of 50 & 40 feet, and a kitchen, 21 x 18 feet, say 1 dwelling house and kitchen and 3 store houses, covered with shingles, and the whole sum paid to the contractor was $3,900. The work was done entirely at their own expense, and they furnished all the materials excepting nails and hinges for the doors and window shutters. We have therefor no reason to complain of the expense, which may be considered exceedingly moderate.[27]

However, a few months later, George Blenkinsop at Fort Colvile noted problems with the route from Fort Shepherd to Fort Hope:

> I regret to say a few observations taken by myself a week or two since prove the barrier of mountains at the back of the New Fort impassable without going into American Territory at least ten miles south of the 49th parallel.

> It is much to be regretted that we are so awkwardly placed at this New Post, it being entirely unapproachable on every side but the wrong one, by Horses; which is equally bad the few acres of it being unfit for cultivation. It is the only place hereabout on the Columbia we could select for a Fur Trade Post within our own lines, to command the Trade in the southern part of this district.[28]

The HBC men were never able to resolve the problems of the trail to and from Fort Shepherd. The fort itself stood for more than a decade, and for most of this time it was a functioning trading post. The HBC men, how-ever, quickly learned that the flat of land on which it was built had no agricultural value, and its location failed to attract the Sinixt hunters from the Arrow Lakes, who were more interested in trading at the Indigenous meeting place at Kettle Falls. Fort Shepherd's trade in furs proved so disap-pointing that it was closed down in 1860. Two years later the post was reopened, but it was closed again in 1870. At the end of 1872 it burned down, and the fort disappeared from history.

⋙ 17 ⋘

1857 BRIGADES: THE GOLD RUSH

As soon as the 1856 fur brigades were safely at their home posts and all was quiet, James Douglas began to think of gold. Early that year he had shipped some specimens to London to be assayed. By return mail he learned the gold was valuable. Miners had already reached Kamloops, and the men in the brigades searched for the mineral as they crossed the mountains. A specimen was found in "a panful of gold taken at hazard from the bed of the stream by one of the [Fort Colvile] party, as he was travelling with the brigade," Douglas reported, and "gold has been discovered in several parts of the Thompson's River district; the River Tranquille, a tributary of Thompson's River about 8 miles from Fort Kamloops, appears to be the most promising gold stream."[1] McLean had already delivered that gold to Douglas at Fort Langley.

Three weeks later Douglas wrote, "We have just heard of the departure of the brigade from Fort Hope on their return to the interior. It is also reported on the same authority that Gold has been found in small quantities in the bed of the Quaqualla [Coquihalla] River, near Fort Hope. The moment I feel assured of gold being found in considerable quantities in the interior I shall order a further supply of Goods from England, as the demand will in that event rapidly increase."[2]

He would be disappointed. In October Douglas told the Secretary of State that:

> the number of persons engaged in gold digging is yet extremely limited in consequence of the threatening attitude of the native Tribes, who being hostile to the Americans have uniformly opposed the entrance of American citizens into their country. The people from American Oregon are therefore excluded from the Gold District, except such, as resorting to the artifice of denying their

country, succeed in passing for British subjects. The persons at present engaged in the search of Gold are chiefly of British origin, and retired servants of the Hudson's Bay Company, who being well acquainted with the natives, and connected by old acquaintanceship and the ties of friendship, are more disposed to aid and assist each other in their common pursuits.[3]

Douglas's report continues:

It is reported that Gold is found in considerable quantities, and that several persons have accumulated large sums by their labour and traffic, but I cannot vouch for the accuracy of those reports, though on the other hand, there is no reason to discredit them, as about 220 ounces of Gold Dust has been brought to Vancouver's Island direct from the Upper Columbia, a proof that the country is at least auriferous. From the successful result of experiments made in washing gold from the sand of the tributary streams of Fraser's River, there is reason to suppose that the gold region is extensive, and I entertain sanguine hopes that future researches will develop stores of wealth, perhaps equal to the gold fields of California.[4]

Douglas regretted that the latest reports from Fort Colvile did not tend to "confirm the belief that Gold is procured in great abundance in that part of the country, while the accounts from Mr. McLean at Thompson's River merely state that he had purchased a small quantity of gold from the Indians, without mentioning the number of ounces."[5] He advised Governor Simpson that he was "quite alive to the advantages derivable from the trade in gold, and prepared to turn them to the best account, by sending in liberal supplies of Goods" whenever it appeared that the amount of gold discovered suggested he should.[6]

Late in the year, McLean reported from Kamloops on the new gold diggings at the Nicoamen River. Douglas's letter to the London Committee, written in early 1857, gives the details of McLean's report. Douglas wrote:

The most interesting item of intelligence from Thompson's River is a further discovery of gold by the Natives of the Chee-whack [Nicola River] and Nicoamen Forks. The sample of gold here forwarded was picked up by those

Nicoamen, Thompson River, British Columbia, ca. 1860s. This is where the first gold was found by a First Nations man stooping to drink the water. Photograph by Frederick Dally, an early photographer known for his images of the Cariboo.

people with their fingers among the stones and gravel in the banks of those streams, a statement corroborated equally by the size of the pieces and the absence of the black oxide of Iron which is invariably mixed up with the scale gold procured by washing. Such being the case, we are led to place a degree of confidence in the further report of those Natives to Chief Trader McLean, to the effect that the precious metal is abundant in those streams and that they would have collected a larger quantity had they been certain that the substance was gold, and conscious of its value. To ascertain the truth of those reports, I lately sent Chief Trader McLean instructions to repair in person to the Chee-wack and Nicoamen with a sufficient party of hands provided with all the necessary implements for digging and washing out Gold, and to employ the local Indian population at that work, buying the gold from them on the spot.

> I sincerely hope that this attempt may prove successful, and become productive of advantage to the concern, which can hardly fail to be the result, whether Gold be found or not in remunerative quantities, as in the latter event it will quiet people's minds and allay the prevalent excitement on the subject of treasure hunting.[7]

In March 1857, James Allen Grahame of Fort Vancouver reported that McDonald "has on hand 168 ounces of gold dust, produce of the Pend'Oreille mines traded from the Indians—and from the few whites who still work there. This in my opinion settles the question as to the prospects of the mines in that region, and we may therefore anticipate doing a good business there in a short time."[8]

Some miners had already moved north from the Pend-d'Oreille, testing every stream for signs of gold. They found it. Grahame learned that a rich mine had been discovered on the Couteaux River (Haines Creek), "which stream I am told flows somewhere between the Okanagan and Thompson's River. Parties are fitting out at The Dalles to explore that region so that whether there is gold or not, the privacy of the Thompson's River District will be invaded."[9]

A Fort Colvile gentleman described the gold he saw. "The Gold in the Couteaux mines, as they are called, that is those of Thompson's River, is certainly of a finer quality and much larger than any found in this District, and it is the general opinion that they will prove quite as rich as many parts of California. A great rush will probably be made towards that country next spring, and lead entirely to the abandonment of these rivers, at least for a time."[10]

Gold was discovered in other parts of the Thompson's River district. McLean investigated new goldfields along Thompson's River, and Douglas reported that, "Owing to the swollen state of the Chee-wack and Nicoamen rivers they could not examine their beds to advantage; at a Rapid however, of Thompson's River, about 2 miles distant from the confluence of the Nicoamen with that stream, he [McLean] found gold in sufficient quantities to induce the belief that the bed of the Nicoamen would prove a remunerative digging. He collected about ½ an ounce of gold at different places before and at the said rapid."[11]

According to Douglas, McLean also reported that a party of "adventurers from Fort Colvile have discovered gold in greater abundance than before known in that part of the country. He goes on to state that about

204 dollars worth of gold dust were washed out by seven men in 2 ½ days at the Falls of the south branch of Thompson's River, making a return of 10 dollars a day for each man's labour."[12] After years of similar reports, Douglas remained skeptical but expressed his willingness "to take advantage of that discovery should it prove real, and for the influx of adventurers from all parts of the country."[13]

At Fort Colvile, Chief Trader George Blenkinsop had temporarily replaced McDonald, who had gone to Fort Vancouver for medical treatment. Blenkinsop arrived at Fort Colvile on May 25, 1857, and within two months he was telling Douglas, "That the country is full of gold there cannot be the least doubt."[14] Miners on the Pend-d'Oreille were making $20 a day. Blenkinsop told Douglas:

> A party arrived a few days since from the Gold Regions of Thompson's River, and gave most favourable accounts of that quarter. There is consequently a great stir at this place amongst all classes, and it has unfortunately extended to the Company's servants, the greater part of whom have left, and will not re-engage on any terms, their contracts having expired on the 1st instant [June]. We are now left with 12 men only for the duties of both establishments, and all the outposts; we will require at least 6 more men by the earliest opportunity.[15]

McDonald recovered from his illness and in June prepared to return to Fort Colvile with the brigades from Fort Langley. Douglas advised Blenkinsop that, like himself, McDonald was now a chief trader. Blenkinsop had been made a chief trader in 1855, and thus was McDonald's superior officer according to HBC community standards. When some men were promoted over others merely because of their connection to certain HBC individuals such as Governor Simpson, it tended to cause conflict in the HBC community they both belonged to. Douglas addressed this problem: "I have explained your position to him as the Senior officer in the District," he wrote to Blenkinsop, "but at the same time given him to understand that in consequence of his long experience in the District he was to conduct the business as heretofore, and that you would principally direct your attention to the affairs of the new Establishment."[16]

Blenkinsop's promotion over McDonald might appear unfair, but Governor Simpson had taken an interest in Blenkinsop's career—and there were limited opportunities for promotion in the company. Although Simpson had reduced the number of highly paid chief factors and created more openings for cheaper chief traders, only a few senior clerks could be promoted to chief trader each year.

George Blenkinsop had joined the HBC as a ship's steward in 1840, and two years later Governor Simpson promoted him to postmaster at Fort Stikine after John McLoughlin Jr.'s sudden death. His subsequent promotions came quickly, at least in HBC terms: he was promoted to clerk in 1846, and in 1855 was made chief trader. Angus McDonald, an older man than Blenkinsop, had taken over Fort Colvile in 1852. He had done a superb job in difficult circumstances, especially at the Flathead Post where competition came from all directions. However, it was not until 1857 that he was made chief trader. By assigning a man who had been a chief trader for a longer period of time than McDonald to the Fort Colvile post, Douglas made McDonald inferior in status to Blenkinsop in his own district. It appeared that promotion from clerk to chief trader depended entirely upon who you knew, as James Anderson, of the Lake Nipigon post, had commented to his brother A.C. Anderson in 1846:

> When all my superiors without exception have agreed in giving one the highest character—and when Sir George [Governor Simpson] has coincided with them, I have a right to assume that I was worthy of promotion—and that in being thus shamefully superseded, I have sustained gross injustice ... If interest is to be the Main channel of Promotion, let it be proclaimed abroad, and let not young men waste their last days in the vain & delusive hope that acknowledged merit, long service, & ability are to be rewarded by promotion in due time.[17]

Anderson was correct when he said that some men were promoted over others better qualified than them, and that promotions depended on recommendations from chief factors who had Governor Simpson's ear. Simpson himself confirmed this when he wrote "that those Gentlemen who have come forward were placed in situations where their services came more immediately under the notice of those on whose recommendations the promotions take place."[18] In fact, James told his brother that he (A.C.) had been made chief trader in 1846 because Peter Skene Ogden had recommended him.[19]

Early in the summer, Douglas reported to the London Committee on the arrival of the outcoming brigade at Thompson's River, where there was sickness. "I have lately received letters from Chief Trader McLean, dated

Thompson's River, the 16th of June," Douglas wrote. "Chief Trader Manson had arrived there with the New Caledonia brigade. There was much sickness at Kamloops, and several deaths had occurred among the children of the establishment from dysentery, which is very prevalent. In other respects, everything was going on favourably, and the brigades were to move [en route] towards Fort Langley on the 18th of June."[20]

Douglas informed Dr. Tolmie at Fort Nisqually that "the dysentery broke out at Kamloops and has prostrated many of the men. Manson and McLean have each lost a child, and five of Manson's children were still suffering from its effects by account received yesterday from Thompson's River."[21] Dysentery is an infection of the intestines, caused by parasites or bacteria. Douglas sympathized with the bereaved fathers and forwarded a supply of medicine to Kamloops.

He was also pondering the replacement of Donald Manson, who was taking furlough but had suggested he might retire. Douglas thought Manson would return to New Caledonia, and "under those circumstances, it was not considered advisable to remove Mr. McLean from Thompson's River, and Chief Trader [Peter] Ogden was therefore appointed to the temporary charge of New Caledonia."[22]

Manson's letter had once again mentioned the shortage of horses, and Douglas responded as tartly as he had always done.

> I observed your remarks on the supply of Horses required for New Caledonia. I think the accounts will show that you cannot reasonably complain of indifference to your wants in that way. The whole country east and west of the mountains has for the last 10 years been ransacked to supply your wants, which appear to be endless, and to absorb the increase of the brood mares at Thompson's River as fast as the animals are produced. Let me ask you, my dear Sir, where Horses are to be got except from our own breeding establishments, and you have from year to year the pick and choice of the band of colts. I admit that those are not equal to thoroughly seasoned horses, but with care the first year they will be found superior to any other horses we could procure in Oregon even at the exorbitant price of 100 dollars a head.[23]

To Yale, Douglas wrote of the expected arrival of the brigade at Fort Langley. "It was intended that the Brigade should leave Thompson's River on the 18th instant [June]," he said, "and they would probably be at Fort Langley about the end of the month. The Waters are high and travelling difficult ... Pray let me know of the arrival of the Brigade with as little delay as possible, and indent for all deficiencies to complete the outfits by that conveyance."[24]

The brigade arrived at Fort Langley towards the end of June, and Douglas made plans to go upriver to the post. There is little information on his time there, but on his return to Fort Victoria he reported on the Fort Colvile arrangements. Douglas wrote:

> I have very lately returned from Fort Langley, where I met the Brigades and made all the necessary arrangement for the business of the coming year. Three Boats were dispatched to Fort Hope with 240 pieces of the Fort Colvile outfit, to meet the Colvile Brigade and enable it to return immediately from that post, in order that there may be time to make a second trip with the remainder of the outfit, and to recruit the transport horses before winter sets in. Chief Trader Angus McDonald, who is now in much better health, took charge of the return brigade, and is to resume his station at Fort Colvile, while Chief Trader Blenkinsop will be stationed at the new establishment which we have named after the Governor [of the London Committee], Fort Shepherd.[25]

Manson arrived at Fort Langley in late July, and in early August was at Fort Victoria, on his way to Fort Nisqually and the Columbia district. When he returned to Fort Victoria in November 1857, he wrote a letter to Governor Simpson, explaining that he had "recently purchased a small property in Oregon Territory, of which I would wish to take possession next summer [1858]."[26] Manson's letter continues:

> I beg to request that you would be pleased to grant me an extension of my furlough until the close of Outfit 1858 [May 1859], when it is my intention to retire from the service. I trust that when you take my long services in the Fur Trade, *say 40 years*, into consideration you will not hesitate in granting me this favour.[27]

Douglas argued in Manson's favour, but Governor Simpson refused the request, as he had refused all such requests over the years. William Gregory

Smith, who had replaced Archibald Barclay as secretary of the London Committee, wrote to Manson that "the Governor and Committee will be glad to learn that you have resolved to return to active service for another year or longer, but should you not wish to do this, they will of course accept your resignation as on the 1st June 1858."[28]

Manson remained at Fort Langley over the winter, and in April was at Fort Vancouver, where he wrote Governor Simpson that he had given up all hopes of further promotion in the fur trade, and "tho' still a poor man, made up my mind to resign my C[hief] Tradership, and to settle down in the Willamette where I can secure a tolerable education for my children."[29] And so Donald Manson was forced into retirement, and Chief Trader Peter Ogden took charge of New Caledonia in his stead.

———

The Thompson's River brigades returned to Kamloops in August 1857, and by August 20 the New Caledonia brigades, under Peter Ogden, were on their way north. In October, Douglas reported that "Chief Trader Ogden mentioned the safe arrival of the New Caledonia brigade at Fort Alexandria and the general welfare of the Company's establishment in that District."[30] From Fort Langley, Douglas heard that the brigades had reached Fort St. James in safety. In his response, Douglas wrote: "I received your letter of the 22nd October with the packet from Thompson's River. The news from the interior are of a mixed character—the brigades had all safely reached their respective homes, but it appears that there is a scarcity of salmon throughout New Caledonia and Thompson's River, which will cause distress among the Indians and prove injurious to the trade."[31]

When the Fort Colvile brigades, under the management of George Blenkinsop, reached Fort Langley, they carried current news of the Pend-d'Oreille gold rush. On his return to Fort Victoria, James Douglas reported to the London Committee that:

> Chief Trader Blenkinsop gives a very favourable account
> of the prospects of the gold mines about Colvile, as you
> will observe by the following extract of his said letter:
> "The Prospects at the mines are just now remarkably good.
> By their present mode of washing the ore by sluices brought
> in some cases three miles, a party of miners will make
> from 12 to 20 dollars a day each man. They are now
> working on the face of the mountain bordering on the

Pend'Oreille River, that the country is full of gold there cannot be the least doubt. It has even been taken from the saw pit at the new establishment [Fort Shepherd] ..."

Such is Mr. Blenkinsop's report, and it is honestly given as the general opinion of the people at Colvile, but that opinion is not supported by any export of gold. I have since seen some of the parties who are mentioned by Mr. Blenkinsop as having lately returned from the gold regions of Thompson's River.[32]

Angus McDonald returned home with the Fort Colvile brigades, and from that post Blenkinsop reported on his robust health: "He is now however gone, quite recovered, and started a fortnight since to examine the country above the upper [Arrow] Lakes to discover, if possible, a road in that direction suitable for the conveyance of Goods from Fort Hope."[33] There was word of a possible trail north of Fort Shepherd, which completely avoided American Territory. While convalescing at Fort Vancouver, McDonald had visited his old friend, A.C. Anderson, from whom he learned of the exploration from Fort Colvile to Okanagan Lake that William Sinclair Jr. had made in 1852 (mentioned in Chapter 16).

Before he left Fort Colvile in 1852, Anderson had sent William Sinclair Jr. to explore for a trail between the Arrow Lakes and Okanagan Lake. Sinclair found a route that went much of the way to Talle d'Épinettes, at the northwest end of Okanagan Lake, via a lake Anderson called the Flat Bow (Mabel Lake).[34] In September 1857, McDonald completed the exploration of a possible new route via Flat Bow Lake, Talle d'Épinettes, Chief N'Kuala's camp [Summerland], Nicola Lake, and Campement des Femmes.[35] Douglas considered this expedition unnecessary. "I place little reliance in Mr. Blenkinsop's astronomical observations," Douglas complained to Angus McDonald, "which with the imperfect means at his disposal could have hardly been correctly ascertained. I conceive it to be quite unnecessary to open a new route by Nicholas [Nicola] Lake, until the boundary line is marked upon the ground by the proper Commissions. Till such time we have a perfect right of passage with our goods to and from the new Establishment."[36]

The search for gold around Kamloops had intensified over the summer. In June, Douglas advised the London Committee that "the Native Indian tribes are opposed to the visits of Strangers, and are reported to have plundered a party of whites at the forks of the Okanagan River near where the boundary line between our Territory and the United States passes."[37] In a second letter Douglas expanded on this. "The Indians object to the entrance of white men into their country," he told Governor Simpson. The Okanagan and Nlaka'pamux refused to allow the miners "to work the auriferous streams, partly with the view of monopolizing the precious metal for their own benefit, and partly from an impression that the Salmon will leave the Rivers and be prevented from making their annual migration from the sea. That disposition on their part is altogether in favour of our interests, and I cannot help admiring the wisdom and foresight of the Indians, and have given directions to the Officers in charge of the Company's Posts to respect their feelings, and to permit them to work the gold for their own benefit, and to bring it in as an article of trade."[38]

A few days later Douglas advised the London Committee that in spite of all the gold discovered in the district, only seven ounces had been traded that year. He also advised them that the miners "speak favourably of the Thompson's River gold district, and they say in fact that gold is abundant, and they would have procured a large quantity had they not been driven off by the Indians who would not suffer them to touch the soil."[39]

If the miners found gold, they were not trading it at the HBC posts, and little gold travelled over the brigade trails to Fort Victoria. The Yakamas and their allies were beginning to lose the war, and American gold miners made their way north to the Pend-d'Oreille goldfields and beyond. So too did the Mexican, Spanish, and American packers who had worked the California mines. From Fort Vancouver, Dugald Mactavish expressed his concern. "As the interior Country is now occupied extensively by petty traders and miners," he informed Governor Simpson, "I have little hope of being able to do much at Colvile for the future, and we may consider ourselves fortunate if we can hold our own there."[40]

In September, Douglas warned Peter Ogden of the difficulties that the gold rush at Thompson's River might cause in his northern department. "I lately heard of your departure from Thompson's River," he wrote, "and of the gold discovered in the Couteaux Country; an event which will give us no end of trouble so far as the Company's servants are concerned; and leave us more than ever dependent upon the natives for getting through with the Brigade and other interior work.

"You must, however, prepare to meet the evil," Douglas's letter continues, "and to devise every possible advantage from the discovery of gold. We have just sent in an additional supply of goods to Thompson's River and Fort Colvile in consequence of our anticipating a large demand for supplies."[41]

Douglas's letters also indicated that gold was found "in the northern district of Thompson's River."[42] This might refer to the gold found on Tranquille River by British gold miner James Houston. In 1856, Houston had stumbled into the Kamloops post more dead than alive and, throwing himself on the mercy of McLean, spent the winter there. In the spring he struck gold and paid McLean for his room and board.[43] This was, in part, the gold that McLean brought to Fort Langley in summer 1857. When McLean returned to Kamloops in August, he found more gold miners awaiting his arrival, with gold in hand. McLean reported that "The Gold Mine appears to be growing profitable. I have traded 49 ounces of Gold Dust since my arrival [from Fort Langley] and could have obtained much more if I had been provided with the proper goods required by the Diggers, such as Sea Boots—Moleskin or Corduroy Trowzers, Navy Blue & Grey Cottons, Serge or [Coarse] Shirts."[44]

These were not items that First Nations miners would demand. By now, the First Nations had allowed retired British and Métis employees from Fort Colvile into the goldfields. As Douglas reported to the London Committee:

> Mr. McLean reports that a party of gold diggers [half-whites] visited the Fort on his return from Fort Langley and informed him that gold was abundant and that they had collected $2,000 worth in less than 6 days. They sold forty-nine ounces of gold dust for supplies at the Company's shop there, a proof that their statements were not unfounded. The richest gold diggings are within twelve miles of the confluence of Thompson's and Fraser's Rivers, where he thinks it will be advisable to commence a small trading establishment for the gold trade; but in respect to that matter, we have not yet come to a decision, as it will require considerable means to carry it into effect, and it may in the end not prove the most convenient position for trade, as the country has been as yet but imperfectly explored, but you may rely that we shall do everything in our power to turn this important discovery to good account.[45]

Writing to McLean, Douglas agreed that the discovery of gold in the Thompson's River district "appears no longer a shadow but a sober reality":

> The quantity you have traded proves that fact beyond a question, and we must now prepare to turn that great

discovery to advantage. You have acted most judiciously in sending the order for additional supplies. Those have been packed and are now to the number of 47 pieces, forwarded per the *Otter* to Fort Langley. Mr. Yale has orders to send them to Fort Hope without delay to meet your people there by the 15th of the present month [September] ...

A pair of gold scales with a set of weights complete are now also sent. We have considered your suggestion with respect to the erection of an establishment at the mouth of Thompson's River; it being forwarded on the impression that it could be supplied by water communication direct from Fort Langley; such, however, is not actually the case, as admitting Fraser's River to be navigable above and below the falls, there must be at that point a land portage of 13 miles, owing to the dangerous character of the rapids, and for the same reason two sets of craft will be required for that transport, one set to run between Fort Langley and the lower end of the Falls. I moreover do not know whether Fraser River be navigable for Boats between the confluence of Thompson's River and the Falls [above Yale], a point which should be ascertained before going to the expense of building a new establishment. We will certainly not be able to commence that establishment this year, but when you have made the necessary enquiries, and discovered that the plan is not seriously objectionable, we shall fall vigorously to work and soon accomplish our object.[46]

McLean was unfamiliar with the hazards of the lower Fraser River, although not unaware of them. Like most of the HBC men, McLean and Douglas had only travelled the section of the river that lay between Fort George (Prince George) and Fort Alexandria. Douglas had heard stories of the canyons that impeded the southern parts of the Fraser but, as always, he believed that most of the HBC men made mountains out of molehills. However, he also knew that Yale had travelled down the Fraser River with Governor Simpson in 1828. McLean's suggestion had merit, and so Douglas asked Yale for advice.

"Chief Trader McLean is strongly in favor of establishing a Post on Thompson's River," Douglas wrote. He suggested the new post might be built about 12 miles from its confluence with Fraser's River, under the impression that Goods might be sent to that place all the way from Fort Langley by water. What is your opinion on the subject? Do you suppose that a Post built there would be supplied from Langley by water? In that case it might become a Depot for the interior far more accessible, and much nearer than Fort Hope. Pray give me your ideas on the subject by the first opportunity, as no one is better qualified to give an opinion in respect to the character of Fraser's River as a navigable stream than yourself. My own impression is that it would be both difficult and expensive to transport Goods over the Falls of Fraser's River.[47]

Yale's response to Douglas's letter is lost, but it is clear he thought that bringing goods up the Fraser might be possible. He also reminded Douglas of the Lillooet River route that Anderson had come down in May 1846 (see Chapter 3).

In the meantime, Douglas arranged for McLean to come out for an additional load of goods in September. "The Steamer *Otter* is now about to proceed to Fort Langley with 46 packages of Goods for the supply of Thompson's River district," Douglas wrote in September. "You will observe by the invoice now forwarded a list of deficiencies, consisting of 25 pairs of Sea Boots, 10,000 percussion caps, and 16 dozen Table Spoons, which I beg of you to complete, if these articles be on hand, from the stock of Goods at Fort Langley, and to add the same to the invoice."[48]

Douglas worried about the mountain route that McLean would be travelling so late in the year. "I hope the goods for Thompson's River will reach Fort Hope in time for the party expected from that District, the road in the mountain is reported to be in a very bad state for the passage of horses, a difficulty which every year appears to increase."[49] According to Douglas, McLean reached Kamloops before the snow fell:

I have lately received a letter from Chief Trader Donald McLean, dated Thompson's River, 19th October last. The additional supply of goods forwarded from Fort Langley in September had been received in good order on the 6th of October, and from that date to the 18th, the trade had produced 80 ounces of gold dust, making a total return for Outfit 1857 of 152 ounces of gold dust.[50]

This shews a gradual increase in the gold returns of the District, and that the Natives are daily becoming more alive to the advantages of gold finding. The prospects of the District are really becoming brilliant, and Mr. McLean writes that in addition to the diggings on Thompson's River, gold has been found in considerable quantities at the following places on Fraser's River, say Fort Yale (100 miles above Fort Langley), and the Pavillon [Pavilion]. In fact the auriferous character of the country is daily becoming more apparent, chiefly through the yet unskillful researches of the natives.

A trading party with an excellent supply of goods under the management of Mr. Robert Todd is kept constantly running among the diggers, to pick up the Gold as fast as it is collected.

We propose hereafter when the mineral character of the country becomes better known, to form a small compact trading Post at some point combining, as far as possible, the advantages of being accessible for the transport of goods from Fort Langley, and to the miners employed in the diggings.[51]

As late as September, Douglas disagreed with McLean on the immediate need to build a small post on the Nicoamen River, where the gold was being found. His instructions changed with the news that Americans were now successfully finding their way into the goldfields and establishing themselves on Thompson's River. Douglas worried for the safety of the First Nations population, who were defending their lands against the American invasion. "I am aware of the feeling of the Indian population in respect to the Americans," Douglas reported to the London Committee,

but I think they will find it impossible to carry out their determination of preventing whites from working in their diggings. Leave them entirely to their own impulses, and be careful not to encourage them to resist the influx of gold diggers, or we may become embroiled in serious difficulties: in short, inculcate upon the Indians the duty of being kind to all white men, our words will at least have a restraining effect if they cannot altogether prevent evil, and at the same time I would take care to inform any white strangers coming into the country that the Indians are dangerous and not to be trusted.[52]

By December, Douglas had received Yale's response to his queries and was prepared to build a permanent post near the junction of Thompson's River and the Fraser. Although bateaux would be necessary for delivery of goods by both the Fraser River and the Lillooet, Douglas appears to have settled on the Fraser River route. He advised Yale that, "We will have to form a transport corps of two officers and 10 white men who with the addition of Indians will form a sufficient force for that purpose. On that service we may employ Mr. [Henry] Peers, who has had much experience in that part of the Country. One of your two present assistants will complete the staff of Officers, and we will beat up for recruits of laboring men in this quarter, though we may find it necessary to increase our present rate of pay, which will be attended with many disadvantages."[53]

At the end of December, Douglas reported to the London Committee on the many challenges he was facing. He reported:

> I am now engaged in devising the ways and means of pouring supplies into the country, but I have not as yet decided whether we shall resort to the land route by Fort Hope: the route by Harrison's River and the Lilliwhit [Lillooet] Lakes to the Great Falls of Fraser's River; or, keeping to Fraser's River, use it as a navigable channel of communication with the Falls of Thompson's River, where it is probable that we shall hereafter build a small trading establishment for the supply of the Gold miners. There is but a choice of difficulties whichever course we take, as the country is everywhere rugged and mountainous, and without comparison the most inaccessible part of the Indian country, but probably the most direct and least expensive route will be that of Fraser's River. I shall have to form a transport corps of two officers and 30 or 40 men, the greater part of the latter will, however, be Indians, as it is impossible to get white men at reasonable rate of wages, to perform the drudgery of inland travelling.
>
> I propose to employ Chief Trader [Henry] Peers in executing that service as he possesses all the requisite qualities for the work.[54]

Henry Peers turned down the opportunity, however, and Douglas was once more stuck for a man to do the work. George Stewart Simpson was the next thought of, "but he, too, I am grieved to say, is not perfectly regular, though he is well disposed to be so and both active, able, and zealous, in the discharge of his duties."[55] Douglas might well be grieved: his letter was addressed to the HBC's Governor George Simpson, father of the "irregular" Simpson now being considered for the difficult work of hauling freight up the Fraser River to the gold mines.

In early 1858, Douglas devised a plan for getting goods and supplies upriver to the new Fort Dallas, now being built on the east bank of the Fraser, a few miles south of its junction with Thompson River.[56] The Fort Langley men were also to rebuild Fort Yale and Simon's House, and improve the road that ran over Douglas's Portage. Douglas told the London Committee how he thought his river transport might work:

> We have now finally resolved on building a small trading Post near the point where the Thompson unites with Fraser's River, and endeavouring to open a water communication for it by Fraser's River for the transport of Goods, and though the difficulties be great, and the River dangerous, as well as being altogether impassible during the summer freshets, yet we hope and shall strive to succeed.
>
> As part of the machinery for that purpose I may here inform you that two lines of River Craft will be required, one to be used between Thompson's River and the upper end of the Falls of Fraser's River, and the other to ply between Fort Langley and the lower end of the same Falls; the intermediate distance between these points (i.e. The upper and lower end of the falls) being about 13 miles, over which the goods will have to pass by land, and it will be further necessary to build a small fort at the lower end of the Portage for storing the goods while in transit.[57]

The thirteen-mile portage was the part of the river between Fort Yale and the Spuzzum village to the north; it was known as Douglas's Portage. The men were sent off from Fort Langley in mid-February, under command of George Simpson and Ovid Allard.[58] In March, Douglas reported that "Mr. Simpson's party had experienced some difficulty above the Falls, and lost two canoes which were dashed to pieces on the rocks, but the property was all saved and no lives were lost."[59] In April, Douglas wrote, "Mr. Simpson has just returned from the Forks with the transport party,

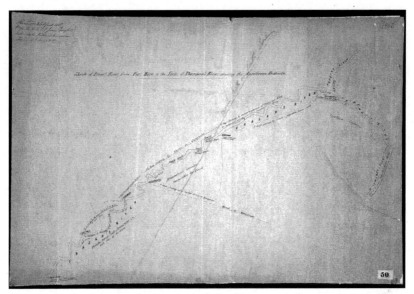

"Sketch of Fraser's River from Fort Hope to the forks of Thompson's River," by James Douglas, 1858. Detail, Hope to Kequeloose [Quayome].

having delivered the property in his charge, about 70 pieces of Trade Goods, into the hand of Chief Trader McLean, who came to that point with horses to meet the transport party from Langley."[60] However, Douglas informed the London Committee, "The river is now on the rise, and we will in consequence have to abandon that route for the present and carry on the summer transport by the Fort Hope Road."[61]

But the spring and summer of 1858 brought changes that no one in the interior was prepared for or wanted. The First Nations peoples in particular were unprepared for the flood of aggressive American gold seekers that would overwhelm their territories in the Columbia district and breach their barricades at the boundary line. They thought the Queen would protect them. But she did not.

❋ 18 ❊

1858 BRIGADES: THE FRASER CANYON WAR

T he gold rushes continued to move north. In the United States, the Spokanes and Yakamas fought the last big battle of the Yakama War, in which the U.S. Army's professional soldiers completely overwhelmed the First Nations warriors. Nothing now prevented the gold miners from pouring into the Thompson's River district via the Okanagan River, and Americans ganged together in groups of men 250-strong to force their way past the First Nations peoples who barred their passage. Most of the Americans brought with them their hatred of the Indian. All of them believed they had an absolute right to take the gold wherever they might find it. The boundary line was not yet marked: they did not know where it was and they didn't care. To them this was American territory and the gold belonged to them.

David McLoughlin, son of retired Chief Factor Dr. John McLoughlin, led one large group of miners north: his party was ambushed on the Okanagan brigade trail in the narrow gully now called McLoughlin's Gulch. A later gang of miners raided an empty Okanagan village, throwing the residents' preserved food into the lake. Some members of that same gang planned an attack on the Okanagans who lived at Rivière à l'Ours (Bear Creek). After the main party had gone ahead, two dozen men remained behind, concealed in a ravine, and murdered the occupants of the village as they returned home.[1] As a result of this attack and others, the Okanagans argued that they must go to war, and they followed the miners to Kamloops. Their chief, N'Kuala, knew the Okanagans could not win a war against these well-armed men and prevented his people from attacking. Instead, he confronted the Americans who had killed his people, berating them for their brutality and cowardice, and shaming them into releasing prisoners they had taken.[2]

At Fort Vancouver, Alexander Caulfield Anderson was besieged by miners asking about routes into the interior, and in May he published his book

Handbook and Map to the Gold Regions of Frazer's and Thompson's River,
which was published in San Francisco. It sold in the thousands of copies
and brought many of the miners north. In the end, more than eight thousand miners travelled north to the goldfields by the Okanagan River, most
arriving in the summer of 1858.

A similar invasion came up the Fraser River, with more than twenty-
three thousand miners entering the goldfields by this route. The miners
were expected to stop at Fort Victoria to buy licenses to mine the gold.
Many avoided that expense by sailing directly to the Fraser River or by
travelling on foot over the Whatcom Trail, a rough road that began in
Bellingham Bay and bypassed Fort Victoria entirely. Nevertheless, many
other miners did pass through the HBC community on Vancouver's Island:
the first major influx of miners bound for the Fraser River arrived at Fort
Victoria in April.

"I have to communicate for the information of the Governor and Committee," Douglas wrote on April 27, "that the Steam vessel 'Commodore'
arrived in this Port on the 25th of Instant [April] direct from San Francisco
with 450 passengers, chiefly gold miners, who have come here with the
intention of working the gold mines of the interior."[3]

As soon as the first group of miners departed for the Fraser, more
arrived. The first widely reported gold strike had taken place at Hill's Bar
on March 12, 1858, but the Nlaka'pamux had already been mining the bar
for months, using gold pans and sluice-boxes carved from cedar. In June,
summer freshets raised the water in the river and drove many miners away
from their gold finds. At Fort Hope, frustrated miners rampaged around,
unable to reach the goldfields because of the freshets. They eyed the First
Nations people who visited the fort, noting that each carried his own little
bag of gold dust. They also noted how well-armed the Nlaka'pamux men
were, and how they appeared to be in league with the HBC. Many American miners threatened to force their way upriver, where, in their own
words, all hell would break loose.

On hearing stories of unrest on the river, and worried about a potential
Indian War, Douglas travelled to the Fraser to see the goldfields and talk
to the miners. Long before he reached Fort Hope, he learned that mining
on the river bars had been suspended as the river was rising. He also discovered the miners were short of provisions and demanded pork, coffee,
and flour. Most could afford to pay the dollar per pound that each of these
items would cost them. The list of needs grew longer the farther he travelled upriver: miners also demanded tea and sugar, nails, clothing such as

Men camped along a river bank, sitting on a log and eating a meal. Photographer unknown.

woollen shirts and stockings, quicksilver, leather boots, rocker irons, long-handled shovels, axes, molasses, yeast powder, and wash pans.

At Fort Hope, Douglas spoke with some of the gold miners, whose tent villages surrounded the post. The HBC men must have heard news of the gold rush as they passed through Kamloops, but when they arrived at Fort Hope in late June they would have had their first glimpse of the thousands of prospectors who had set up camp outside the fort walls. To remove the voyageurs from the bubbling excitement that surrounded the post, Douglas likely met the brigades there and travelled downriver with them to Fort Langley. Some HBC employees may have expressed an interest in deserting the trade for the gold rush. To encourage them to return to the interior with the brigades, Douglas increased their wages: "New Caledonia, an increase of 10 on all classes of servants which will bring the rate of wages to £35 for the boutes, £30 for the middlemen, and £45 for guide & boat builder."[4]

In the meantime, a group of heavily armed miners had set up camp on Thompson's River near the Nicoamen River. It was mid-June, and because of the freshets they were unable to pan for gold. They decided to leave after a First Nations woman warned them that white men had been killed downriver. The miners made their way to China Bar (near Spuzzum), where they reported that twenty-six of their members had been killed in running battles with the Nlaka'pamux. At the Spuzzum village itself, miners shot thirty-six Nlaka'pamux, including five or more chiefs. News of these battles reached Fort Yale when bodies of nine mutilated white men floated down the Fraser. Jason Allard wrote:

> Those were troublesome times. Bodies were picked out of the river, and Indians were blamed for murdering the white men who had been drowned through inexperience of the difficult waters of the river. My father [Ovid Allard] repeatedly warned white men against the dangers of such a fate. Agitations were started to clean up the Indians. The climax came when the body of a headless white man was found floating in a back eddy of the river, and near it the body of a white woman, both stripped of clothing. Then war was declared against the Indians. Mass meetings were held at which wild speeches were made and two companies of troops were formed and officers selected. Captain Snyder and Lieutenant Graham and an officer named Donelly were among the officers elected. The Indians were at this time in the mountains, gathering and drying food for the winter, and my father explained this and the probable cause of the deaths of the whites to the infuriated miners. But to no purpose. The irregular troops started out for vengeance in military form, the stars and stripes at their head. A week later they straggled back, arriving at midnight with the story that now a war of extermination was essential. They appeared to be in a very ugly mood, created a terrible commotion.

Allard's story concludes with the note that "later it developed that two officers had been shot during a scouting tour by their own men who mistook them for Indians."[5]

Captain Snyder was Captain H.M. Snyder, an American Army man, well known in San Francisco and commander of the Pike Guards on the Fraser River. "Lieutenant" Graham was commander of the Whatcom Guards, another American force set up at Fort Hope. It is likely that "Donelly" was a former chief of the San Francisco Police named B.C. Donellan, who in July, on what he named "Washington Bar," arranged a pact with the Nlaka'pamux that would allow him and his companions to pan for gold during the day while the Nlaka'pamux fished for salmon in the mornings and evenings.

On August 18, the troops described by Allard ascended the river. Their goals differed: while Snyder wanted to sign peace treaties with the First Nations people, Graham wanted to kill them all. On August 21, Snyder met with Chief Spintlum (Sexpinlhemx) at Lytton, telling him and his chiefs that if he had to come again to force peace, he would come with thousands of men. As the Nlaka'pamux were aware of what had happened on Okanagan Lake and in the United States, they believed him. Spintlum was prepared to negotiate for peace.

In the meantime, at Fort Hope, the miners panicked when rumours that forty-nine white men had been killed on the upper Fraser reached them; additional false stories of 150 men murdered on the newly opened Harrison–Lillooet Trail contributed to their alarm. On August 21 they held meetings at Fort Hope, addressing a report to Governor Douglas on the "Indian difficulties."

Douglas arrived at Fort Hope on September 3, accompanied by thirty-five red-jacketed Royal Engineers. These were members of the Boundary Commission, soldiers who were to carve the boundary line between the United States and British territories all the way to the Rocky Mountains. By luck, they had arrived at Fort Victoria on July 12.[6] Douglas was also accompanied by militia men from HMS *Satellite*.

On August 30, Lieutenant Charles Wilson of the Royal Engineers, who remained behind at Fort Victoria, described the departure of his companions for the Fraser River:

> In consequence of the very bad reports from the mines up Fraser river, Major Hawkins has gone up with a body of men, to help the Governor to keep the peace. I volunteered several times to go up as a little fighting would be much more to my taste than this work ... I am very anxious for news of the party, as there has been a good deal of fighting up there & wise heads in these matters say we are going to have a regular Indian war.[7]

But there was no war on the Fraser River, much as Lieutenant Wilson wanted it to happen. As early as May 1858, Douglas had reached the conclusion that "it is almost impossible to prevent people from entering the British possessions in search of gold, as long as there is a prospect of finding it."[8] He hoped that if the diggings did not prove remunerative, the miners would abandon the country and return home. While he may have hoped for this, in the meantime he must deal with these frustrated gold prospectors. Douglas, backed by the Royal Engineers, made it clear to the Americans that the HBC was in power here, and that they had the connections to use their power. He made it understood that the Americans were now in British Territory and must behave. He represented the HBC communities with a show of strength that was more fragile than he would have liked, but in doing so he prevented the chaos that would have occurred had he been more cautious.

His message to the First Nations communities up and down the river would have been different: "The Queen is looking after you." The remainder of his message would have echoed Peter Skene Ogden's speech to the Cayuse in 1847, after the Waiilatpu Massacre. "But if you go to war, we cannot help you."

There is, however, little record of what he actually did and said. Douglas's journal of his visit to Fort Hope in September does not report that he was accompanied by both Royal Engineers and militia men. He may have impressed the Americans with the power of the British law, but the waters of the Fraser River were also subsiding, which meant the gold miners were able to proceed upriver from Fort Hope. The problem solved itself.

EPILOGUE: 1859 BRIGADES AND BRITISH COLUMBIA'S FUTURE

T he second group of Royal Engineers arrived at Fort Victoria in November 1858. Lieutenant Henry Spencer Palmer arrived with the third group in December. These later arrivals, consisting of 150 sappers in addition to officers, were to act both as law enforcement and road builders in the new Colony of British Columbia. In summer 1859, Lieutenant Palmer was assigned the duty of riding over the brigade trail with Angus McDonald, surveying its route and assessing whether a wagon road could be built over the mountain.[1]

The Fort Colvile brigade left Fort Hope on September 17, with one of its members reporting that McDonald's brigade party consisted of "some dozen Indians & mules."[2] In his own journal, Palmer wrote an excellent description of the brigade trail that the HBC men had used for the past decade. His journal begins on September 17, when "I left Fort Hope, in company with Mr. Angus McDonald of the Hudson's Bay Company, and commenced my journey up the Coquihalla Valley."[3] The country was "level and lightly timbered, and covered in places with an abundance of brush and young trees" (81). Three miles east of Fort Hope,

> two conical hills, from 600 to 800 feet high, obstruct the otherwise generally straight course of the river, and have forced it to find a passage between them and the mountain mass skirting the southern limits of the valley. To avoid this unnecessary circuit, the trail crosses the Coquihalla [River] 1 ½ miles from Hope, and leaving it to the right, follows the level country to the base of the first hill. Near this spot lies a pretty little lake [Kawkawa Lake], to which I could see no outlet or inlet, and which was apparently

fed by springs and the drainage from the mountains. Towering above its opposite shores were the steep rocky cliffs of "Ogilvy's" [Ogilvy Peak] and adjacent peaks so close as to be clearly reflected in the dark still water of the lake, and a tiny cascade stealing down the crooked crannies of the mountain with a scarcely perceptible motion added to the picturesque beauty of the spot. (81)

Palmer's journal continues:

Leaving the lake, we crossed the two conical hills before us, and rejoined the Coquihalla three miles further on. While traversing the southern slope of the second of these two hills, Mr. McDonald drew my attention to what was apparently a large defile in the mountain range, bearing S.E. about 20 miles, and leading, as far as I could judge from that distance, through the main Cascade Range eastward. (81)

This defile was the opening of the Nicolum Creek valley that Anderson had followed from the mouth of the Coquihalla River to the summit of the Tulameen Plateau in July 1846. Lieutenant Palmer's journal continues. "After rejoining the Coquihalla, we travelled along its right bank [descending] for about one miles [*sic*], and then, leaving the Boston Bar trail trending north up the valley of the river, we crossed to its left bank a mile west of the foot of the most prominent spur from the Manson Range" (81).

The Boston Bar Trail had been cut by Royal Engineer Lieutenant A.R. Lempriere in summer 1859. It led from Hope to Boston Bar Creek, then over a high pass to Anderson's River, and allowed access to the goldfields in summertime. The route was tortuous, with the trail subject to landslides, and the pass was covered with snow many weeks longer than trails at lower levels.

Palmer goes on:

On arrival at the foot of this spur, we commenced the ascent on the southern slope in a direction parallel, or nearly so, to its crest, leaving the mass of the mountain intervening between us and the Coquihalla. Here the road, which thus far has been tolerably good, deteriorated to an extent anything but pleasant, a rude, rocky track wound its way along the steep sides of the mountain over hundreds of fallen logs and amongst masses of fragmentary rock that has from time to time been detached from the precipice above, and

on attaining a high elevation, mud, one of the few dis-
agreeables of a mountain journey in the Cascades, and deep
enough to debar any but Indian horses from forcing their
way through it, rendered travelling a matter of considerable difficulty, and added a scarcely agreeable feature to a
landscape already somewhat limited. (81)

"The Coquihalla River," painted by Henry F. Tasker-Taylor, n.d.

Six miles of rough travel brought the brigades "to the first camping place [Manson's Camp], where a slight opening in the woods enabled me to discover the feature of the country through which the latter part of our route had lain" (81). Palmer's journal continues:

> We appear to have been travelling up a mountain pass walled in by two slightly converging spurs from the Manson Range, whose slopes, although separated at the opening of the pass by a considerable space, here meet and form a rocky defile, down the bed of which a swift brook [Peers Creek] forces its way, and fed on its passage by numerous small streams and waterfalls, swells to the magnitude of a mountain torrent, and rushes into the Coquihalla a short distance below the point where we last crossed. (81)

Most of the trail to Manson's Camp has been obliterated by logging roads: Manson's Camp itself was logged in 1969 and its exact location lost. But in 1859, what lay directly ahead of Palmer was Manson's Mountain (now Manson's Ridge), with Mount Outram on his right hand. "To the east I saw towering above us the steep portion of the main Manson Range [Manson's Ridge]," Palmer wrote, "over which lay our to-morrow's journey, its crest running nearly North and South, and connecting the two spurs above mentioned" (81). Fortunately, "wood and water were of course abundant, but the horses had to be fed on barley brought for the purpose, there being no grass in the neighbourhood or indeed anywhere on the mountain slopes" (81).

The next day they tackled Manson's Mountain. In August 1971 some modern-day explorers hiked the trail from east to west and described their journey over the ridge to Manson's Camp:

> Clear and warm, another excellent day. Up at 5. Off on the trail by 8.10. It is clearly marked with first the original HBC blazes, gray and deep inset in the core wood with the bark doing its best to grow over the damaged tissues ... The trail climbed about 1,000 feet from Fool's Pass [on the north side of the ridge] to the divide at the lowest point of the Manson Ridge. It was not a long journey but it was over the most rugged terrain we've traversed so far. No wonder so many horses perished on

this particular part for an unsure footing, a slip or a slide would send you skidding down the steep rocky slope. The trail is clearly marked and deeply worn ...

We reached the summit in time for lunch on a green alpine meadow with the high snow-streaked slopes of Manson's Mt. as a backdrop ...

The trail down the western slopes of Manson's Ridge was undoubtedly the most rugged of the entire journey. In a relatively short distance we had to lose 2,000 feet. So the trail wound its way by switchbacks back and forth in the search for footings that could afford a way for the HBC horses. I marvel that any could survive as we staggered along narrow rocky ledges then crossed rock-strewn creek beds and skidded down gravel slopes that taxed the agility of the best of us ... In many places the ground was worn down by the pounding of countless horses' hooves and the trench-like depression was in marked contrast to the usual terrain; then to our utter amazement the blazes would thin out and the deep trail seemed to disappear. So it would go, alternatively a well-marked trail and a wandering sparsely designated open mountain-side.[4]

In his journal, Lieutenant Palmer describes the climb over the same ground, although he is travelling from west to east:

We rose at dawn, and soon commenced the laborious ascent of the mountain by a zig-zag trail, very steep and rocky, but, fortunately for ourselves and the horses, free from mud. After struggling up this difficult mountain path for an hour and a half we reached the summit of the pass, the magnificent view from which fully compensates the traveler for the labour of the ascent. Looking north, south, and east, the view embraced mountain scenery of a description scarcely to be surpassed. As far as the eye could reach, an endless sea of mountains rolled away into blue distance, their sides clothed almost to the summits with an impenetrable forest of every species of pine, and their peaks and recesses lit up by the rays of the early sun,

too early yet to lighten the gloomy valley below us. Here
and there a rugged naked peak towered up to bold relief
some 1,000 feet or more above the summits of the adjacent ranges, spotted with occasional patches of snow in
crevices never perhaps penetrated by the sunlight and so
complete was the network of mountains in which we
were enveloped, that the question of "How were we ever
to get out of them," which naturally occurred, appeared
to me somewhat difficult of solution. (81–82)

From the heights, Palmer looked down into the sloping valley of
Sowaqua Creek, "a steep glen or forest bottom, not free from mountains,
it is true, but nevertheless a valley, down which pours a considerable
stream" (82). The trail climbed the floor of the valley, crossing Colvile,
Bushby, O'Reilly, and Matthew Creeks (named in 1971). After fording
the Sowaqua, the brigaders climbed over the steep flanking ridge of Mount
Davis, where they reached a height of six thousand feet above sea level.
Campement du Chevreuil was just east of that highest point of travel, and
one day's journey beyond Manson's Camp.[5]

Lieutenant Palmer's journal continues with his journey up Sowaqua
Creek valley to Campement du Chevreuil. "The trail follows this bottom
for about five miles in a general south-south-easterly direction, a distance
it took us 3 ½ hours to travel, and then plunging into a deep glen crossed
the previously mentioned tributary of the Coquihalla [Sowaqua]" (82). In
his journal, Palmer also described the western slope of the dividing ridge,
which fell "almost perpendicularly into this stream and though less muddy
than those of Manson Mountain [Ridge], and tolerably free from rock,
except in places where huge masses of debris detached from the summit
have found a lodgement on the side of the hill, it is if anything steeper than
the latter, though not so trying to animals" (81). The mountainsides were
clothed with a thick forest of spruce and brush was becoming scarce. "The
trail winds up the face of a huge spur from the mountain mass [Mount
Davis], jutting out in a south-westerly direction and, steep though it was,
our horses appeared to ascend with much greater ease than they did on the
rocky muddy slopes of Manson's Mountain" (82).

In two hours, the horses approached the top of the mountain, where there
was "a considerable decrease in the density of the forest, and the appearance
of short grass and mountain heather told me we were nearing the summit;
the timber shortly almost entirely disappeared, and as both men and horses

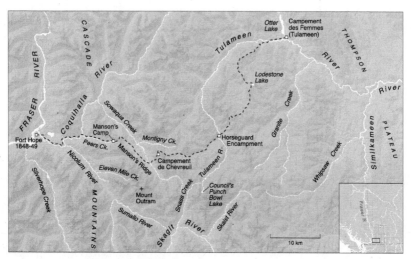

Map 14: The HBC Brigade Trail (also seen on page 134).

were by this time tired, we camped towards evening in a pretty sheltered spot 600 feet below the summit known as the 'Campement du Chevreuil'" (82).

"Everyone seems to like Campement du Chevreuil, both in the days of 1859 and now," brigade trail historian Harley Hatfield wrote in the early 1970s. He goes on:

> It is a truly beautiful campsite, a dimple in the vast sweep of the mountainside. A small ice-cold stream [Chevreuil Creek] comes out of the talus slope at the back and runs through the camp in a half circle and just below is a waterfall and the pool where [Arthur Thomas] Bushby in his time and we in ours enjoyed a bath, in our case at least a very quick one. At the back on the eastward side the final ridge of the Cascades with its scattered alpine trees curve around like a protecting hand.[6]

Palmer's journal continues with his record of the next day's journey, rounding the northern slopes of Mount Davis and riding down the long hill to Podunk Creek—Palmer's Tulameen River. "At Mr. McDonald's suggestion I gave the mountain we stood on the Gaelic name 'Stuchd-a-choiré' from the beautiful 'choiré' or recess situated about half way down its eastern slope" (83). In the Gaelic language that McDonald spoke, *stuchd* means "peak," and *choiré* translates as "corrie," which is a round hollow in a hillside.

Palmer's journal includes a description of a lake later named for him:

> On the summit, and invisible except [for] the rocks [that] immediately surround it, lies a pretty sequestered little lake [Palmer Pond], guarded by one solitary stunted oak, and lower down on the eastern slope is a larger one [Jacobson Lake], on whose banks, there being plenty of firewood, travelers from the eastward frequently camp.

> The "Campement du Chevreuil" is, however, the usual camping place going westward. About 10 a.m. the horses having arrived, we commenced our journey down the eastern slope of "Stuchd-a-choiré," a matter easily accomplished owing to the gradual nature of the descent. (83)

Here Lieutenant Palmer noticed that the mountains that separated the waters of the Fraser from those of the Columbia also drew a dividing line in the characteristics of the country. In the alpine meadows that now surrounded the men of the brigades, the trees were smaller, the forest more open, and grass abundant. "After descending some 800 feet from the summit," Palmer wrote, "we struck a small stream [Podunk Creek] fed by still smaller forks branching off into ravines and clefts in the hills. These are the headwaters of the 'Tulameen,' the main tributary of the Similkameen River" (83).

In his journal, Palmer noted that "for the first seven or eight miles the road, though excellent for travel, passed through a forest of small burnt timber, and the scarred and blackened trunks, devoid of foliage, presented a dreary and monotonous landscape" (83). It is known that First Nations peoples burned the woods to destroy underbrush and encourage the growth of edible bulbs such as the avalanche and glacier lily, spring beauty, and large camas, all harvested in these alpine forests. The HBC men used the same practice to encourage the growth of grass for their horses, as Anderson did in 1846 when he climbed the south side of the Tulameen Plateau. Douglas confirmed this practice when in 1850 he reported that the woods had been partially cleared by fire (mentioned in Chapter 10). Palmer noted that the many tracts of burnt wood were contained by rocky mountain spurs and bends in the river, which suggest the fires were purposely set.

His journal continues, with the brigade reaching the main stream of the Tulameen atop the plateau:

> About 12 miles by trail from the point where we first struck it [Podunk Creek], the Tulameen takes a long sweep to

the northward, and crossing it here at a ford where it was about 15 yards broad and 18 inches deep, we camped on the opposite bank. The camp, designated No. 3, is about 15 miles by the trail from the "Campement du Chevreuil," and contains an abundance of firewood and water. The horses were driven again across the river to feed, but as grass was very scarce they had to pick what they could from the wild vetches and other plants, on which Indian animals alone can subsist. (83)

The brigades were now on the Tulameen River, where Horseguard Camp had been established a short distance downstream from the mouth of Podunk Creek, and fifteen miles from Campement du Chevreuil. Modern-day explorers describe the Tulameen as having crystal-clear waters, and they remove trousers and socks "to slip and slide barefooted across the refreshing river."[7]

In the morning the brigades began their journey to Lodestone Lake from the Horseguard. Crossing the Tulameen, Palmer and his companions mounted a steep slope to ride "across a heavy bush country and over soggy moss-covered streams—slipping and sliding."[8] But as they approached Lodestone Lake, the terrain became an "easy open-timbered country."[9] Palmer's journal reads:

September 20th—Commenced cloudy and cold with light rain. From the point where we were camped the Tulameen takes a large horse-shoe bend to the northward, resuming its easterly course about 10 miles from us in a straight line near the completion of the shoe. The bend is filled up by an elevated plateau 1,000 feet high, whence numberless low, sharp, broken spurs jut out in every direction towards the stream.

Over this plateau lay our to-day's journey, the trail taking this route to avoid the long detour made by the Tulameen. Four miles travel in a north-easterly direction up a steep defile [Packers Creek], between two of the spurs, brought us to the summit, and we emerged on a large open undulating down [plateau], where the timber nearly disappeared, and was replaced by quantities of yellow furze and mountain heath. (83)

The Fort Colvile brigades now made their way up the side of Lodestone Mountain, which stood sixty-two hundred feet above sea level. Palmer continues:

> Preserving a general north-easterly direction we continued our journey across the plateau. The soil became very peaty and the trail rocky in some places, though generally good for travel. Ponds and marshes frequently occurred, grass in the latter growing to a considerable height, though on the drier portions of the plain it was scarcely long enough for a horse to nibble at, and five miles from the commencement of the plateau timber (fir) again became plentiful. A short way farther on a trail from "Whatcom," cut last year by miners anxious to reach "Thompson's River," forks with that on which we were now travelling. On the exact route it takes, or the extent of which it is practicable for travel, I could collect no reliable information; but I believe it crosses the Cascades at the vicinity of the [49th] parallel, and is generally a better trail than that over Manson Mountain. (83)

The Whatcom Trail followed Anderson's 1846 trail up the Tulameen Plateau from the Sumallo River. Once it reached Council's Punch Bowl, however, it took a different path across the plateau, joining the brigade trail a few miles south of Lodestone Lake.[10] Despite Palmer's assertion that it was an easier trail to follow, it was not. It reached the Sumallo by crossing the height of land at the headwaters of the Chilliwack River, and the clamber up the sides of the box canyon surrounding Chilliwack Lake made the trail so difficult that no prospector used it twice.

Palmer's journal continues, as the brigades mounted the heights of Lodestone Mountain:

> At 2 p.m., after a short day's journey we camped near the eastern extremity of the plateau, on the borders of a small, nearly circular, lake [Lodestone Lake]. In the evening a storm of snow and sleet gave us reason to congratulate ourselves on having snug tents and good camp fires ...
>
> [The] morning broke, cold, raw, and muggy; and the snow, which was some four or five inches deep, and still continuing to fall, scarcely contributed to the general

comfort of either ourselves or our animals. We decided not to move till the storm was over, which the Indians told us would be about noon, and their prediction proved correct; as shortly after that hour the snow ceased, the sky brightened, and we started as quickly as possible, anxious to reach "Campement des Femmes" before nightfall ...

We travelled this afternoon in a generally north-easterly direction over a tract of country, lightly timbered and grassy on the uplands, but heavily timbered in the valleys. The trail rose and fell over a succession of low and rather precipitous ranges of hills, among the recesses of which the noisy waters of numerous small rivulets wind their tortuous paths, and uniting here and there in considerable streams force their way to various points on the Tulameen. (83–84)

The first stream they encountered was Blakeburn Creek, which joins Arrastra Creek and flows into the Tulameen River east of Coalmont. The stream the brigades followed north to Campement des Femmes was Collins Gulch Creek. Lieutenant Palmer's journal continues, as the brigades reached the summit of the final steep descent to the Tulameen River: "Opposite the spot where we stood extends a broad thickly timbered valley leading to the Nicholas [Nicola] Lake, and thence to Fort Kamloops" (84). As he reached Campement des Femmes with the Fort Colvile Brigades, Palmer noted:

Descending the hill we shortly reached the river, and leaving the Kamloops trail to our left traversed the right [south] bank for a few hundred yards. Then, crossing at a ford, readily distinguishable, we pitched our tents at the "Campement du Femmes," so named from a custom prevalent among the Indians en route for Fort Hope of leaving their women and children here while they perform the journey across the mountains.

The fine evening, and its position in a mild and pleasant valley, made camp 5 contrast agreeably with our last night's quarters, and some tolerable bunch grass afforded the horses a better meal than they had had since leaving Fort Hope. (84)

The Royal Engineers, who were both soldiers and engineers, were responsible for surveying the boundary line, keeping order in the new colony, and building its roads. They widened the Harrison–Lillooet Trail built by the gold miners, turning it into a good wagon road. They also cleared and rebuilt the abandoned brigade trail that led over the mountain to Anderson's River, although they reported its high pass was subject to landslides in wintertime. Finally, they blasted a good road out of the cliff faces between Yale and Boston Bar, and by autumn 1862 their road reached Lytton.

All of these newly built trails provided routes for the miners into the goldfields. Men came from all over the world to make their fortune in the territory, where the HBC had already made a small fortune from the furs the First Nations traded. The HBC adapted and made another small fortune from the gold miners. New posts were built to serve them, and a new business burst into existence—storekeeping. In 1866 the company established a short-lived post in Hazelton and built a store in Quesnel, and in 1867 it purchased an existing store in Barkerville.[11]

The HBC also continued to pack its own goods, packing in the coffee, flour, washing pans, gum boots, shovels, and other tools the miners demanded. Other HBC men packed from Fort Hope to the new Similkameen post and Fort Shepherd, and eastward as far as Wild Horse Creek on the Columbia River.

Jason Allard told stories of the times when the HBC men used trickery to avoid the American customs agents at their Little Dalles post on the Columbia River north of Fort Colvile. While Allard and his hired gamblers diverted the agents with rounds of liquor and a lucrative card game, his First Nations employees confiscated the boats on the customs agency's side of the river. Then, while the Americans stood helpless on the wrong side of the river, shaking their fists in anger, the HBC men hustled their horses past the agency at a fast trot.[12]

The gold miners needed more provisions and equipment than the HBC could provide, and some men quit their employment with the company and became packers. Henry Shuttleworth, who in 1857 had abandoned the HBC in disgust after Douglas criticized him, carried mail by pack train through the Similkameen valley, from Fort Hope to Wild Horse Creek, for many years after he left the company.

First Nations peoples also took up packing. When the gold miners came they had the most to lose. It is not known how many thousands of First Nations people died at the hands of the American gold miners, nor how many villages were burned to the ground. Later, when the Royal

Climbing the hill from Kettle River. L.H.S. Leading pack train

"Lawrence H. Sitwell leading a pack train up the hill from the Kettle River," photographer unknown, 1902.

Engineers built roads through their fishing stations, they lost once again. Their culture was attacked when their traditional fisheries were destroyed, and it became difficult for them to fish for their winter food. Loss of their fisheries might also have forced them to fish in places they were not welcomed by other First Nations, with whom they had always been enemies.

The Similkameen, Nlaka'pamux, and Stó:lō peoples, however, had always been a ready source of labour for the HBC brigades, and they had the survival skills and local knowledge needed to navigate the rough back-country trails the brigades passed through. Now the First Nations began to run the pack trains for the HBC. For many years Black-eye or his son packed trade goods for the Kamloops post, probably travelling over the Coquihalla trail from Fort Hope and delivering goods to Kamloops and its outlying post, Fort Dallas. Women also worked in the brigades; an Upper Similkameen woman named Nora Yakumtikum ran her own pack trains across the trail for a number of years.[13] According to James Douglas's report of April 1860, First Nations packers were indispensable for carrying goods over various trails from the coastal forts into the interior at any time of year:

> The roads leading into the country from Hope and Yale
> have, in consequence of the great depth of snow in the
> mountain passes, been impassible since the beginning of
> Winter, to any other mode of transport than by Indian
> packers, who, with singular force and power of endur-
> ance, toil through mountain trails at that trying season,
> with loads of one hundred pounds each, but that mode
> of transport is not even attempted in winter by the Hope
> trail, which is hermetically sealed to travel from the inte-
> rior, between the months of October and June.[14]

Some Royal Engineers remained in the colony after their companions had left, taking up the business of packing: John K. Lord, who had worked on the Boundary Commission, wrote a book about the experience. Mexican packers who came north from the California goldfields—men like Rafael Carranza, Jesus Garcia, Jose Marie Tresierra, Pancho Gutierrez, Manual Alvarez, and others—continued to pack in the interior for many years after 1858.[15] Jean Caux (Cataline) came from France and packed until 1912: he is perhaps the most famous of all the packers. Some Chinese gold miners or storekeepers went into packing; in 1861, six different Chinese outfits worked out of Lytton.[16] Jason Allard of Fort Yale wrote of another Chinese man named Nie-Tie who in 1867 started off with a pack train of thirty-five horses for the Kootenays. He never arrived and was presumed to have been murdered for his goods and animals.[17] Frank Laumeister and Charles Gowan imported twenty-three Bactrian (double-humped) camels into the territory for use on the Cariboo Road. The camels carried massive loads but their presence created chaos as pack horses and mules panicked, scattering in all directions.[18]

Although history changed the HBC, many things stayed the same. The gentlemen came from many different backgrounds, but most common over the years were the Scots, the majority of them from Canada, who continued to make up the bulk of chief factors and chief traders over the years that followed. Their work remained the same. Chief traders managed the forts in the interior and had their own specialized work to do at headquarters: picking out their trade goods for the winter that followed, attending the meetings, receiving their instructions from the chief factors, and communicating the difficulties they were experiencing in the interior.

But there was always conflict, at least in the years before the gold rush. Chief Factor James Douglas was a prickly man who desired to control everyone and everything. He forced change on everyone, whether the change worked or not. The chief traders themselves caused some of the difficulties, quarrelling with each other or with their employees. But the stress that these men worked under was what brought them to blows. That stress was caused by their inability to control or solve many of the problems they encountered: not enough horses, not enough food, not enough rest.

Because of the constant disappointment and conflict, many HBC gentlemen retired early and looked for opportunities in communities outside the HBC. For most, however, their strong connections to the HBC did not disappear. Alexander Caufield Anderson settled on the Columbia River in 1855, coming to Fort Victoria in spring 1858. Donald Manson retired in anger and disappointment in 1857; after spending a winter at Fort Langley, he took up land in the Willamette Valley, south of Fort Vancouver. Douglas himself gave up his chief factorship in November 1858 when he became governor of British Columbia.

Suffering under these irritable and violent chief factors and traders were the clerks, many of whom were underpaid "half-gents," with fathers who had worked for the company east of the Rockies and mothers who were Métis or First Nations. Few of the mixed-blood clerks could aspire to become a chief trader, and even fewer became chief factors. Peter Ogden was one who managed a promotion, chiefly because his father was Chief Factor Peter Skene Ogden. Ferdinand McKenzie was another. He was put in charge of Fort Alexandria in the mid-1850s, and he is the "Red River" McKenzie described in packer Frank Sylvester's manuscript *The Old Brigade Trail in '59.*[19]

But the Canadien and Métis voyageurs were always the unrecognized backbone of the brigades; it was they who did all the work of getting the furs out to the coast, and the trade goods in. In some years they had horses to ride; in others they walked over the trails on foot because of a shortage of horses. They had little control over the decisions the gentlemen made, and they made the best of the bad decisions and complained, or resisted, when situations became too difficult. Some years they deserted the brigades, hoping to make it to the gold mines in California even when they knew they could not. It was they who suffered the most from the conflicts that were rampant in many of the HBC communities over these years.

Then the gold mines came to them, and many quit their jobs at the end of their contracts, cutting their connections with the HBC and moving north with the gold finds, following where the gold might lead them. Others settled close to the fort they had worked at or made new lives for themselves at Fort Victoria or in communities that sprang up around Fort Vancouver. What they did not do, for the most part, was return to their homeland, the Saskatchewan and Red River districts. Instead, they remained in the new Colony of British Columbia or in Washington Territory, establishing new lives here.

Even the Iroquois, who had come from Montreal, remained in the west. Their descendants maintained their traditions until those traditions were absorbed by the new community that surrounded them. Like the Canadiens, they spoke the French language until their children or their children's children scorned the language. For many years they kept their culture alive—until their children were no longer interested.

For the mixed-blood children of the gentlemen who lived at Fort Victoria, things were different. The British people who came to British Columbia after 1858 were far less adaptable, and far less tolerant, than any invader that had entered the territory in the fifty years that preceded the gold rush. HBC men who had worked in the territory for fifty years were criticized for the choices they had made: Royal Engineer turned packer John K. Lord was harshly critical of the HBC men for not using mules for their pack trains, seemingly unaware mules were not available before the Mexican packers came north.

At Fort Victoria, many colonists appeared to hate the retired members of the HBC communities, bullying them, criticizing them, and snubbing them and their wives. Mixed-blood daughters and sons of the HBC men were saddened to learn that they were viewed as second-class citizens by the colonists in their own community because they had First Nations or Métis mothers. Many never married because no British settler would marry them. Others endured snubs and gossip, even from the Royal Engineers who remarked on their ancestry. One of James Douglas's daughters was surprised to find that she was considered a "squaw" by a British midshipman.[20]

But many other HBC daughters married successfully, although their children faced similar prejudice, even from their own family members. When my English grandmother Emmy May Christmas married my Métis grandfather, son of Alexander Caulfield Anderson, Emmy's brother never spoke to her again. My mother, granddaughter of A.C. Anderson and his Métis wife, spoke of her Indigenous blood when she moved to a new home at Manson's Landing. Long-time residents who were children of the original settler, Michael Manson, spread the news that she was Indian and bullied her. The lesson was learned: when she moved away from Cortes Island, she never mentioned her ancestry again. As a result of the racism she faced most of her life, she did not tell her children that they had a little Indigenous blood.

To my unending surprise, this racism exists even today. I face it on occasion, when people I know read my first book, or when I tell people I am Métis. But I am fortunate to live in British Columbia, where this racism is less tolerated than in other communities. If I lived in Saskatchewan, as a Métis woman I would be forty-nine times more likely to go to jail than a white female descendant of a settler. I find that shocking.

In June 2019, I was interviewed on my family history by the Métis Nation of British Columbia. I was to speak of my family but was not allowed to refer to notes of any sort. The interviewer was amazed that I had eight generations of Métis people who lived west of the Rocky Mountains. Unlike other families who lived in the west, my family has long generations, and I knew these other families would have at least two more generations in the west than my family does. Still, when I thought a bit more about this, I realized my family has lived west of the Rocky Mountains for two centuries. Two hundred years. I have history here. My Métis homeland may be at Red River, but I am at home in British Columbia.

ACKNOWLEDGMENTS

I thank both the British Columbia Archives and the Hudson's Bay Company Archives for making available the many documents, journals, and letters that I accessed to write this book. This list includes Alexander Caulfield Anderson's journals of his cross-country expeditions in 1846 and 1847, and Henry Newsham Peers's journals of the disastrous 1848 brigade from Fort Langley to Kamloops.

So many other people helped me over the years!

I thank Angie Bain, a researcher for UBCIC, for her interest in my search for Black-eye's story and for locating an A.C. Anderson document in the archives of the Smithsonian Institute, which gave details about the brigade trails that no one here had.

I thank Kelly Cook of Princeton, B.C., who ensured I had a copy of Lieutenant Henry Palmer's journal of his journey from Fort Langley to Fort Colvile in 1859. She also answered many other questions about the brigade trail when I got lost.

More information came from various descendants of other men, whether European, Canadian, or First Nations: this list includes Ronnie Harris, descendant of Chief Pahallak, Anderson's Stó:lō guide; and Sally Nault, descendant of Black-eye, who was Anderson's Upper Similkameen guide. Sally told me the story that gave me the perfect ending for this book, and for this I especially thank her.

I also thank Roxanne Salinas of Lone Butte for information on Green Lake and area, and Ruth Bleuer of Falkland, for her information on birch trees, the habits of horses, and the old NWC brigade trails through the Grand Prairie.

I especially thank David Gregory for that golden day in the bench lands above Summerland: a visit that showed me the reason why the brigade trails did not closely follow the creeks that flooded in the springtime.

More than anyone else, I have to thank my editor, Audrey McClellan, of West Coast Editorial Associates, whose work has again improved my writing.

Thank you.

NOTES

INTRODUCTION

1   Frank Sylvester, "The Old Brigade Trail in '59," unpublished manuscript, AR281, Frank and Cecilia Sylvester family fonds, University of Victoria Archives.

2   Augustus Richard Peers, "Journal, 1842–52," 43 (transcript), E/B/934, British Columbia Archives (hereafter BCA).

3   Peers, "Journal, 1842–52," 63.

4   Alexander Caulfield Anderson, "British Columbia," draft unpublished manuscript, 27–28, Mss. 559, volume 2, folder 8, BCA.

5   Peers, "Journal, 1842–52," 63.

PROLOGUE

1   It was a two-year journey from London to Fort Vancouver and return. Two ships were always underway, while one remained in London for repairs.

2   Charles Wilkes, *Life in the Oregon Country Before the Emigration*, ed. Richard E. Moore (Ashland: The Oregon Book Society, 1975), 126–27.

3   Alexander Ross, *The Fur Hunters of the Far West*, ed. Kenneth A. Spaulding. (Norman: University of Oklahoma Press, 1956) All quotations in this section are from this journal unless otherwise indicated. Folio numbers are given for the quotations.

CHAPTER 1

1   William Connolly, "Journal of the Brigade from New Caledonia to Fort Vancouver, 1826," B.188/a/8, Hudson's Bay Company Archives (hereafter HBCA). All quotations in this section are from Connolly's journal unless otherwise indicated. Folio numbers are given for the quotations.

2   Peter Warren Dease, "Journal of the Brigade from New Caledonia to Fort Vancouver and Return, 1831," fo. 10, B.188/a/17, HBCA.

3   The barrier was probably a fish weir, but the river might have been named because it was a barrier to the brigades.

4   Two separate historical events appear to have affected the water table around Westwold. First, one of the San Francisco earthquakes lowered the water table, and the valley is much drier now than it used to be. In addition, a ditching project, undertaken by a local rancher in the early 1960s, drained the Salmon River marshes and created the grasslands and hayfields that we now see there.

5   Lac Vaseux was sometimes called Oak Lake, for the poison oak that grew there.

6   Gloria Griffen Cline, *Peter Skene Ogden and the Hudson's Bay Company* (Norman: University of Oklahoma Press, 1974), 130.

7   John Work, "Journal July 19 to October 25, 1823," 38 (transcript), A/B/40/W89.1A, BCA.

8   Dease, "Journal of the Brigade from New Caledonia to Fort Vancouver and Return, 1831," fo. 10, B.188/a/17.

9   Email conversation with David Gregory, December 19, 2021.

10   Alexander Ross, *The Fur Hunters of the Far West*, 113.

11   Email conversation with Sam Pambrun, June 15, 2020.

12   Bruce McIntyre Watson, *Lives Lived West of the Divide: A Biographical Dictionary of Fur Traders Working West of the Rockies, 1793–1858* (Kelowna: Centre for Social, Spatial and Economic Justice, University of British Columbia, Okanagan, 2010), 43; and "Fort St. James Post Journal, 1840–1846," fo. 83, B.188/a/19, HBCA.

CHAPTER 2

1   McDonald's journal was published with notes in Malcolm McLeod, ed., *Peace River: A Canoe Voyage from Hudson's Bay to Pacific, by the Late Sir George Simpson, in 1828* (Ottawa: J. Durie and Son, 1872), 1. All quotes in this section are from this account unless otherwise indicated. Folio numbers are given for the quotations.

2   E.E. Rich, ed., *Simpson's 1828 Journey to the Columbia* (London: Hudson's Bay Record Society, 1947), 38–39.

3   Fort Nisqually, on Puget Sound, was not built until 1832.

CHAPTER 3

1   Alexander Caulfield Anderson, "History of the Northwest Coast," 49–50, Mss. 559, box 2, folder 3, BCA.

2   In 1846, John McLoughlin retired from the company, and Chief Factor John Work took his place.

3   Peter Skene Ogden, "Extract from C.F. Ogden's letter to Chief Traders Tod & Manson, dated Colvile, 22nd Oct. 1845," A/B/40/Og2, BCA. Edited for clarity and to remove 50 million commas.

4   "Fort Alexandria Journal, 1845–1848," fo. 14, B.5/a/7, HBCA.

5   Alexander Caulfield Anderson, "Journal of an Expedition under command of Alex C. Anderson of the Hudson's Bay Company, undertaken with the view of ascertaining the practicability of a communication with the interior, for the import of the annual supplies, 1846," fo. 1, Mss. 559, volume 2, folder 1, BCA.

6   Alexander Caulfield Anderson to Board of Management, May 25, 1846, Mss. 559, volume 1, folder 5, BCA.

7   This map is A.C. Anderson's: "A New Route Proposed for the Horse Brigade from New Caledonia via the Harrison River, 1845," fo. 2, B.5/z/1, HBCA.

8   James Murray Yale to Governor Simpson, December 18, 1847 (transcript), A/B/20/L3A, BCA.

9   Anderson to Board of Management, May 25, 1846.

10   Douglas Hudson, personal communication with author, May 6, 2013.

11   Anderson, "Notes on the Indian Tribes of British North America and the Northwest Coast," *Historical Magazine* 7, no. 3 (March 1863), 77–78, http://archive.org/details/cihm_16598/page/n5.

12   Anderson to Board of Management, May 25, 1846.

CHAPTER 4

1   Alexander Caulfield Anderson, "Journal of an Expedition, 1846," fo. 11. Other quotations in this chapter are from the journal unless otherwise indicated. Page numbers are given for the quotations.

2   Accessioned Map 18941A, BCA.

3   Lieutenant Henry Spencer Palmer, "Report on the Country between Fort Hope on the Fraser and Fort Colvile on the Columbia River," 81. Great Britain, Colonial Office. Papers Relative to the Affairs of British Columbia, No. 33.

4   Alexander Caulfield Anderson, "Notes on the Indian Tribes," 80.

5   Alexander Caulfield Anderson to Board of Management, June 23, 1846.

6   Brian Thom, "Ethnographic Overview of Stó:lō People and the Traditional Use of the Hudson's Bay Company Brigade Trail Area" (Report prepared for Chilliwack Forest District, Ministry of Forests, for Contract No. 12015-20/CS96DCK-002, August 1995; written while working at Stó:lō Nation, Chilliwack, B.C.), 5–6.

7   Anderson's Bible, with its preserved flower, is in the Royal British Columbia Museum.

8   National Gallery of Canada, *Paul Kane's Frontier* (Toronto: University of Toronto Press, 1971), 129–30.

9   "Fort Alexandria Journal, 1845–1848," fo. 14, B.5/a/7.

10   Peter Skene Ogden and James Douglas to Alexander Caulfield Anderson, January 12, 1847, A/B/20/V, BCA.

CHAPTER 5

1   "Fort Alexandria Journal, 1845–1848," fo. 28, B.5/a/7.

2   Alexander Caulfield Anderson, "Journal of an Expedition to Fort Langley via Thompson's River, Summer of 1847," in "History of the North West Coast," 77, Mss. 559, Box 2, File 3 (B.A. McKelvie version), BCA. Other quotations in this chapter are from the journal unless otherwise indicated. Page numbers are given for the quotations.

3   The Petite Forks referred to the junction of the Nicola River with the Thompson.

4   Alexander Caulfield Anderson, "Supplement to Handbook and Map to the Gold Region, 1858," 2, (typescript), Mss. 559, volume 2, folder 2, BCA.

5   Samuel Black, Map, "Southern District of British Columbia," CM/B2079, BCA.

6   Malcolm McLeod, ed., *Peace River,* 37.

7   Alexander Caulfield Anderson, *Handbook and Map to the Gold Regions of Frazer's and Thompson's River* (San Francisco: J.J. LeCounte, 1858), 21.

8   Richard C. Bocking, *Mighty River: A Portrait of the Fraser* (Vancouver: Douglas & McIntyre, 1997), 170.

9   Alexander Caulfield Anderson to Governor Simpson, February 24, 1848, fo. 291, D.5/21, HBCA.

10   Anderson to Governor Simpson, February 24, 1848, fo. 292, D.5/21.

11   Alexander Caulfield Anderson, "Notes on the Indian Tribes," 77.

12   Anderson, "Notes on the Indian Tribes," 78.

13   Anderson, "Notes on the Indian Tribes," 78.

14   Anderson, "Notes on the Indian Tribes," 78.

15   Anderson to Governor Simpson, February 24, 1848, fo. 292, D.5/21.

CHAPTER 6

1   Alexander Caulfield Anderson, "Journal of an Expedition, Summer of 1847. Upward Journey," fo. 85. Other quotations in this chapter are from the journal unless otherwise indicated. Page numbers are given for the quotations.

2   Pahallak's village was situated on either Ruby or Mahood Creek.

3   Alexander Caulfield Anderson, *Handbook and Map to the Gold Regions of Frazer's and Thompson's River*, 23.

4   Alexander Caulfield Anderson to Governor Simpson, February 24, 1848, fo. 292, D.5/21.

5   Anderson to Governor Simpson, February 24, 1848, fo. 292, D.5/21.

6   Alexander Caulfield Anderson to E.A. Meredith, July 21, 1877, Canada. Department of Indian Affairs. Black Series. RG10, Volume 3651, File 8540, BCA.

7   James Douglas to James Murray Yale, June 26, 1847, A/B/20/V2D, BCA.

8   John Lee Lewes to Governor and Council, September 21, 1847, fo. 280, D.5/20, HBCA.

9   James Douglas and John Work to Governor and Committee, November 6, 1847, fo. 86, B.223/b/36, HBCA; also A/B/20/V2D, BCA.

10   Douglas and Work to Governor and Committee, November 6, 1847, fo. 86, B.233/b/36.

11   Douglas and Work to Governor and Committee, November 6, 1847, fo. 86, B.233/b/36.

12   Douglas and Work to Governor and Committee, November 6, 1847, fo. 86, B.233/b/36.

13   James Murray Yale to Governor Simpson, December 18, 1847, A/B/20/L3A.

14   Yale to Governor Simpson, December 18, 1847, A/B/20/L3A.

15   Anderson to Governor Simpson, February 24, 1848, fo. 291, D.5/21.

16   Joseph William McKay to William Fraser Tolmie, October 31, 1867, Mss. 557, volume 1, folder 1, BCA.

CHAPTER 7

1   Board of Management to Governor and Committee, November 2, 1846, fo. 2, B.223/b/34, HBCA.

2   Board of Management to Governor and Committee, November 2, 1846, fo. 2, B.223/b/34.

3   Board of Management to Governor and Committee, November 2, 1846, fo. 2, B.223/b/34.

4   Board of Management to Governor Simpson, March 16, 1848, fo. 7, B.223/b/37, HBCA.

5   Board of Management to Governor Simpson, March 16, 1848, fo. 7, B.223/b/37.

6   Thomas Lowe, "Journal of a Trip from Vancouver to York Factory per York Factory Express, Spring 1847," November 14, A/B/20.4/L95, BCA.

7   Lowe, "Journal of a Trip, Spring 1847," November 17, A/B/20.4/L95.

8   William McBean to Board of Management, November 30, 1847, in *Oregon Spectator Newspaper*, vol. 11, no. 23, December 9, 1847.

9   Nicholas Finlay, son of Jaco Finlay (a North West Company engagé who had been a scout for David Thompson on the latter's journeys through the Rocky Mountains and along the Columbia River), had married a Cayuse woman and lived near the mission-house, where he was sometimes employed.

10   Peter Skene Ogden, *Traits of American Indian Life and Character, by a Fur Trader* (London: Smith Elder & Co., 1853), 110.

11 Thomas Lowe, "Private Journal Kept at Fort Vancouver, November 1, 1846–March 20, 1848," December 6, 1847, volume 3, E/A/L95.9, BCA.

12 Lowe, "Private Journal, November 1, 1846–March 20, 1848," December 7, 1847, volume 3, E/A/L95.9.

13 Board of Management to Governor Simpson, March 12, 1848, fo. 434, D.5/21, HBCA.

14 Peter Skene Ogden to Reverend Elkiah Walker, December 13, 1847, in Frederick Merk, "Snake Country Expedition, 1824–5: An Episode of Fur Trade and Empire," *Oregon Historical Quarterly*, 35, no. 2 (June 1934): 398.

15 Lowe, "Private Journal, November 1, 1846–March 20, 1848," January 8, 1848, volume 3, E/A/L95.9.

16 Lowe, "Private Journal, November 1, 1846–March 20, 1848," January 17, 1848, volume 3, E/A/L95.9.

17 Board of Management to Governor Simpson, March 16, 1848, fo. 7, B.223/b/37.

18 Board of Management to James Murray Yale, March 23, 1848, A/B/20/V2 Od, BCA.

19 Board of Management to Governor Simpson, March 16, 1848, fo. 3, B.223/b/37.

20 Alexander Caulfield Anderson, *Dominion of the West: A Brief Description of the Province of British Columbia, Its Climate and Resources* (Victoria: Richard Wolfenden, 1872), Footnote, 97–98.

CHAPTER 8

1 "Fort St. James Post Journal, 1846–1851," fo. 48–49, B.188/a/20, HBCA. Castoreum is a rank-smelling oil secreted from the beaver's castor glands, used by the beaver to mark its territory. In the 1840s, castoreum was considered a medicine that treated headache, fever, and hysteria. Even today it is used in perfumes.

2 Alexander Caulfield Anderson, "History of the Northwest Coast," fo. 51.

3 Alexander Caulfield Anderson to Donald Manson, August 24, 1848, fo. 46, B.223/b/37, HBCA.

4 Board of Management to Governor and Committee, December 4, 1848, in Hartwell Bowsfield, ed., *Fort Victoria Letters, 1846–1851* (Winnipeg: Hudson's Bay Record Society, 1979), 30–31; and Ken Favrholdt, "The Cordilleran Communication: The Brigade System of the Far Western Fur Trade" (master's thesis, UBC, 1998, 106, Koerner Library AW5 B71-1998-0334).

5 Alexander Caulfield Anderson to Governor Simpson, April 17, 1849, fo. 120, D.5/25, HBCA.

6 George Stewart Simpson to Governor Simpson, April 3, 1849, fo. 13, D.5/25 HBCA.

7 Anderson, "History of the Northwest Coast," fo. 51.

8 "Fort Victoria Post Journal, 1846–1850," fo. 94, B.226/a/1, HBCA.

9 Board of Management to Archibald Barclay, September 18, 1848, fo. 52, B.223/b/38, HBCA. Archibald Barclay was secretary at Hudson's Bay House between 1843 and 1855.

10 Alexander Caulfield Anderson to Governor Simpson, February 24, 1848, fo. 291, D.5/21.

11 Board of Management to James Murray Yale, May 21, 1848, A/B/20/V2 Od, BCA.

12 James Murray Yale to Governor Simpson, March 18, 1849, fo. 417, D.5/24, HBCA.

13 "Fort Yale, Bill of lading, Summer Brigade 1848," fo. 1, A/B/20/Y1, BCA.

14 Alexander Caufield Anderson, *Handbook and Map to the Gold Regions of Frazer's and Thompson's River*, 5–6.

15 Henry Newsham Peers, "Private Journal of Henry Peers from Fort Langley to Thomson's River, Summer 1848," fo. 1 (transcript), E/A/P34, BCA. Other quotations from Peers in this chapter are from the journal unless otherwise indicated. Page numbers are given for each quotation.

16 Donald Manson to Board of Management, August 24, 1848, fo. 45, B.223/b/37, HBCA.

17 Anderson to Governor Simpson, April 14, 1849, fo. 120, D.5/25.

18 Anderson, *Handbook and Map to the Gold Regions of Frazer's and Thompson's River*, 6.

19 Yale to Governor Simpson, March 18, 1849, fo. 417, D.5/24.

20 Anderson to Governor Simpson, April 17, 1849, fo. 120, D.5/25.

21 Anderson to Governor Simpson, April 17, 1849, fo. 120, D.5/25.

22 Manson to Board of Management, August 24, 1848, fo. 43, B.223/b/37.

23 Manson to Board of Management, August 24, 1848, fo. 43, B.223/b/37.

24 Anderson, *Handbook and Map to the Gold Regions of Frazer's and Thompson's River*, 7.

25 Governor Simpson to Board of Management, June 30, 1849, fo. 262, D.4/70, HBCA.

26 Anderson to Donald Manson, August 24, 1848, fo. 46, B.223/b/37.

27 Manson to Board of Management, August 24, 1848, fos. 45–46, B.223/b/37.

28 Manson to Board of Management, August 24, 1848, fo. 46, B.223/b/37.

29 John Tod to Governor Simpson, March 20, 1849, fo. 445, D.5/24, HBCA.

30 Tod to Governor Simpson, March 20, 1849, fo. 446, D.5/24.

31 Yale to Governor Simpson, March 18, 1849, fo. 416, D.5/24.

32 Yale to Governor Simpson, March 18, 1849, fo. 416, D.5/24.

33 Simpson to Governor Simpson, April 3, 1849, fo. 13, D.5/25.

34 "Fort Alexandria Journal, 1848–1851," fo. 13, B.5/a/8, HBCA.

35 "Fort St. James Post Journal, 1846–1851," fo. 61, B.188/a/20.

36 Donald Manson to Governor Simpson, February 20, 1849, fo. 274, D.5/24, HBCA.

37 Alexander Caulfield Anderson to Board of Management, June 21, 1847, in "History of the Northwest Coast," fo. 192.

38 Alexander Caulfield Anderson, "Journal of an Expedition, Summer of 1847," fo. 80.

39 George Stewart Simpson to Governor Simpson, April 3, 1849, fo. 13, D.5/25. In this letter, George Simpson Jr. is repeating to his father information he received from Peers at Kamloops.

40 James Douglas and John Work to Governor and Committee, December 4, 1848, in Hartwell Bowsfield, ed., *Fort Victoria Letters*, 30–31.

41 James Douglas to James Murray Yale, October 30, 1848, fo. 8, B.113/c/1, HBCA.

42 Douglas to Yale, October 30, 1848, fos. 8–9, B.113/c/1.

43 Douglas to Yale, October 30, 1848, fo. 9, B.113/c/1.

44 Simpson to Governor Simpson, April 3, 1849, fo. 14, D.5/25.

45 Jason O. Allard, "Reminiscences," fo. 4, E/C/Al5A, BCA.

46 Allard, "Reminiscences," fo. 4, E/C/Al5A. Although Jason said this happened in winter 1847–48, Fort Hope was built in 1848–49.

47 Yale to Governor Simpson, March 18, 1849, fo. 415, D.5/24.

CHAPTER 9

1 Peter Skene Ogden to Donald Ross, March 6, 1849, Mss. 635, file 143, BCA.

2   "Fort Alexandria Journal, 1848–1851," fos. 29–30, B.5/a/8.

3   James Murray Yale to Governor Simpson, December 28, 1850, fo. 414, D.5/29, HBCA.

4   Alexander Caulfield Anderson, *Handbook and Map to the Gold Regions of Frazer's and Thompson's River*, 7.

5   Yale to Governor Simpson, December 28, 1850, fo. 414, D.5/29.

6   Donald Manson to Governor Simpson, February 25, 1850, fo. 362, D.5/27, HBCA.

7   Manson to Governor Simpson, February 25, 1850, fo. 362, D.5/27.

8   James Douglas to Archibald Barclay, September 3, 1849, in Hartwell Bowsfield, ed., *Fort Victoria Letters*, 44–45.

9   Peter Skene Ogden to Governor Simpson, September 15, 1849, fo. 93, D.5/26, HBCA.

10   James Douglas to Governor Simpson, February 23, 1850, fo. 342, D.5/27 HBCA.

11   Manson to Governor Simpson, February 25, 1850, fo. 362–63, D.5/27.

12   Manson to Governor Simpson, February 25, 1850, fos. 363, D.5/27. Manson seems to write his letters in a barely controlled fury, and his hard-to-read handwriting is also typical of his reports.

13   Alexander Caulfield Anderson to Governor Simpson, September 15, 1849, fo. 93, D.5/26, HBCA.

14   Alexander Caufield Anderson to Governor and Council, April 18, 1850, fo. 107, D.5/28, HBCA.

15   George Stewart Simpson to Governor Simpson, April 18, 1850, fo. 96, D.5/28, HBCA.

16   Eden Colvile to Governor Simpson, October 15, 1849, fo. 286, D.5/26, HBCA.

17   John Keast Lord, *At Home in the Wilderness: What to Do There and How to Do It* (London: Hardwick & Bogue, 1876), 62–64.

18   "Fort Alexandria Journal, 1848–1851," fo. 39, B/5/a/8.

19   "Fort Alexandria Journal, 1848–1851," fo. 38, B.5/a/8. Manson's family travelled in with him, but according to Anderson's son, James Robert, the family had spent the summer at Kamloops.

20   Donald Manson to Governor and Council, February 25, 1850, fos. 357–58, D.5/27, HBCA.

21   Manson to Governor and Council, February 25, 1850, fo. 358, D.5/27.

22   Eden Colvile to Governor and Committee, October 21, 1852, in E.E. Rich, ed., *London Correspondence Inward from Eden Colvile, 1849–52* (London: The Hudson's Bay Record Society, 1956), 168.

23   Paul Fraser to Governor Simpson, March 1, 1850, fo. 384, D.5/27, HBCA.

24   Eden Colvile to Sir J.H. Pelly, October 15, 1849, in E.E. Rich, *London Correspondence*, 3.

25   Colvile to Sir Pelly, October 15, 1849, in E.E. Rich, *London Correspondence*, 3.

26   Colvile to Sir Pelly, October 15, 1849, in E.E. Rich, *London Correspondence*, 3.

27   Victor Wilson, "HBC Trek, July 31 to August 8, 1971, Victor Wilson's Journal," *Thirty-Sixth Annual Report of the Okanagan Historical Society*, 1972, 29–30.

28   Colvile to Sir Pelly, October 15, 1849, in E.E. Rich, *London Correspondence*, 3–4.

29   Colvile to Sir Pelly, October 15, 1849, in E.E. Rich, *London Correspondence*, 4.

30   Colvile to Sir Pelly, October 15, 1849, in E.E. Rich, *London Correspondence*, 4.

31 Colvile to Sir Pelly, October 15, 1849, in E.E. Rich, *London Correspondence*, 4.

32 Douglas to Governor Simpson, February 23, 1850, fo. 342, D.5/27.

33 Eden Colvile to Governor Simpson, July 10, 1849, fo. 376, D.5/25, HBCA. In 1849, Francis Ermatinger was chief trader at Fort Chipewyan, a post that Colvile would have passed through on his way to Peace River.

34 Peter Skene Ogden to Governor Simpson, March 10, 1849, fo. 365, D.5/24, HBCA.

35 Peter Skene Ogden to Governor Simpson, March 16, 1850, fo. 456, D.5/27, HBCA.

36 Douglas to Governor Simpson, February 23, 1850, fo. 342, D.5/27.

CHAPTER 10

1 "Fort St. James Post Journal, 1846–1851," fo. 100, B.188/a/20.

2 James Robert Anderson, "Notes and Comments on Early Days and Events in British Columbia, Washington, and Oregon, written by himself," 136 (transcript), in possession of author. Further quotes from this account in the chapter are indicated in the text by [JRA, page number].

3 Named for Frank Richter, who ran the HBC's Similkameen post in the 1860s.

4 Alexander Caulfield Anderson, *Handbook and Map to the Gold Regions of Frazer's and Thompson's River*, 14–15.

5 James Douglas to Archibald Barclay, July 16, 1850, in Hartwell Bowsfield, ed., *Fort Victoria Letters*, 109.

6 Alexander Caulfield Anderson, "Statement Re: Boundary Question, 1871," fo. 2, K/RN/An2, BCA.

7 Quoted in Bruce A. McKelvie, "Jason Allard: Fur-Trader, Prince, and Gentleman," *British Columbia Historical Quarterly* 9 (1945): 246.

8 James Douglas to Governor Simpson, October 15, 1850, fo. 57, D.5/29, HBCA.

9 Douglas to Barclay, August 17, 1850, in Hartwell Bowsfield, ed., *Fort Victoria Letters*, 110–11.

10 Alexander Caulfield Anderson to Governor and Council, September 20, 1850, fo. 624, D.5/28, HBCA.

11 Douglas to Barclay, August 17, 1850, in Hartwell Bowsfield, ed., *Fort Victoria Letters*, 110–11.

12 Peter Skene Ogden to Governor Simpson, September 18, 1850, fo. 51, B.223/b/39, HBCA.

13 Ogden to Governor Simpson, September 18, 1850, fo. 51, B.223/b/39.

14 Lieutenant Henry Spencer Palmer, "Report on the Country," 84. Further quotes from this account in the chapter are indicated in the text by [Palmer, page number].

15 "Map of the Route from Fort Hope to Fort Colvile," 3T2 Miscellaneous, BC Lands and Titles.

16 Jason Allard, "Enclosed Sketches of Early Life in B.C.," fo. 17, E/D/Al50, BCA (Note that the l is a small L, not a capital I or the number one).

17 Alexander Caulfield Anderson to Governor, Chief Factors and Chief Traders, September 20, 1850, fo. 624, D.5/28, HBCA.

18 Paul Fraser, "Fort Kamloops Journal Kept by Paul Fraser, 1850–55," 1, A/C/20/K12A (transcript), BCA.

19 "Fort Alexandria Journal, 1848–1851," fo. 60, B.5/a/8.

20 "Fort St. James Post Journal, 1846–1851," fos. 112–14, B.188/a/20.

21 Fraser, "Fort Kamloops Journal, 1850–55," 3.

22 Fraser, "Fort Kamloops Journal, 1850–55," 3.

23 Fraser, "Fort Kamloops Journal, 1850–55," 4.

24 Fraser, "Fort Kamloops Journal, 1850–55," 7.

25 Anderson to Governor and Council, September 20, 1850, fo. 624, D.5/28. In April 1850, Eden Colvile had arrived at Fort Colvile with the outgoing York Factory Express. Anderson took the opportunity to speak to him about the need for a fresh supply of horses.

26 Alexander Caulfield Anderson to Governor and Council, March 21, 1853, fo. 478, D.5/36, HBCA.

27 Donald Manson to Governor Simpson, February 11, 1851, fos. 233–34, D.5/30, HBCA.

28 James Douglas to Peter Skene Ogden, February 14, 1851, fo. 61, B.226/b/3, HBCA.

29 James Douglas to Paul Fraser, July 11, 1851, fo. 114, B.226/b/3, HBCA.

30 Douglas to Barclay, August 17, 1850, in Hartwell Bowsfield, ed., *Fort Victoria Letters*, 110–11.

31 Douglas to Fraser, February 10, 1851, fo. 54, B.226/b/3.

32 Manson to Governor Simpson, February 11, 1851, fos. 234–35, D.5/30.

33 Peter Skene Ogden to Governor and Council, March 20, 1851, fo. 445, D.5/30, HBCA.

CHAPTER 11

1 The trail might also have followed Goose Creek to Lily Pad Lake.

2 Alexander Caulfield Anderson, "Report on the Country between the Fraser River and Stuart Lake, 1865," fo. 8, William Dall Papers, Accession SIA RU007073, Box 18, Folder 4, Smithsonian Institution Archives, Washington, DC.

3 Sometimes called Eightythree Mile Creek.

4 Alexander Caulfield Anderson, "British Columbia," 15–16.

5 Alexander Caulfield Anderson, "Notes Connected with the Accompanying Map of British Columbia," fo. 3, Mss. 559, volume 2, folder 9, BCA.

6 George Mercer Dawson, "Report on the Area of the Kamloops Map Sheet, British Columbia" (Ottawa: Geological Survey of Canada, 1895), 297–98.

7 David Douglas, "Book of Sketch Maps," MS-0622, BCA. From Kamloops, the cattle travelled along the south shore of Kamloops Lake and crossed the Thompson River at the west end of the lake. The men drove the cattle westward to the mouth of the Bonaparte River and followed its valley north to Scottie Creek. Scottie Creek led them to a point where they passed behind a rocky height to reach Loon Creek, which they crossed. Following Loon Creek to the east, they travelled along the north shore of Loon Lake to its far end. There they joined the 1843 trail (described in this chapter), which brought them north to Green Lake. The cattle drive, however, travelled along the south shore of Green Lake to its eastern end, where a curving trail eventually led them north to Horse Lake. Any portion of this route might have been a section of the North West Company's old provisioning trails to Kamloops, discussed in the prologue.

8 Anderson, "Report on the Country between Fraser River and Stuart Lake," fo. 8.

9 Now Painted Bluffs Provincial Park. Batholithic rocks are intrusions of magma from the Earth's interior.

10 Anderson, "Report on the Country between Fraser River and Stuart Lake," fo. 8.

11 "Fort Alexandria Journal, 1848–1851," fos. 71–72, B.5/a/8.

12 James Douglas to Paul Fraser, March 15, 1851, fo. 69, B.226/b/3.

13 Paul Fraser, "Fort Kamloops Journal Kept by Paul Fraser, 1850–1855," 18–19.

14 James Douglas to James Murray Yale, June 23, 1851, fo. 111, B.226/b/3, HBCA.

15 Fraser, "Fort Kamloops Journal, 1850–55," 20.

16 Fraser, "Fort Kamloops Journal, 1850–55," 20.

17 James Douglas to Donald Manson, July 11, 1851, fo. 114, B.226/b/3, HBCA.

18 Quoted in letter from John Ballenden to Governor Simpson, January 3, 1852, fo. 26, D.5/33, HBCA.

19 Douglas to Manson, July 11, 1851, fo. 115, B.226/b/3.

20 Douglas to Manson, July 11, 1851, fo. 115, B.226/b/3.

21 James Douglas to Archibald Barclay, July 22, 1851, in Hartwell Bowsfield, ed., *Fort Victoria Letters*, 201.

22 "Invoice of Grass Seeds Forwarded per Canoe to Fort Langley, July 23," fo. 37, B.113/z/1, HBCA. The watermark on the paper is 1850. The New Caledonia men might have left Fort Langley by the time the grass seed arrived, but it is likely the Fort Colvile men were still there.

23 Douglas to Barclay, July 22, 1851, in Hartwell Bowsfield, ed., *Fort Victoria Letters*, 201.

24 Fraser, "Fort Kamloops Journal, 1850–55," 21. John Simpson was George Stewart Simpson's half-brother and another son of Governor George Simpson.

25 "Fort Alexandria Journal, 1851–1855," fo. 1, B.5/a/9, HBCA.

26 James Douglas to Archibald Barclay, October 31, 1851, in Hartwell Bowsfield, ed., *Fort Victoria Letters*, 224.

27 Donald Manson to Governor Simpson, February 25, 1852, fo. 238, D.5/33, HBCA.

28 Donald Manson to Governor and Council, February 20, 1852, fo. 224, D.5/33, HBCA.

29 Alexander Caulfield Anderson, "British Columbia," 69.

30 Alexander Caulfield Anderson to Governor and Council, September 29, 1851, fo. 546, D.5/31, HBCA.

31 Alexander Caulfield Anderson to Governor Simpson, April 21, 1851, fo. 635, D.5/30, HBCA.

32 Anderson to Governor Simpson, April 21, 1851, fo. 635, D.5/30.

33 John Ballenden to Archibald Barclay, December 5, 1851, fos. 93–94, B.223/b/39, HBCA.

CHAPTER 12

1 James Douglas to Alexander Caulfield Anderson, March 16, 1852, fo. 59, B.226/b/4, HBCA.

2 Eden Colvile to Governor and Committee, October 21, 1852, in E.E. Rich, *London Correspondence*, 170.

3 Alexander Caulfield Anderson to Governor and Council, April 22, 1852, fo. 448, D.5/33, HBCA.

4 James Douglas to Eden Colvile, March 16, 1852, fo. 38, B.226/b/6, HBCA.

5 Douglas to Colvile, March 16, 1852, fos. 38–39, B.226/b/6.

6 Rockweed or Black Tree Lichen is a long, hair-like lichen that grows on trees and was used as a food by every First Nations group in the interior.

7 James Douglas to Archibald Barclay, April 18, 1852, fo. 64, B.226/b/6, HBCA.

8 James Douglas to James Murray Yale, April 14, 1852, fo. 79, B.226/b/4, HBCA.

9 "Fort St. James Post Journal, 1851–1856," fo. 31, B.188/a/20, HBCA.

10 "Fort Alexandria Journal, 1851–1855," fo. 9, B.5/a/9.

11 "Fort Alexandria Journal, 1851–1855," fo. 9, B.5/a/9. Toutlaid was a First Nations man who worked at Fort Alexandria.

12 Paul Fraser to Eden Colvile, March 16, 1852, A/C/40/F862, BCA. Colts were young male horses that would be used in the brigades.

13 Eden Colvile to Governor and Committee, July 21, 1852, in E.E. Rich, *London Correspondence*, 148.

14 Bruce McIntyre Watson, *Lives Lived West of the Divide*, 664.

15 "Fort Alexandria Journal, 1848–1851," fo. 21, B.5/a/8.

16 Donald Manson to Governor and Council, February 20, 1853, fo. 323, D.5/36, HBCA.

17 During the Chilcotin War of 1864, Donald McLean refused to duck when he heard the snick of a gun, and as a result was shot and killed by a Tsilhqot'in man.

18 Douglas to Barclay, July 12, 1852, fo. 93, B.226/b/6.

19 Douglas to Barclay, July 12, 1852, fo. 93, B.226/b/6.

20 James Douglas to John Ballenden, August 3, 1852, fo. 121, B.226/b/4, HBCA.

21 Manson to Governor and Council, February 20, 1853, fo. 324, D.5/36.

22 "Fort Alexandria Journal, 1851–1855," fo. 15, B.5/a/9.

23 "Fort Alexandria Journal, 1851–1855," fo. 15, B.5/a/9.

24 "Fort Alexandria Journal, 1851–1855," fo. 15, B.5/a/9.

25 "Fort Alexandria Journal, 1851–1855," fo. 15, B.5/a/9.

26 "Fort St. James Post Journal, 1851–1856," fo. 43, B.188/a/21.

27 James Douglas to Donald Manson, July 6, 1852, fo. 110, B.226/b/4, HBCA.

28 Manson to Governor and Council, February 20, 1853, fo. 323, D.5/36.

29 James Douglas to John Ballenden, November 1, 1852, fos. 35–36, B.226/b/7, HBCA.

30 Douglas to Barclay, February 17, 1853, fo. 171, B.226/b/6.

31 Manson to Governor and Council, February 7, 1853, fo. 320, D.5/36.

32 Governor Simpson to Donald Manson, June 18, 1853, fo. 1, B.188/c/1, HBCA.

33 Paul Fraser to James Murray Yale, August 9, 1853, A/C/40/F862, BCA.

34 James Douglas to Donald Manson, April 7, 1857, fo. 80, volume 1, A/C/20/Vi4A, BCA.

35 Douglas to Manson, July 10, 1857, fo. 150, volume 2, A/C/20/Vi4A.

36 James Murray Yale to Governor Simpson, October 22, 1852, fo. 81, D.5/35 HBCA; also A/C/40/Ya2, BCA.

CHAPTER 13

1 James Douglas to Archibald Barclay, May 12, 1853, fo. 218, B.226/b/6.

2 Donald Manson to Governor Simpson, March 1, 1853, fo. 334, D.5/36, HBCA.

3 "Fort St. James Post Journal, 1851–1856," fo. 60, B.188/a/21.

4 "Fort St. James Post Journal, 1851–1856," fo. 60, B.188/a/21.

5 "Fort Alexandria Journal, 1851–1855," fo. 30, B.5/a/9.

6 Ferdinand McKenzie to James Murray Yale, June 15, 1853, fo. 40, B.113/c/2, HBCA.

7   Margaret A. Ormsby, ed., *A Pioneer Gentlewoman in British Columbia: The Recollections of Susan Allison* (Vancouver: UBC Press, 1999), 9–10.

8   Lieutenant Henry Spencer Palmer, "Report on the Country," 81.

9   Douglas to Barclay, July 4, 1853, fos. 226–27, B.226/b/6.

10   Douglas to Barclay, July 4, 1853, fo. 227, B.226/b/6.

11   James Douglas to James Murray Yale, June 30, 1853, fo. 42, B.113/c/1.

12   James Douglas to J.W. McKay, July 20, 1853, fo. 133, B.226/b/7, HBCA.

13   James Douglas to Donald Manson, November 20, 1853, fo. 55, B.226/b/10, HBCA.

14   Governor Simpson to Donald Manson, June 18, 1853, fos. 1–2, B.188/c/1.

15   Valemount Historical Society, *Yellowhead Pass and Its People* (Valemount: D.W. Friesen & Sons, 1984), 2.

16   A.G. Morice, *The History of the Northern Interior of British Columbia, Formerly New Caledonia (1660 to 1880)* (Smithers: Interior Stationery Ltd., 1978), 279–80.

17   James Robert Anderson, "Notes and Comments on Early Days and Events in British Columbia," 164.

18   Paul Fraser to James Murray Yale, August 9, 1853, A/C/40/F862.

19   James Douglas to Paul Fraser, September 1, 1853, fo. 14, B.226/b/10, HBCA.

20   "Fort Alexandria Journal, 1851–1855," fo. 36, B.5/a/9.

21   "Fort Alexandria Journal, 1851–1855," fo. 36, B.5/a/9.

22   "Fort St. James Post Journal, 1851–1856," fo. 71, B.188/a/21.

23   Peter Skene Ogden to Governor Simpson, April 20, 1853, fo. 6, B.223/b/41, HBCA.

24   Angus McDonald to Governor and Council, September 26, 1853, fo. 779, D.5/37, HBCA.

25   John Work to Peter Skene Ogden and Dugald Mactavish, November 24, 1853, fo. 46, B.226/b/10, HBCA.

CHAPTER 14

1   James Douglas to Donald Manson, April 12, 1854, fo. 110, B.226/b/10.

2   Quoted in Terry Pettus, "Frolic at Fort Nisqually," *Beaver Magazine*, Summer 1961, 11.

3   "Fort St. James Post Journal, 1851–1856," fo. 86, B.188/a/21.

4   "Fort Alexandria Journal, 1851–1855," fos. 52–53, B.5/a/9.

5   Frank Sylvester, "The Old Brigade Trail in '59," fos. 19–20.

6   "Fort Alexandria Journal, 1851–1855," fo. 52, B.5/a/9.

7   "Fort Alexandria Journal, 1851–1855," fos. 52–53, B.5/a/9.

8   "Fort Alexandria Journal, 1851–1855," fo. 55, B.5/a/9.

9   James Douglas to Paul Fraser, August 1, 1854, fo. 142, B.226/b/10.

10   Margaret A. Ormsby, *A Pioneer Gentlewoman in British Columbia*, 9.

11   Ormsby, *A Pioneer Gentlewoman in British Columbia*, 9.

12   James Douglas to William Henry McNeill, August 12, 1854, fo. 145, B.266/b/10, HBCA.

13   James Douglas to James Murray Yale, November 7, 1854, fo. 63, B.113/c/1.

14   Douglas to Manson, August 1, 1854, fo. 142, B.226/b/10.

15   "Fort Alexandria Journal, 1851–1855," fo. 57, B.5/a/9.

16   "Fort Alexandria Journal, 1851–1855," fo. 58, B.5/a/9.

17 "Fort Alexandria Journal, 1851–1855," fo. 58, B.5/a/9.

18 "Fort Alexandria Journal, 1851–1855," fo. 58, B.5/a/9.

19 "Fort Alexandria Journal, 1851–1855," fo. 58, B.5/a/9.

20 "Fort St. James Post Journal, 1851–1856," fo. 95, B.188/a/21.

21 "Fort St. James Post Journal, 1851–1856," fo. 96, B.188/a/21.

22 Douglas to Manson, September 19, 1854, fos. 158–159, B.226/b/10.

23 Douglas to Yale, September 19, 1854, fo. 159, B.226/b/10.

24 Paul Fraser to James Douglas, undated, 1–2, A/C/40/F862, BCA.

25 Peter Skene Ogden and Dugald Mactavish to Archibald Barclay, July 21, 1854, fo. 48, B.223/c/2, HBCA.

26 Governor Simpson to Board of Management, June 28, 1854, fo. 100, B.223/c/2, HBCA.

27 Governor Simpson to Board of Management, September 7, 1854, fo. 111, B.223/c/2, HBCA.

28 Mactavish, who had been Peter Skene Ogden's assistant at Fort Vancouver, took over Ogden's position when the latter was too sick to do his job. Ogden died in September 1854.

29 James Sinclair to Dr. Cowan, January 3, 1855, Letter #3, E/B/Si6, BCA. Sir G. is Sir George Simpson, governor of the HBC.

30 Alexander Caulfield Anderson, "British Columbia," 27–28.

CHAPTER 15

1 "Fort Alexandria Journal, 1851–1855," fos. 75–76, B.5/a/9. In 1854 they had taken out 106 packs of furs.

2 Paul Fraser, "Fort Kamloops Journal Kept by Paul Fraser, 1854–1855," 44, part two.

3 Fraser, "Fort Kamloops Journal, 1854–1855," 18, part two.

4 Fraser, "Fort Kamloops Journal, 1854–1855," 45, part two.

5 Fraser, "Fort Kamloops Journal, 1854–1855," 45–46, part two.

6 James Douglas to William G. Smith, July 10, 1855, fo. 16, B.226/b/13, HBCA. William Gregory Smith was the secretary at Hudson's Bay House between 1855 and 1871.

7 Douglas to Smith, July 10, 1855, fo. 16, B.226/b/13.

8 Douglas to Smith, July 10, 1855, fo. 17, B.226/b/13.

9 Douglas to Smith, August 1, 1855, fo. 18, B.226/b/13.

10 "Fort Alexandria Journal, 1851–1855," fo. 80, B.5/a/9.

11 A.G. Morice, *The History of the Northern Interior of British Columbia*, 280.

12 Harley H. Hatfield, "The Proposed Cascade Wilderness," *Okanagan Historical Society Report*, November 1, 1980, 13.

13 Lieutenant Henry Spencer Palmer, "Report on the Country," 82.

14 James Douglas to Governor Simpson, August 7, 1855, A/C/20/Vi5, BCA.

15 "Fort Alexandria Journal, 1851–1855," fo. 80, B.5/a/9.

16 "Fort Alexandria Journal, 1851-1855," fo. 80, B.5/a/9.

17 "Fort St. James Post Journal, 1851–1856," fo. 115, B.188/a/21, HBCA.

18 Donald McLean to James Murray Yale, September 19, 1855, fo. 82, B.113/c/1, HBCA.

19 Glanders or farcy was a serious infectious disease caused by the bacterium *Burkholeria mallei*. Although now uncommon, in the 1800s it was usually fatal.

20 Douglas to Smith, December 11, 1855, fos. 32–33, B.226/b/13.

21 Dugald Mactavish to William G. Smith, June 23, 1855, fo. 81, B.223/b/41, HBCA.

22 George Dickey, ed., "The Journal of Occurrences at Fort Nisqually" (Fort Nisqually Association), Section 10, 42.

23 Terry Pettus, "Frolic at Fort Nisqually," 11.

24 Dugald Mactavish to Governor Simpson, July 31, 1855, fo. 84, B.223/b/41, HBCA.

25 Dugald Mactavish to Governor Simpson, July 23, 1855, fo. 305, D.5/40, HBCA.

26 Pettus, "Frolic at Fort Nisqually," 13.

27 Pettus, "Frolic at Fort Nisqually," 13–14.

28 Pettus, "Frolic at Fort Nisqually," 14.

29 Dickey, "The Journal of Occurrences at Fort Nisqually," Section 10, 43.

30 Pettus, "Frolic at Fort Nisqually," 14.

31 Alexander Caulfield Anderson, "History of the Northwest Coast," 54–55.

32 James Douglas to Right Honourable William Molesworth, Secretary of State for the Colonies, November 8, 1855, 244, C/AA/10.1/7, BCA. The Duke of Newcastle was Secretary of State for the Colonies until June 1854, and Sir William Molesworth took over his position.

33 Mactavish to Governor Simpson, September 5, 1855, fo. 430, D.5/40.

34 Douglas to Smith, July 10, 1855, fos. 16–17, B.226/b/13.

35 Douglas to Smith, August 1, 1855, fo. 18, B.226/b/13.

36 H.L. Cairns, "Notes on Road History of British Columbia, 1953," 3–4, Legislative Library 971.1 C136.

37 James Douglas to James Murray Yale, October 2, 1855, fo. 88, B.113/c/1.

38 James Douglas to James Murray Yale, June 6, 1856, fo. 73, B.226/b/12, HBCA.

39 Douglas to Smith, July 8, 1856, fo. 68, B.226/b/13.

CHAPTER 16

1 Alexander Caulfield Anderson, "History of the Northwest Coast," 53.

2 James Douglas to Secretary of State, Great Britain, April 16, 1856, [Executive No 10], C/AA/10.1/3, BCA.

3 James Sinclair to Dr. Cowan, July 5, 1855, fo. 1, Letter #4, E/B/Si6, BCA.

4 Sinclair to Cowan, July 5, 1855, fos. 2–3, Letter #4, E/B/Si6.

5 Dugald Mactavish to William G. Smith, June 30, 1855, fo. 83, B.223/b/41.

6 Douglas to Secretary of State, Great Britain, July 22, 1856, [Executive No. 15], C/AA/10.1/3.

7 James Douglas to Donald McLean, March 29, 1856, fo. 39, B.226/b/12, HBCA.

8 James Douglas to William G. Smith, May 15, 1856, fo. 59, B.226/b/13.

9 James Douglas to Angus McDonald, April 30, 1856, fos. 54–55, B.226/b/12, HBCA.

10 Douglas to McDonald, May 5, 1856, fo. 59, B.226/b/12.

11 Douglas to McDonald, July 7, 1856, fo. 83, B.226/b/12.

12 Douglas to Smith, July 8, 1856, fo. 67, B.226/b/13.

13 Peter H. Burnett to James Douglas, May 5, 1848, fo. 288, B.223/c/1, HBCA.

14 James Douglas to Governor Simpson, December 22, 1856, fo. 90, B.226/b/13, HBCA.

15 James Douglas to Henry Shuttleworth, July 2, 1856, fo. 85, B.226/b/12, HBCA.

16   Dugald Mactavish to Governor Simpson, September 25, 1856, fo. 121, B.226/b/12, HBCA.

17   Douglas to McLean, September 25, 1856, fo. 119, B.226/b/12.

18   Eden Colvile to Sir George Simpson, July 10, 1849, in E.E. Rich, *London Correspondence*, Appendix, 175.

19   Douglas to Smith, July 8, 1856, fos. 66–67, B.226/b/13.

20   Douglas to Smith, July 8, 1856, fo. 67, B.226/b/13.

21   Douglas to Smith, July 8, 1856, fo. 67, B.226/b/13.

22   Douglas to Smith, July 29, 1856, fo. 71, B.226/b/13.

23   James Douglas to James Murray Yale, August 6, 1856, fo. 102, B.113/c/1.

24   Douglas to Smith, September 20, 1856, fos. 78–79, B.226/b/13.

25   Douglas to McLean, September 25, 1856, fo. 118, B.226/b/12.

26   James Douglas to Donald Manson, September 25, 1856, fo. 120, B.226/b/12, HBCA.

27   James Douglas to William G. Smith, July 20, 1857, fo. 2, B.226/b/15, HBCA.

28   George Blenkinsop to Governor Simpson, September 18, 1857, fo. 299, D.5/44, HBCA.

CHAPTER 17

1   James Douglas to William G. Smith, July 8, 1856, fo. 67, B.226/b/13.

2   Douglas to Smith, July 29, 1856, fo. 71, B.226/b/13.

3   James Douglas to Secretary of State, Great Britain, October 29, 1856, [Executive No. 28], C/AA/10.1/3.

4   Douglas to Secretary of State, Great Britain, October 29, 1856, [Executive No. 28], C/AA/10.1/3.

5   James Douglas to Governor Simpson, December 23, 1856, fo. 91, B.226/b/13.

6   Douglas to Governor Simpson, December 23, 1856, fo. 91, B.226/b/13.

7   Douglas to Smith, February 19, 1857, fo. 98, B.226/b/13.

8   James A. Graham to Governor Simpson, March 25, 1857, fo. 130, B.223/b/41, HBCA.

9   James A. Graham to Governor Simpson, March 9, 1857, fo. 279, D.5/33.

10   George Blenkinsop to Governor Simpson, September 18, 1857, fos. 315–16, D.5/44.

11   Douglas to Smith, May 26, 1857, fo. 114, B.226/b/13.

12   Douglas to Smith, June 27, 1857, fo. 117, B.226/b/13. The word "Falls" referred to rapids.

13   Douglas to Smith, June 27, 1857, fo. 117, B.226/b/13.

14   Blenkinsop's report quoted in letter, James Douglas to William G. Smith, July 20, 1857, fo. 3, B.226/b/15.

15   Quoted in letter, Douglas to Smith, July 20, 1857, fo. 3, B.226/b/15.

16   James Douglas to George Blenkinsop, July 8, 1857, fo. 144, volume 2, A/C/20/Vi4A, BCA.

17   James Anderson to Alexander Caulfield Anderson, December 24, 1846, A/B/40/An32, BCA.

18   Anderson to Anderson, April 20, 1847, A/B/40/An32.

19   Anderson to Anderson, December 24, 1846, A/B/40/An32.

20   Douglas to Smith, June 27, 1857, fos. 117–18, B.226/b/13. Dysentery is an infection of the intestines caused by parasites or bacteria.

21 James Douglas to William Fraser Tolmie, June 25, 1857, fo. 133, volume 2, A/C/20/ Vi4A, BCA.

22 Douglas to Smith, July 20, 1857, fo. 3, B.226/b/15.

23 James Douglas to Donald Manson, February 14, 1857, fo. 5, volume 1, A/C/20/ Vi4A, BCA.

24 James Douglas to James Murray Yale, June 24, 1857, fo. 129, volume 2, A/C/20/ Vi4A, BCA.

25 Douglas to Smith, July 20, 1857, fo. 2, B.226/b/15. As explained in Chapter 16, the post was named for the newly minted governor of the HBC's London Committee, John Shepherd.

26 E.E. Rich, ed., *Black's Rocky Mountain Journal, 1824* (London: The Hudson's Bay Record Society, 1955), 239.

27 Rich, *Black's Rocky Mountain Journal, 1824*, 239. An outfit ran from June 1 of the year mentioned to May 31 of the year that followed.

28 Rich, *Black's Rocky Mountain Journal, 1824*, 239.

29 Rich, *Black's Rocky Mountain Journal, 1824*, 240.

30 Douglas to Smith, October 11, 1857, fo. 15, B.226/b/15.

31 James Douglas to James Murray Yale, November 7, 1857, Mss. 537, BCA.

32 Douglas to Smith, July 20, 1857, fos. 2–3, B.226/b/15.

33 George Blenkinsop to Governor Simpson, September 18, 1857, fo. 314, D.5/44.

34 Alexander Caulfield Anderson, "The Proposed New Route to Kootenay," *Colonist Newspaper*, February 16, 1869.

35 Blenkinsop to Governor Simpson, September 18, 1857, fo. 314, D.5/44.

36 James Douglas to Angus McDonald, September 21, 1857, 192, volume 2, A/C/20/ Vi4A, BCA.

37 Douglas to Smith, June 27, 1857, fo. 118, B.226/b/13.

38 James Douglas to Governor Simpson, July 17, 1857, fo. 32, D.5/44, HBCA.

39 Douglas to Smith, July 20, 1857, fo. 2, B.226/b/15.

40 Dugald Mactavish to Governor Simpson, August 19, 1857, fo. 140, B.223/b/41.

41 James Douglas to Peter Ogden, September 21, 1857, fo. 98, volume 2, A/C/20/ Vi4A, BCA.

42 James Douglas to Donald McLean, September 10, 1857, fo. 183, volume 2, A/C/20/ Vi4A, BCA.

43 Ron Hatch, Elisabeth Duckworth, Sylvia Gropp, and Sherry Bennett, *Kamloops: Trading Post to Tournament Capital* (Kamloops: Thompson Rivers History and Heritage Society, 2012), 37.

44 Donald McLean to James Murray Yale, August 20, 1857, fo. 110, B.113/c/1.

45 Douglas to Smith, September 1, 1857, fo. 6, B.226/b/15.

46 Douglas to McLean, September 10, 1857, fo. 183–84, volume 2, A/C/20/Vi4A.

47 Douglas to Yale, November 23, 1857, fo. 238, volume 2, A/C/20/Vi4A.

48 Douglas to Yale, September 10, 1857, fo. 182, volume 2, A/C/20/Vi4A.

49 Douglas to Yale, November 17, 1857, fo. 18, B.226/b/15.

50 In 1859, Lieutenant Spencer Palmer of the Royal Engineers rode over the trail with Angus McDonald (see the epilogue). As he reached the eastern side of the high mountain ridge, he reported that "Mr. McLean of the Hudson's Bay Company, who

crossed in 1857 or 1858, on the 16th of October, had a very disastrous trip, and lost 60 or 70 horses in the snow." This did not occur in 1857.

51 Douglas to Smith, November 17, 1857, fo. 18, B.226/b/15.

52 Quoted in letter, Douglas to Smith, November 17, 1857, fo. 18, B.226/b/15.

53 James Douglas to James Murray Yale, December 26, 1857, fo. 113, B.113/c/1.

54 Douglas to Smith, December 28, 1857, fo. 26, B.226/b/15.

55 James Douglas to Governor Simpson, January 4, 1858, fo. 28, B.226/b/15.

56 Douglas to Smith, March 25, 1858, fo. 46, B.226/b/15.

57 Douglas to Smith, January 14, 1858, fos. 29–30, B.226/b/15.

58 Jason Allard, "Enclosed Sketches of Early Life in B.C.," fo. 12, E/D/Al50.

59 Douglas to Smith, February 18, 1858, fo. 38, B.226/b/15.

60 Douglas to Smith, March 25, 1858, fo. 46, B.226/b/15.

61 Douglas to Smith, April 19, 1858, fo. 50, B.226/b/15.

CHAPTER 18

1 Daniel Marshall, *Claiming the Land: British Columbia and the Making of a New El Dorado* (Vancouver: Ronsdale Press, 2018), 149.

2 Ken Mather, *Trail North: The Okanagan Trail of 1858–68 and Its Origins in British Columbia and Washington*, (Victoria: Heritage House, 2018), 86.

3 James Douglas to William G. Smith, April 27, 1858, 70 (transcript), A/C/20/Vi3A, BCA.

4 James Douglas, "Private Papers," first series, 64 (transcript), B/20/1858, BCA.

5 Jason Allard, "Enclosed Sketches of Early Life in B.C.," fos. 12–13, E/B/Al59. His father was Ovid Allard of Fort Yale.

6 George F.G. Stanley, ed., *Mapping the Frontier: Charles Wilson's Diary of the Survey of the 49th Parallel, 1858–1862* (Toronto: Macmillan of Canada, 1970), 23–24.

7 Stanley, *Mapping the Frontier*, 32.

8 Douglas to Smith, May 18, 1858, 70, A/C/20/Vi3A.

CHAPTER 19

1 Sappers were soldiers responsible for building or repairing roads or bridges.

2 "From the Journal of Arthur Thomas Bushby," *Okanagan Historical Society Journal*, November 1, 1972, 26.

3 Lieutenant Henry Spencer Palmer, "Report on the Country," 81. All quotations in this chapter are from the report unless otherwise indicated. Page numbers are given for the quotations.

4 Victor Wilson, "Journal, HBC Trek, 1971," 35–36.

5 Harley H. Hatfield, "Brigade Trail, Fort Hope to Campement des Femmes," *Okanagan Historical Society Journal*, November 1, 1972, 39.

6 Hatfield, "Brigade Trail, Fort Hope to Campement des Femmes," 40.

7 Wilson, "Journal, HBC Trek, 1971," 30.

8 Wilson, "Journal, HBC Trek, 1971," 30.

9 Wilson, "Journal, HBC Trek, 1971," 30.

10 Harley H. Hatfield, "The Proposed Cascade Wilderness," 9.

11 Ramona Boyle and Richard Mackie, "The Hudson's Bay Company in Barkerville," *B.C. Studies*, no. 185 (Spring 2015): 79–107.

12   Jason Allard, "Enclosed Sketches of Early Life in B.C.," fos. 22–23, E/D/Al50.

13   "Heritage Context Study of the 1849 Hudson's Bay Brigade Trail between Peers
     Creek Forest Service Road and the Tulameen Plateau, B.C." (Stó:lō Research
     and Resource Management Centre, December 2010), 18–19.

14   James Douglas to Duke of Newcastle, Secretary of State for the Colonial
     Department, April 23, 1860, fo. 103, C/AB/10.1A/5, BCA.

15   Roderick J. Barman, "Packing in British Columbia: Transport on a Resource
     Frontier," *Journal of Transport History* 21, no. 2 (2000).

16   Barman, "Packing in British Columbia."

17   Jason Allard, "Enclosed Sketches of Early Life in B.C.," fo. 2, E/D/Al50.

18   John Mantz, "Camels in the Cariboo," *Canadian West Magazine* 7, no. 1 (Spring
     1991): 19–27.

19   Frank Sylvester, "Old Brigade Trail in '59," fo. 19.

20   Lisa Phillips, "Transitional Identities: Negotiating Social Transitions in the Pacific
     NW 1825–1860s," *Canadian Political Science Review* 2, no. 2 (June 2008): 34.

ILLUSTRATION CREDITS

Page 2 Tremayne Album 1, British Columbia, 1897–1898. Herbert A. Tremayne fonds. Hudson's Bay Company Archives [HBCA], 1979/53/154, Archives of Manitoba

Page 5 John Innes, "The Hudson's Bay Fur Brigade Passing Down the Okanagan," A.D. 1825–1835. Original oil painting: SFU Art Collection. Gift of Post #2, Native Sons of British Columbia, 2004. Photograph: London Album, 42-0021, HBCA

Page 10 Mikan 2897241, Library and Archives Canada [LAC], C-040856

Page 11 A-01637, courtesy of the Royal BC Museum, BC Archives

Page 13 A-01876, courtesy of the Royal BC Museum, BC Archives

Page 25 PDP03731, courtesy of the Royal BC Museum, BC Archives

Page 28 Courtesy of Glenbow Archives, NA-1274-17

Page 30 Mikan 3336072, LAC, PA-032334

Page 31 B-05547, courtesy of the Royal BC Museum, BC Archives

Page 34 Courtesy of Glenbow Archives, NA-1214-4

Page 36 PDP02186, Courtesy of the Royal BC Museum, BC Archives

Page 38 Courtesy of Glenbow Archives, NA-4140-70

Page 39 Courtesy of Glenbow Archives, NA-843-14

Page 45 A-01075, courtesy of the Royal BC Museum, BC Archives

Page 49 Noted in Dr. Richard Ruggles, *A Country So Interesting: The Hudson's Bay Company and Two Centuries of Mapping, 1670–1870*, 94 [Ruggles, 95. 273A] HBCA, B.5/z/1, fo. 2 (N4748)

Page 54 A-00900, courtesy of the Royal BC Museum, BC Archives

Page 56 Noted in Ruggles, *A Country So Interesting*, 95 [Ruggles, 12B]. Accessioned Map 18941A, [Detail]. Courtesy of the Royal BC Museum, BC Archives

Page 73 Part of the Frank Cyril Swannel fonds, 1909. 1-333272, courtesy of the Royal BC Museum, BC Archives

Page 75 Mikan 3308494, LAC, C-088895

Page 79 Courtesy of Glenbow Archives, NA-3740-55

Page 83 Courtesy of Glenbow Archives, PD-326-10

Page 92 PDP02225, courtesy of the Royal BC Museum, BC Archives

Page 93 A-01233, courtesy of the Royal BC Museum, BC Archives

Page 97 PDP05241, courtesy of the Royal BC Museum, BC Archives

Page 101 Mikan 2834221, LAC

Page 104 A-01813, courtesy of the Royal BC Museum, BC Archives

Page 109 Courtesy of the American Antiquarian Society, 434451_Warre_0031

Page 117 PDP02438, courtesy of the Royal BC Museum, BC Archives

Page 122   A-08377, courtesy of the Royal BC Museum, BC Archives. Published in *The Canadian Illustrated News, vol. 5, no. 2 (May 18, 1872)*. The Canadiana Collection Identifier is http://canadiana.ca/oocihm.8_06230_133

Page 126   HBCA, A.11/72, fo. 174 [Detail]. Circa. 1860. Surveyor General's Vault, Land Title and Survey Authority of British Columbia, Plan 12 Tray 3 Miscellaneous. Permission granted by the Surveyor General of the Land Title and Survey Authority of British Columbia

Page 137   Ruggles numbered this map 153C in his book, *A Country So Interesting*, 95, and said that Henry Newsham Peers drew it. It might also have been drawn by Deputy-Governor Eden Colvile. HBCA, B.113/c/1.

Page 142   Mikan 3309494. Geological Survey of Canada/LAC/PA-052732

Page 144   PDP01236, courtesy of the Royal BC Museum, BC Archives

Page 149   Mikan 3308292. Geological Survey of Canada/LAC/PA-039784

Page 150   D-03815, courtesy of the Royal BC Museum, BC Archives

Page 154   Courtesy of the American Antiquarian Society, 434451_Warre_0068

Page 165   Courtesy of Glenbow Archives, NA-3934-16

Page 170   Courtesy of Glenbow Archives, NA-1274-19

Page 182   A-00901, courtesy of the Royal BC Museum, BC Archives

Page 183   Courtesy of Glenbow Archives, PA-1374-1

Page 195   PDP00019, courtesy of the Royal BC Museum, BC Archives

Page 211   Courtesy of Glenbow Archives, NA-1274-18

Page 220   HBCA, P-165

Page 222   A-01495, Courtesy of the Royal BC Museum, BC Archives

Page 241   Ruggles numbered this map 534A in his book, *A Country So Interesting*. [Detail]. HBCA, Map G.1/318.

Page 246   Courtesy of Glenbow Archives, NA-674-24

Page 261   National Archives, Kew, Foreign Office, Reference FO 925/1608. Mentioned by Ruggles in *A Country So Interesting*, 108

Page 264   Courtesy of Glenbow Archives, NA-1338-18

Page 270   PDP02526, courtesy of the Royal BC Museum, BC Archives

Page 280   Mikan 3194139, LAC PA-111926

INDEX

Page numbers of photographs and maps are in bold

ABOUT THE AUTHOR

Nancy Marguerite Anderson is Métis, and an accepted member of Métis Nation British Columbia. She is descended from a North West Company voyageur known to have lived and worked in Red River District for many years; a man who crossed the Rocky Mountains with explorer David Thompson, and whose daughter married a Scottish gentleman in the west. Because of her Scottish ancestors' involvement with the York Factory Express and the HBC Brigades on the Pacific Slopes, she has (to her surprise) become a transportation historian of sorts, writing about the journeys that the Hudson's Bay Company men made both east and west of the Rocky Mountains. nancymargueriteanderson.com